The kind of text which we need in the education system in this country – a rich and wide-ranging resource for teachers and learners.

Tim Oates – Group Director, Cambridge Assessment

The idea at the heart of this work is extremely valuable; there is excellent material here.

Bruce Gillham – Former President, UK Reading Association

Awesome – clear, easily accessible, interesting and a friendly tone. Fabulous stuff!

Liz – tutor

You have led me back to the classroom, prepared to learn this time.

James – 18

An extremely useful manual for secondary pupils, adults and tutors alike.

Julia – teacher.

My son's school predicted a U failure at GCSE: with Peter's help he tackled the first six chapters in six lessons and passed with a C. I would recommend Peter's book to anyone struggling with English.

Lisa – mother.

With grateful thanks to Ben Cornwell and Ben Franklin,
without whom this book would not have been written.

WHAT, HOW AND WHY

A MANUAL OF
BETTER ENGLISH

For anyone concerned about better English – *parents,
tutors, teachers, employers and students.* For anyone
who wants to help.

Peter Inson

The Book Guild Ltd

First published in Great Britain in 2021 by
The Book Guild Ltd
9 Priory Business Park
Wistow Road, Kibworth
Leicestershire, LE8 0RX
Freephone: 0800 999 2982
www.bookguild.co.uk
Email: info@bookguild.co.uk
Twitter: @bookguild

Typeset in 11pt Adobe Garamond Pro

Printed and bound in the UK by TJ Books LTD, Padstow, Cornwall

ISBN 978 1913913 175

British Library Cataloguing in Publication Data.
A catalogue record for this book is available from the British Library.

LET'S GET STARTED

You may be reading this because you are concerned about your English.
You may be reading this because someone else is concerned about your English.
Does English matter?
Yes. It matters a lot.
English, our language, is what allows us to communicate everything we know.
If we fail to communicate clearly, whatever we know is lost.
This is something by which other people judge us, especially employers.
This manual will help you understand the way that we use our language so that you read and write effectively, as an educated adult who writes confidently and can check his or her own work.

Now you can be as good as anyone else.

Look, my first car, a Ford Prefect which cost me £10.

I neglected it – no oil.
Bought a replacement engine.
Dismantled it to see
how it worked.

Piston rings – replaced to
reduce oil consumption.
Exhaust valves – reground.
Engine – decoked to
improve performance.

Twenty-four hours later I had reassembled the engine. I pulled the starter and the engine sprang into life: one of my proudest moments.

**IF YOU CAN FOLLOW THIS YOU WILL SUCCEED
WITH THE REST OF THE BOOK.**

A TASTE OF
WHAT'S TO COME

Look at Three Sentences...

To study your own language is different from studying anything else. An engineer can leave a machine in pieces and forget it when he goes down to the pub but we have to continue using our language even when we are studying it. So, I'd like a pint.

Let's look at the final, short sentence, *So, I'd like a pint*. This is what is important:

- It follows a sentence which is long and complicated. A break is welcome, a short sentence with a single, simple idea.
- The capital S at the start reminds us that we have come to a new sentence, that we might have to take a breath if we are reading aloud, and that a pause will allow more of the previous, long sentence to sink in.
- The word *So*, followed by a comma, commands attention before the speaker tells everyone what he or she would like to drink.
- The full stop at the end makes it clear that there is nothing more to say. The speaker could have gone on to say just what was wanted: a pint of orange squash, tea or a favourite beer. Perhaps there was no need to say exactly what was wanted because he or she was among friends.

Not one of these points is difficult. These are not new ideas. These are ideas that you carry around with you because you carry the English language with you. I couldn't explain these things to you if you didn't.

> All I have done is to help you to understand
> what you already know.

THINGS YOU CAN DO TO IMPROVE YOUR ENGLISH

- **Read** for a minimum of ten minutes every day.
- Choose a newspaper or magazine, a book – conventional or electronic, fiction or non-fiction. If you can't get on with it after ten minutes find something else for tomorrow. Read things with ordinary-sized print, not pages of pictures or headlines. Further help can be found later in the book.
- **Write** for five minutes a day – a mini-blog, perhaps. Try to write in complete sentences – just few lines of your own thoughts or observations about anything you like. Read it aloud to yourself; then keep it as a diary or throw it away.

> **Whatever else you do:**
>
> Ignore anyone who tries to tease, mock, embarrass or ridicule you about this; you are doing something important to help yourself. These people will not be around when you need a job or opportunities to make something of your life. Adults make their own choices for their own reasons, not other people's.

CONTENTS

WELCOME TO PART ONE

CHAPTER ONE

WORDS AND
THEIR WORK – 1

Sounds that mean something and become words.
Different jobs for different words – parts of speech.

Words are the basic units of language with which we communicate. Sometimes a word is enough on its own: **"Stop."** Someone is telling you what to do. There might be a crash or simply an appearance in court if you don't, but stop you must. Just one word.

Sometimes a lot more words are used in a sentence. Count the words in each sentence in the first paragraph: eleven, nine, seven, eighteen and three. <u>No</u>, the last three words in the paragraph do not form a sentence but I have made them look like one. I will explain later, but for now it's important to realise that sentences can be very short, or very long. One of the longest ever, over a page long, can be found in *Ulysses* by James Joyce.

I will return to sentences, clauses and phrases later. Now we must go back to basics, to words.

Words – not just noises but noises with an agreed meaning. In English we have forty-four sounds represented by means of twenty-six letters.

Words are sounds, or groups of sounds, that enable us to mean things and communicate these meanings to other people. Some of our ancestors found that they could change and vary basic animal sounds so that we have far more sounds to use as signals. By stretching and twisting our mouths and our tongues we can form human or **articulate** speech. (Think of a bird's-eye view of an articulated lorry swerving sharply one way then another.)

Try making simple animal sounds. You will find that most animal sound is represented by the five letters which we call vowels, *a, e, i, o, u*. A good one to try is the mooing of a cow. (The best way to imitate the sound of a cow mooing is to open your mouth but let the sound come down your nose – most cows leave out the *m*.)

Then try reading this paragraph aloud, very slowly, very clearly and very carefully, like a television newsreader, or like someone who is trying to make a deaf person understand. Now you are also using, very carefully, the sounds represented by the remaining twenty-one letters of the alphabet. These letters represent the ways that we shape our mouths when we speak. These letters we call *consonants* – with the sound. They tell us how to shape our mouths as we make the sounds of our language.

Try looking at your mouth in a mirror and watch closely, as you say, "Tit," "Bumble," then, "Lilly." Essentially, these twenty-six letters, our alphabet, enable us to write down the sounds of speech, to make a visual record of what we say.

Written words – faster communication.

As you read this you are actually using a sophisticated system for converting visual signs into speech. Your brain reacts to these signs so quickly that you do not have time to speak them aloud, but you understand them as clearly as if you were listening to someone speaking aloud. Time yourself reading a page of a book silently, to yourself. You'll probably take about a minute, possibly less, to read three hundred words. Then try reading the page aloud. To do this you will take about three minutes, a speed of only one hundred words per minute.

Remember – your brain works faster than your mouth.

Some years ago, Angela Rippon, then a well-known newsreader on BBC television, had to be slowed down once her reading speed reached 120 words per minute. Up to that speed viewers could take in what she was telling them. When you read silently, you are taking in words three times as quickly, something we have only been able to do in English for about six hundred years, although we have been writing and reading English for about fifteen hundred years. For nine hundred years all reading was done aloud.

> **What you are doing now is incredibly clever.**
> **Your brain can think much faster than your mouth can speak.**
>
> The written language is very important.
> It enables us to take in information incredibly rapidly.
> It communicates despite the writer's absence.
> It provides a record.

Now we are back to your concern to use the written language as well as you can, and the basics. Words.

> **Nouns** – names of things.

Words work together in phrases or sentences to carry meaning. Some words, such as "pencil", have an obvious meaning – we can point to pencils and say the word and we have conveyed the idea even to someone who does not speak English. Similarly we can point to a sheep and teach the name for it, but how then would we teach someone the word "animal"?

If a foreigner points at the sheep and says, "animal", we cannot shake our heads and tell him that he is wrong. That would be confusing for him; it's not his fault that he doesn't realise that we want him to use the word for this particular animal, sheep. So, how are we going to teach both words so that the foreigner learns to use each of them properly? Remember, the key is to set things up so that he cannot get things wrong. This is where we are now trying to stand outside our language, thinking about it in a different way, learning how it works.

Finding answers to this sort of question is something that teachers enjoy, a challenge to the brain. If I were teaching on a farm or in a zoo it would be easy to show that all of the creatures there could be called animals, but only particular animals, those with long snouts, big ears and curly tails, and called

Percy, could be called pigs. One answer would be to use pictures, in a book, on a sketch pad or on a whiteboard.

Try thinking up ideas of your own and sketching them out – that way you will be getting outside your language and be able to think about the way it works.

Four animals. Just to be technical for a moment, *animal* here is a general word used to bring together several particular words such as *goat* and *sheep*. At another level, *animal* can be used as a particular word, along with *bird* and *reptile*, while we are using *creature* as a general word. Just as goats, pigs and sheep are all animals, so animals, reptiles and birds are all creatures. General words hold together groups of particular words.

Brain hurting yet? Just think of all these animals running about in a classroom full of children. Not much teaching would get done. For that we need simple pictures of the animals and the names of the animals, labels, written underneath.

What I'm trying to show you here is the range of jobs that words can do on their own before they start to operate with other words. So far we have dealt with only one kind of noun, the **common noun**. There are also **proper nouns**, **collective nouns** and **abstract nouns**.

> **Common nouns name ordinary things:**
> *school, teacher, label, noun.*

Nouns are all names of things. I want you to imagine being at school, at the age of about twelve. A slightly mad young teacher has handed each of you some **old-fashioned card luggage labels**, the sort that has a hole at one end so that you can tie it to something. The teacher has been talking about nouns and naming or labelling things and asks you to write as many of the names of things in the room as you can, each on a separate label. When you have finished you are going to fasten the labels to the things to which they apply. The teacher has extra string, Sellotape and Blu Tack to help you with this.

So, decide now, which nouns are you going to fix as labels on things that are in the room?

This is where we find out whether you were **trouble at school**. The teacher walks around the class, looking at your choices of nouns. If you have written words like *door*, or *desk* or even *student*, that's fine and you can fasten your labels onto something or someone straight away.

However, if you have prepared labels saying things such as *freak*, *nerd* or *slob*, then you will be made to wait to one side with your labels. Later, your teacher will tell you to give up the label to someone else in the class who will then be able to label you with these words!

Someone has written *friend* on his label, but no one wants to be his friend so the teacher gets the boy to give the label to one of the girls who finds another girl to stand still long enough for her to tie the label to her wrist, long enough to be her friend.

Someone has written *class*. The teacher pauses for a moment, then reaches for the string and snips off a long, long piece. He gives it to the student who hands one end to another student who is standing at the edge of the room. While the others watch he walks around all of them, letting out the string as he goes. Back to the first student, he takes both ends of the string and pulls them as tightly as he can.

Could this be you, the class joker? His victims wriggle and try to push each other onto the floor but they are tied together in a group, a class, and the joker is absolutely right with his label.

Collective nouns: flocks, squadron, team.

Class is a collective noun. It refers to a group or collection of things, in this case pupils or students. **Collective nouns** are easy to identify – *herds* of cows, a *platoon* of soldiers.

It could have been one of the nerds, or perhaps some smart kid, wanting to catch out this new teacher, but it's one of the girls this time. Her word is *bored*. She stands in front of the teacher all wriggle and pout and hands on her hips: **"Sort this out then, clever clogs."** You can imagine her saying the words, but she doesn't. The teacher takes her label and picks up a pencil. He changes the word – *boredom*. "That do?" he asks, and the girl nods.

"Charlie!" Charlie is one of nature's artists – his cartoons appear in the school magazine, and other places when no one's watching. "Charlie – can you help us out, mate?" You remember, teachers, always friendly when they want a favour.

The teacher explains something to Charlie, who gets to work on the large whiteboard. Soon two students are sitting in front of you, one of them slumped, fast asleep; the other student pats his mouth. Someone has bored them. Your teacher hands back the girl's altered label and she sticks it on the whiteboard.

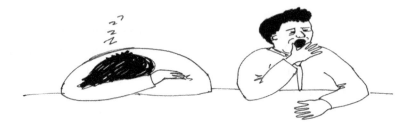

Even someone who did not speak English would realise what was what. The word is like the label on a painting or a photograph and we know that it tells us about the <u>idea</u> that the picture or photograph suggests, not about the things that are in the picture. It depends on our understanding of what we can see, of knowing that bored people put their heads down and yawn. It's an abstract idea, pulled away from the actual things that we can see.

Abstract nouns: luck, honesty, tension, germination.
They all depend on our understanding what's going on.

Then the teacher tells the class to pick up one more blank label each and write their names on them. When they have done this he collects them up, shuffles them and walks around the room, sticking them onto windows, walls and doors, turned so the names cannot be seen. Now each student has to find his or her label and there is chaos for several moments. Eventually everyone has the right one. Some of them cling to their labels as if they are their personal property and refuse to show the others and the class realises that there is only one place for each label.

> **Proper nouns:** Heathrow Airport, Toronto, Fred, Sophie, the University of Sydney, Sony, Ford.

"Each of you," says the teacher, "has your own piece of property." They are puzzled – so the school is giving away luggage labels – but they listen as he explains what proper nouns do: they name particular individual's things, in your case, your name.

> ### What Have You Learnt from This?
>
> There are four kinds of nouns.
>
> **Common nouns** refer to ordinary things such as *mushrooms*, *stars* and *tables*.
>
> **Collective nouns** refer to groups of things: *herds* of cows, *packs* of wolves.
>
> **Abstract nouns** refer to our understandings of things: *boredom*, *friendship*, *justice* and *liberty*.
>
> **Proper nouns** are like property; they belong to particular people, *John Smith*, or to particular places such as *New York*, or to particular things such as *Barclays Bank*.

EXERCISE ONE

Ask yourself how well you think you have followed things so far. If you complete this exercise successfully you should feel confident and that will help you move along more quickly. You will find the answers at the end of the chapter.

1. Identify the nouns in these sentences and decide which type each one represents.

    a. Aeroplanes are expensive.
    b. Aeroplanes are expensive items.
    c. Fleets of aeroplanes are very expensive.
    d. British Airways' shares are cheap.
    e. British Airways have been praised for their efficiency.

2. Still unsure? Test and teach yourself. Make your own list of nouns, decide in which category each one belongs then check with a dictionary.

3. Now try something a little more demanding.

    a. All cows eat grass.
    b. Teachers of music use this sentence as a mnemonic (pronounced nemonic) to help their pupils remember the notes on lines of written music.
    c. Players in a band have to respond to melody, harmony and rhythm if they are to succeed. If they do this well the result can be great enjoyment; if not there is chaos.

(You should have found a total of eighteen nouns in section 3, counting one noun twice. Answers can be found at the end of this chapter; do check that you understand any mistakes you have made.)

By now I hope that you are getting the hang of my way of explaining things. We need to move on. We still have to examine seven more kinds of words – *parts of speech*, to be technical.

Adjectives – words used to describe things.

Imagine a handful of pencils, green pencils and yellow pencils. The words *yellow* and *green* are used to describe the pencils. Adjectives provide additional information about things – some of the pencils were yellow, others were green. Adjectives are said to <u>qualify</u> nouns, to tell us more about them; an *intelligent* horse, a *comfortable* chair, an *incredible* teacher.

EXERCISE TWO

1. Identify the adjectives in these sentences.

    a. Tigers are impressive animals.
    b. They stacked the wooden chairs.
    c. Fleets of aeroplanes are very expensive.
    d. From the air they could see the grey water below them.
    e. His curly hair impressed the girl.

A little complication now – there are always complications with our language – *this* and *that*, *these* and *those*.

In class I would point to one student and say something like, *This boy at the front of the class and that boy at the back of the class may go home early.* There would follow an argument about just which boys I meant, for they would all want to go home early. The words **this** and **that** simply enable me to demonstrate exactly which boys are to go home early, just as *yellow and green* enabled me to indicate particular pencils. **These** and **those** are the plural forms of **this** and **that**: they are **demonstrative adjectives.** **These girls**, here at the front of the class, can have an early lunch. **Those girls**, up there at the back of the class, are excused homework.

Now try something a little more demanding. Each of these sentences contains more than one adjective. Some of them are not straightforward like matters of shape or colour.

2. Identify the adjectives in these sentences.

    a. The best aeroplanes are expensive.

b.   All the men helped to stack the wooden chairs.

c.   Future requirements for the military will be difficult to justify.

d.   Buy cheap; sell dear.

e.   British Airways have been praised for their efficiency.

> **Verbs** – action words at the heart of a sentence.

Do you remember "**Stop**"? When I ask students how many words you need to form a sentence the answers can be great fun. I rarely get the correct response, "One, one verb." We can't stop now but we do need at least to slow down while we deal with this very important kind of word, the <u>verb</u>. **This is the word that tells us what is happening or has happened, or will happen.** There is of course an exception here; the verb *to be* tells us something about the state of the world – *Boys and girls <u>are</u> different* – rather than about an action.

> The odd one out – the verb **to be**. It's more like an equals sign **=**

You are about to be thrown in at the deep end, but you are capable, determined and learning fast. Tell me, can you try identifying the verbs in the previous paragraph that begins, "Do you remember…"? There are sixteen of them.

Here is the same paragraph with the verbs underlined.

<u>Do (you) remember</u> "<u>Stop</u>"? When I <u>ask</u> kids how many words you <u>need to form</u> a sentence the answers <u>can be</u> great fun. I rarely <u>get</u> the correct response, "One, one verb." We <u>can't stop</u> now but we <u>do need (at least) to slow down</u> while we <u>deal</u> with this very important kind of word, the verb. This <u>is</u> the word that <u>tells</u> us what <u>is happening</u> or <u>has happened</u>, or <u>will happen</u>. There <u>is</u> of course an exception here; the verb *to be* <u>tells</u> us something about the state of the world, rather than about an action.

EXERCISE THREE

Underline the verbs in the following sentences:

a.   Fill the kettle, switch it on, put a teabag in a mug or a cup, pour the boiling water into the mug, leave it for two minutes, remove the teabag, stir in milk, and sugar if required.
b.   He fills the kettle, switches it on, puts a teabag in a mug, pours the boiling water into the mug, leaves it for two minutes, removes the tea bag, stirs in milk and adds sugar if required.
c.   He filled the kettle, switched it on, put a teabag in a mug, poured the boiling water into the mug, left it for two minutes, removed the teabag, stirred in milk and added sugar if required.

There are three questions about verbs which we need to ask now.

The first question concerns the grammatical sense of "action". This does not simply mean some physical event that we can see or hear. It can also refer to a mental action, for example, when we <u>think</u> about something. The words, *we do need at least to slow down* from the last paragraph, show that I had thought about something, the speed with which I was presenting ideas to you. That was why I decided to slow down. My mind had been active. In grammar, the idea of an action is much wider and includes events that would not be thought of as action in the ordinary, common-sense sort of way, such as eating or smiling.

Grammatical action – I <u>hope</u> West Ham…

The second question involves the "verbs" that follow the word *to. To form* and *to slow*. (Worry about *down* later.) These are very straightforward. They are the names of actions. We call them <u>infinitives</u> and they are incomplete verbs, incomplete because there is no indication whether the action has already taken place, is taking place or will take place, and there is no indication of who or what it was that did the action. They are best regarded as the names of the verbs which are incomplete. Verbs such as *I* <u>whistled</u>, *you* <u>sing</u>, *he* <u>will run away</u>

indicate past, present and future as well as the agent, the person or thing that does the action, the subject of the verb. (Ask who whistled, who sings and who will run away.) These are finite verbs.

> **The infinitive** – a verb's name or title.
> The verb *to call.*

(The word finite is related to the French word *fin*, which means end, and our word *final* – originally Latin, *finis*.)

Some of the verbs in the first paragraph of this section are single words, *stop, ask, need, get, deal, is, tells.* Here is the same paragraph again with all the verbs **emboldened**.

Do you **remember** "Stop"? When I **ask** students how many words you **need** to form a sentence the answers **can be** great fun. I rarely **get** the correct response, "One, one verb." We **can't stop** now but we **do need** at least to slow down while we **deal** with this very important kind of word, the verb. This **is** the word that **tells** us what **is happening** or **has happened**, or **will happen**. There **is** of course an exception here; the verb *to be* **tells** us something about the state of the world, rather than about an action.

These are actions that happen and are no trouble to us; what happened? He or they or we stopped, asked, needed, etc.

The third question concerns the puzzle I left for you which comprises the verbs that are formed with more than one word, that appear in a phrase: *do (you) remember, can be, can't stop, do need, is happening, has happened, will happen.* Here there is more than just the simple action.

Do is a verb in its own right – we do things. Combined with the word that tells us who or what is doing the action, in this case *you*, and the word that identifies the action, *like*, they form a question such as, "Do you like ice cream?"

Another example, *Can he swim?* uses a different verb, the verb to be able – I can, etc. In the case of *has happened*, the additional verb is the verb *to have* which marks a past tense – something that has taken place already.

"She has texted him five times this morning and it's only half past seven."

These extra verbs are used as **auxiliary verbs**. (*Auxilium* – Latin for help or assistance.) Auxiliary verbs, combined with an ordinary verb, form **compound verbs**, e.g. *was working, is trying* and *will succeed.*

Before we go on: my putting words in brackets, like (*Auxilium*) in the paragraph above – or <u>underlining</u> them or putting them in *italics*. These are my way of using the language at the same time that I am trying to analyse it.

EXERCISE FOUR

Here are a few sentences with <u>compound verbs</u>; identify the auxiliaries then ask yourself about the information or understanding that the word brings to the sentence.

a.   William was smiling.
b.   They don't smile here.
c.   He couldn't wait.
d.   She might have waited.
e.   Can it be?

If you enjoy this sort of thing, look for more compound verbs in newspapers, magazines and books. If you don't, make sure that you understand this before you continue, even if that means rereading the section on verbs or reading *Essentials for Students Chapter One.* Sometimes another way of explaining something will do the trick.

Remember, the verb in a sentence is like the engine in a car; it is the part that moves the car along.

You are making good progress with this most important of words, the verb.

Nothing happened is a sentence and, like all sentences, it depends on having a verb. In this case the verb is *happened*, which tells us what happened, grammatically, although, as we are told, nothing really did happen. What happened, grammatically, is that a statement was made, *nothing happened*, and this statement told us that nothing had occurred or taken place.

By the time you reach the end of this section you will have been studying several types of word. Tell me, how many auxiliary verbs did I use in the previous sentence? The answer is three; *will* and *have* indicate that the action of this verb *study* will be complete at some time in the future and *been*, with *studying*, rather than *study* alone, tells us that the action was continuous, that it will have been going on for some time by the time you reach the end of this section.

By next week I <u>will</u> <u>have</u> <u>been</u> **enjoy**<u>ing</u> ice cream for over fifty years.

In the sentence above we have the future past continuous tense. Yes, that's quite right: future – *will*, past – *have*, continuous – *been* and the *ing* at the end of *enjoying*. We can say these things and we can write them down. With a bit of practice we will do so without thinking or worrying about them.

Tenses

The word simply means time: past, present or future.

Verbs are built up with auxiliary verbs added to the root verb to show actions in the past, present or future, and to indicate whether they are complete or continuous. Changes to the root verb – *teach* and *taught* – can also indicate the past tense. *(Taught is an inflection of teach.)*

I have eaten another ice cream. The perfect tense – a completed action in the past. I could continue and boast, *and I am going to eat some more.*

I ate another ice cream. The past tense – an action in a period of time which is complete. We say *Yesterday I ate another ice cream.*

However if the action occurred today I have to say, <u>Today</u> I <u>have eaten</u> *another ice cream.*

The present has three versions, simple – *I eat ice cream every day,* continuous – *I am eating ice cream today,* and emphatic, to make it clear that something happens – *I do eat ice cream.*

The future is formed in more than one way: *I will eat* or *I am going to eat.* In Ireland *shall* is often used to form the future tense. In the UK we use *shall* when we want to emphasise an intention – *I shall be there, don't you worry.*

Transitive and intransitive verbs

We are comfortable saying: *I shovel ice cream on Tuesdays,* but not, *I shovel on Tuesdays.* *Shovel* is a transitive verb which always requires an object. Here the object is *ice cream,* something that is shovelled.

We are comfortable saying: *I laugh all the time,* but we cannot say, *We laugh jokes.* *Laugh* is an intransitive verb and does not take an object.

Because *breathe* can function as a transitive or an intransitive verb we are comfortable saying: *I breathe all the time* or *I breathe great mouthfuls of air when I am running.*

This, I hope, is **as difficult as things will get**.

In this chapter I am simply trying to show the different kinds of words that we use. The trouble is that words get mixed up with each other very quickly and, if we are not careful, we lose control of the things and we say things that we did not mean to say. This can be embarrassing or just plain annoying, but it happens and we would like it to happen less often. Perhaps that's why we are studying the language.

My aunt's neighbour once placed a small ad in her local paper.

> **Wanted** *Home for cross collie. Walks on lead.*
> *Clean. Easy to feed.*

A day or two later my aunt phoned her neighbour and said that she was from the RSPCA, a UK animal charity. Why, she demanded to know, why was the collie cross?

Adverbs – describe actions and modify adjectives.

We are going to remove the <u>adverb</u> from the sentence that follows.

Mr Smith resigned cheerfully.

Now look again.

Mr Smith resigned.

How did he resign? *Cheerfully.*

Doubtless you could find replacements: *hastily, sneakily, craftily, honourably.*

These adverbs can all be used to **qualify** the verb *resigned.* (Remember **qualify**?) If you want to qualify the noun, *Smith* – what kind of noun? That's right, a proper noun – you could qualify *Smith* with an adjective so that we would read, *Cheerful/hasty/sneaky/crafty/honourable Mr Smith resigned.*

How do you study? *Carefully? Determinedly?*

To concentrate on the man we use adjectives. To concentrate on the way he does things we use adverbs. The adverb, *cheerfully*, adds to what the verb tells us, that he resigned. Now we know how he resigned, *cheerfully.*

Obviously the sort of people we are and the way we do things are linked, but we can choose to shift the emphasis from person to action. We could go further: *Crafty Mr Smith resigned cheerfully.*

EXERCISE FIVE

1. Identify the adverbs in these sentences and indicate what they qualify.

    a. She limped slowly along the road.
    b. Cautiously he approached his mother-in-law.
    c. It was cooked well.
    d. He drove carelessly and ended up in the ditch.
    e. She picked up the ice cream tenderly then spread it firmly across his face.

There is another function that adverbs have, to <u>modify</u> adjectives and other adverbs. I have italicised the adverbs in the next two sentences.

"This shirt is *clearly* red," my wife tells me; she thinks I'm colour blind. I put down the shirt *very slowly* and ask myself why I have agreed to go shopping with her.

The shirt is not *simply* red, it is *obviously* red, or should be to anyone who is not colour blind, and is *clearly* unsuitable, as my wife has tried to point out. (Here three adverbs, *simply*, *obviously* and *clearly*, are modifying the adjectives, *red* and *unsuitable*.)

Very and *slowly* are both adverbs. *Slowly* qualifies the verb *put down*; it tells us how I put down the shirt. *Very* is an unusual adverb – it is only used to modify adjectives and other adverbs. It functions as an <u>intensifier</u>; here it tells us how slowly indeed I put down the shirt, which I really liked, of course.

Ordinary adverbs also work like this, as modifiers. For example, *fairly* in:

The shirt is not totally unsuitable, for the colour will fade *fairly* quickly, as I work out in the garden whenever I can.

> **Slightly** hurt, **almost** perfect.

You should note that adverbs are often formed from adjectives; quick/quickly, charming/charmingly. In these and many other examples, the suffix *ly* is added to the end of the adjective to form the adverb. Endings like this one are the remains of a link to the German suffix *lich* which means *like*. In both German and English the noun *friend* – German *Freund* – becomes the adjective *friendly* or *freundlich*. **Well done. Adverbs, finished – well, almost.**

EXERCISE FIVE

2. Identify the adverbs in these sentences and indicate what they qualify.

    a. Fleets of aeroplanes are very expensive.
    b. He is almost completely bald.

    c.   The teacher was barely breathing.
    d.   The teacher was barely alive.

Note how sentences c. and d. seem to say almost the same thing. For our purposes it is important to see how the language can be used like this. In the first sentence our attention is directed towards the lack of breathing, perhaps as a nurse or a doctor might observe a patient. In the second sentence the writer might be anticipating a death or a surprising recovery.

There remain: pronouns, prepositions, conjunctions, articles, exclamations and things that sound like words. As we shall see in the next chapter, where there will be **a sort of fancy-dress party for words**, all these different kinds of words have their jobs to do. For the moment I am simply going to identify them as quickly and as easily as possible.

> **Pronouns** – stand in for nouns.

Mummy took away Billy's ice cream. He cried. One day he would be stronger than her.

He and *her* are pronouns. They stand for nouns. (*Pro* Latin – *for* or *on behalf of, noun* – name.) Without pronouns speech would be very laborious – try reading the next sentence **aloud**.

Mummy took away Billy's ice cream. Billy cried. One day Billy would be stronger than Mummy and then Billy would have to look after Mummy and buy Billy's own ice creams.

One of the reasons that this sounds like baby talk is that children learn more slowly about pronouns and continue to use ordinary nouns, especially proper nouns, rather than pronouns. Even with pronouns where we would normally find them this little piece still sounds rather creepy, but it is now an adult voice, even if it has put some strange ideas into a young man's head. (Think of Roald Dahl's children's books.)

Try reading the passage again and identify the extra pronouns.

Mummy took away Billy's ice cream. He cried. One day he would be stronger than her and then he would have to look after her and buy his own ice creams.

Mummy, Billy – **proper nouns**.

He, she, him, I, me, my, mine, you, yours – **pronouns**.

That's it really. *I*, *me*, *my* and *mine* are words that we all use in reference to ourselves when we do things, when things are done to us, when we refer to something that belongs to us. **You can imagine a mad teacher who has an ice cream fetish:**

I like ice cream. Give *me* one and *I* will probably let you leave school early. Yes, that's *my* ice cream, not *yours*. Yes, and all those are *mine* too.

EXERCISE SIX

Besides the six italicised pronouns in the above sentence, there are four others. Can you identify them? Remember they all stand for something or someone.

Earlier we met the four demonstrative adjectives, *this*, *that*, *these* and *those*. We talked about this boy and that boy. Now look at another way of using these words.

That's the one I'd like.

Automatically, we look for someone to point at something, to indicate which bunch of flowers, or picture, or ice cream that has been chosen. These four words function as pronouns, standing in for a noun, but also enabling us to demonstrate which particular one we are talking about. This ice cream is delicious; this is rubbish.

This ice cream is delicious (**demonstrative adjective**). *This* is rubbish (**demonstrative pronoun**).

Coupled with a noun, these words are demonstrative adjectives; alone, they are demonstrative pronouns.

Then how about:

Who won the prize? The woman who cooked the best pizza.

When we ask the question, *Who won the prize?* we need a word that stands in for someone we don't know. The word *who* does just that. Here it functions as an **interrogative pronoun**. Other words can function in this way: *whom*, *whose*, *which* and *what*, e.g.

Whose watch is this? (Tracey's.)

Whom do you prefer? (Kerry.) Many people just say, <u>Who</u> *do you prefer?*
What do you want? (An ice cream.)
Which one? (The vanilla, please.)

> **Interrogative pronouns:** Words to form questions –
> Who? Whom? Whose? Which? What?

A reminder; we are examining our language to see how the components, words, work together. We don't have to memorise all this but we should be able to follow what is being explained. It should make sense. That's all. Now we must move on and see what Billy is up to. I wonder how Mummy's getting on. Read this:

a. Billy remembered the moment when Mummy took away his ice cream and he had fired at her with a water pistol. He was later found abandoned behind the nursery where she had left him. He was discovered by his best friend who had seen the water pistol which he had hidden in the push-chair. Billy's probation officer, who he had attacked with a banana only the previous week, came, smiling, to take him away.

Some Questions
What are we told about?

*   The moment Billy remembered
*   The nursery
*   His best friend
*   The water pistol
*   His probation officer

Now try removing this additional information from the passage.

b. Billy remembered the moment (when Mummy took away his ice cream and he had fired at her with a water pistol). He was later found abandoned behind the nursery (where she had left him). He was discovered by his best friend (who had seen the water pistol) (which he had hidden in the pushchair). Billy's probation officer (who he had attacked with a banana only the previous week) came, smiling, to take him away.

And you are left with:

Billy remembered the moment. He was found abandoned behind the nursery. He was discovered by his best friend. Billy's probation officer came, smiling, to take him away.

All the pieces of additional information, which I have now removed from the passage, are related to the main part of each sentence. They are joined by relative pronouns: *when, where, who, which* and *whom*. These words are acting just like components in an engine. They bring together bits of our language and enable it to work more efficiently. Without them this is what we would have to struggle to read, especially if we try to read it **aloud**.

c.   Billy remembered the moment. Mummy took away his ice cream and he had fired at her with a water pistol. He was found abandoned behind the nursery. She had left him. He was discovered by his best friend. His best friend had seen the water pistol. Billy had hidden the water pistol in the pushchair. Billy's probation officer came, smiling, to take him away. Billy had attacked him with a banana only the previous week.

Count the number of sentences in versions a. and c. Without the relative pronouns version c. has only two additional words but is much more difficult to read than the original above. Now count the number of sentences in each version. How many times must you stop in each version? Can you now see how, with the relative pronouns, version a. is so much easier to read (aloud)?

Now we are due in court. "Is this the weapon that you found in the push-chair?"

The judge nodded at the water pistol which had required two baby-minders and a traffic warden to wrestle it from Billy's grasp. It lay there in front of a packed courtroom.

That can also function as a relative pronoun. Here it relates the hidden weapon to the pushchair. This is important for the prosecution will need to link the two. It is not any weapon; it is that particular one. *Which*, on the other hand, makes less important connections; the water pistol happens to be on the table and it happened to require three adults to take it away from Billy. What is important is that it was the weapon <u>that was found in the pushchair.</u>

We will deal more thoroughly with the effects of using particular words in particular ways in a later chapter.

Prepositions – link things and actions.

Well, start by thinking about (pre) position. What position are you in? Sitting probably, but on something, a chair, a settee, perhaps a table or a bed, or standing, perhaps, in a bookshop or at a bus stop. There may be someone sitting next to you, or beside you, and the lamp above you may be a good one, but not as good as the one which is throwing light through the doorway, over there where your friend is leaning against the wall waiting for you to go down to the pub.

Off the table – not for discussion.
On the table – an offer.
Under the table – drunk.

You would not have been through the chair, but you might have been in the bed and possibly spread along the settee. You might even have been under the table. Let's start now by removing one word from this last sentence, *under*.

You might even have been the table.

This sentence makes sense, but only grammatically. We know of course that you could never really be a table, so for the sentence to make practical sense another word is needed, a word such as *above*. This word, or others like it, *under*, *next to* (a phrase that functions as a preposition), *by*, *opposite*, would all make sense. They are prepositions which tell us about the position of things, *on* the table, *behind* the door and so on. These prepositions link two nouns or pronouns; we saw *him* <u>on</u> *the bike.*

Other prepositions tell us about movement.

The lamp which was throwing light *through* the doorway. (It could have been *past* the doorway.)

Instead of location, this type of preposition tells us about movement, about direction: *along, up, down, towards.* These prepositions link verbs, in this case *was throwing,* with nouns or pronouns, in this case, *the doorway.*

An answer here for those of you who like to ask awkward questions. No, the preposition *through* does not link *light* and *the doorway.* "Right," you say, "tell us just what job the word *light* does do here?"

For a moment I pause, not because I haven't got the answer right up my sleeve, but because I am a kind teacher and, just for a second or two, I will allow you to think that you have caught me out.

But you haven't. The word *light* tells me what the lamp was throwing. Light is the <u>object</u> of the verb *was throwing* and the lamp is the <u>subject</u> of the verb, and this should be enough to keep you quiet until we encounter these terms again in a later chapter.

Now the rest of you can pay attention again so that we can finish prepositions.

What is the difference between falling *in* the shower and falling *into* the shower? Could the shower door remain closed in both cases? How would you get Charlie, the class cartoonist, to draw each scenario? *In* is a preposition of location while *into* is a preposition of direction or movement. Falling *in* the shower is possible without the door being opened whereas the door would have to be open if someone was going to fall into the shower, for the movement, the fall, would have to begin outside the shower and finish inside. I am assuming here that there is some sort of roof or top to the shower. If this is beginning to sound like something from a detective novel it might just be that words and the ways that we use them can be a very important matter.

"May it please Your Honour." Counsel for the defence was not having an easy day. He let his hands rest on (**preposition of location**) the table in front of him and turned his gaze towards (**preposition of movement**) the defendant.

"The evidence put before you shows quite conclusively that the door of the shower had jammed and that the deceased's fall took place inside (**preposition of location**) the shower. I put it to Your Honour that the accused could not have pushed the deceased into (**preposition of movement**) the shower even had he wanted to."

> Walk **into** the swimming baths, **from** the bus stop and swim **in** the pool once you get there.
>
> While she swims **in** the pool he is jumping **into** the pool.

I once dreamt about ice cream.

What did my dream concern? It was about ice cream. *About* links the verb *dreamt* with the noun *ice cream*. This is clearly nothing to do with position or movement but with something more abstract, about ideas and understanding, rather like abstract nouns.

That's it. Now I will go and relax in the garden while you complete the following…

EXERCISE SEVEN

Try identifying all the prepositions in this paragraph which you have already met, and decide which type they are.

Well, start by thinking about position. What position are you in? Sitting probably, but on something, a chair, a settee, perhaps a table or a bed, or standing, perhaps, in a bookshop or at a bus stop. There may be someone sitting next to you, or beside you, and the lamp above you may be a good one, but not as good as the one which is throwing light through the doorway, over there where your friend is leaning against the wall waiting for you to go down the road to the pub.

Next we have:

> **Conjunctions** – join words and groups of words.

Read this next paragraph **aloud**.

I dreamt once that ice cream tasted of fried tomatoes. This had a devastating effect on me. For months afterwards I was unable to eat the stuff. Eventually I had to force myself to buy an ice cream to break the dream. Then I returned enthusiastically to Rossi's ice cream parlour. Rossi's had been my favourite maker of ice cream for years.

We can improve things:

I dreamt once that ice cream tasted of fried tomatoes and this had a devastating effect on me. For months afterwards I was unable to eat the stuff so, eventually, I had to force myself to buy an ice cream to break the dream. Then I returned enthusiastically to Rossi's ice cream parlour because Rossi's had been my favourite for years and I no longer dreaded eating ice cream.

Three words, ***and***, ***so*** and ***because***, make this passage easier to read. The first two sentences are simple statements of fact and we can absorb them more quickly once they are linked by *and*, and we no longer have to pause after the word *tomatoes*. *So* links two sentences in which the action in the second sentence follows from the (grammatical) action in the first. In the third pair, *because* links the action in the first part of the sentence with the reason for that action, which we find in the second part of the sentence; because Rossi's had been my favourite ice cream parlour I had returned there. Like prepositions, conjunctions provide easier reading.

In this second version, separate sentences, which stand alone at first, are combined.

Just remember that *and* is also used to join the last two items in a list. As we read, it signals the end of the list and we are ready to stop. Read the rest of this sentence **aloud**; so far we have tackled nouns, adjectives, adverbs, verbs, pronouns, prepositions *and* conjunctions.

Conjunctions done.

Articles – so easy that some languages don't bother with them.

We have touched already on the business of articles in the introduction so all we have to do now is make sure that we have dealt with all four of them: *a*, *an*, *some* and *the*. Articles precede nouns to indicate whether particular things are being referred to or not.

I am afraid that you are due in court again.

A court official holds up *a* large, old-fashioned feather duster.

"Is this," asks the judge, "is this *the* feather duster you kept at home and which, the prosecution claims, was used by you to attack the prime minister?"

You are relieved for it is simply *a* feather duster and not your old feather duster which had a green handle, not a red one, and you explain that *the* feather duster which you kept under the stairs at your home was destroyed at a fancy-dress party weeks before the alleged attack. Wonderful – you're not guilty. They can't touch you. As the judge dismisses the case *some* police officers enter the court. That's all right – they're just coppers. Then you notice that among them are *the* officers who you attacked with a banana the night you were arrested in Downing Street, outside the prime minister's home.

The, the definite article which refers to particular things, *the* feather duster with the red or green handle, or *the* particular police officers who you did not want to meet again.

The indefinite articles: *a* indicates here any feather duster which is not yours and *some* any police officers who were not attacked by you when you were armed with a banana in Downing Street.

(*An* is simply used instead of *a* when the word that follows begins with one of the five vowels. Try saying *a orange*. The word comes from the Spanish, *naranja*, so perhaps we should say, *a norange*. You can imagine somebody in the market: "*Lovely noranges. Four for a quid!*")

For you it was important to convince the court that *the* feather duster shown in evidence was not *the* feather duster which lived under your stairs. As you leave the court you will probably take care to avoid any police officers, especially *the* officers who you met in Downing Street that night.

Case dismissed. And finally—

Exclamations, interjections and swear words – reactions to things.

Exclamations, interjections, reactions to things, that sound like words.

This section contains words and expressions that we often hear and see but which some of us dislike.

They are part of the language, even if we only notice them, uncontrolled, in public places. It is a fact that some people express themselves excessively in language which other people find coarse or foul, or blasphemous, but these are words and the way they are used needs to be understood as part of an examination of our language.

To do this we need to refer to these words, even if we do not use them. Think of them clinically, like a disease if you like, that we need to study, however unpleasant it may be.

"Oh, shit!"

You have stepped backwards into the wet concrete that you have just laid and staggered all over it. The footprints that you have left behind laugh at you and so do your mates. Or, you have just realised that you have left the keys inside the car which you locked before you shut the rear door. Sometimes it is different, quicker.

"Shit!"

An own goal in extra time, or the slipping of a sharp knife in the kitchen.

Links between words and meanings are not always fixed, and a dictionary will tell of *shit's* basic meaning – *excrement*. (*Poo* in baby vocabulary or *turds* if you don't want to sound posh.) The word *shit* is more often met in speech, where there is greater flexibility, rather than in writing. In speech it is rarely used to stand for excrement.

"Look at all that shit."

Here the word is obviously a noun, standing for something, but what? A pile of manure, a place full of rubbish or something we don't like? Then try:

"That was a shit goal."

A sports fan suffers disappointment and uses the word as a sort of adjective, but it tells us little about the goal, whether it was easy, or the result of a mistake. All we know is that for some reason that is not clear to us, the speaker was not impressed with this goal.

"Oh, shit! They missed."

Here the word is nothing to do with them or what they missed; it's simply a reaction to the fact that they missed.

Like *indeed, damn, really* or *God*, the word has a meaning, something to which it refers. Later I will return to the origin and influence of words such as these. But for the moment it is sufficient to recognise that here they are simply used as a reaction to something and we call them **exclamations**, words that are called out in reaction to something. (Latin: *ex = out* and *clamo = I call.* Our modern *clamour = a lot of noisy calling out.*)

Interjections are sounds or words that are thrown in between "real" words. Imagine that you are in very serious trouble. You are very young and very keen not to be caught out. This could so easily have been two of us at school, playing firemen in the boys' toilet which had no roof, at the age of five. Soon we found ourselves outside the headmistress's office while she spoke to an angry woman who had been showered as she walked along the pavement outside. You struggle to explain and there is a loud, *Hmmmm,* from one of the adults and you realise that you are simply digging yourself into deeper trouble. (*Hmmmm* – a warning that someone does not believe you and that you might as well own up straight away and save everyone a lot of time.)

Er, a good one for really awkward questions and direct accusations, *Oooh,* for a large bill and a really well-timed coughing fit can of course bring a difficult conversation to a complete halt.

Just before you move on – **determiners**.

You may come across this word in connection with parts of speech. Simply be aware that a determiner is a word which indicates which person or object, or the number of people or objects, to which someone is referring. Think of them as working like adjectives, telling us more about something.

e.g. <u>That</u> book, <u>my</u> book, <u>each</u> book, <u>which</u> book, <u>three</u> books.

ANSWERS TO THE QUESTIONS IN CHAPTER ONE

EXERCISE ONE

1.

    a.   Aeroplanes (common).

    b.   Aeroplanes, items (both common).

    c.   Fleets (collective), aeroplanes (common).

    d.   British Airways (proper), shares (common).

    e.   British Airways (proper), efficiency (abstract).

3.

    a.   Cows (common), grass (common).

    b.   Teachers, music, sentence, mnemonic, pupils, notes, lines, music (all common).

    c.   Players, band, melody, harmony, rhythm, result, (all common except enjoyment and chaos which are abstract).

EXERCISE TWO

1.

    a.   Impressive.

    b.   Wooden.

    c.   Expensive.

    d.   Grey.

    e.   Curly.

2.

    a.   Best – *a superlative – better than anything else*. Expensive.

    b.   All – *number – every one*. Wooden.

    c.   Future, difficult.

    d.   Cheap, dear.

e. Praised, their – *a possessive adjective which tells us whose efficiency is involved.*

EXERCISE THREE

a. (What is he told to do?) <u>Fill</u> the kettle, <u>switch</u> it on, <u>put</u> a teabag in a mug or a cup, <u>pour</u> the boiling water into the mug, <u>leave</u> it for two minutes, <u>remove</u> the teabag, <u>stir</u> in milk, and sugar if required.

b. (What does he do?) He <u>fills</u> the kettle, <u>switches</u> it on, <u>puts</u> a teabag in a mug, <u>pours</u> the boiling water into the mug, <u>leaves</u> it for two minutes, <u>removes</u> the teabag, <u>stirs</u> in milk and <u>adds</u> sugar if required.

c. (What did he do?) He <u>filled</u> the kettle, <u>switched</u> it on, <u>put</u> a teabag in a mug, <u>poured</u> the boiling water into the mug, <u>left</u> it for two minutes, <u>removed</u> the teabag, <u>stirred</u> in milk and <u>added</u> sugar if required.

EXERCISE FOUR

a. Was – indicates an action in the past.

b. Don't (do not) – negates the verb – smiling is something they do not do.

c. Couldn't (could not) – indicates an inability to do something in the past. He may be able to do it now. (Can you see how I have used a similar construction here to explain the answer? *May* indicates the possibility that he can wait now.)

d. Might have – indicates a possibility in the past.

e. Can – indicates an ability in the present. Reversing the order of *Can* and *it*, the sentence is made into a question.

EXERCISE FIVE

1.

    a. *Slowly* – qualifies *limped.*

    b. *Cautiously* – qualifies *approached.*

    c. *Well* – qualifies *cooked.*

    d. *Carelessly* – qualifies *drove.*

e.   *Tenderly* – qualifies *picked up. Firmly* – qualifies *spread.*

2.

a.   *Very* – qualifies the adjective *expensive.*

b.   *Almost* – qualifies the adverb *completely* which qualifies the adjective *bald.*

c.   *Barely* – qualifies the verb *was breathing.*

d.   *Barely* – qualifies the adjective *alive.*

EXERCISE SIX

The additional pronouns are: *one* (also functions as a noun and as an adjective), you, that (in *that's*) and *those. That* and *those* both refer to ice creams.

EXERCISE SEVEN

by	links the verb *start* with *thinking*
about	links the verb *thinking* with the noun *position*
in	links the verb *are* with the noun *position*
on	links the pronoun *you* (implied, from the previous sentence) to the pronoun *something* (location)
in	links *you* (the same *you*) to *bookshop*
at	links *you* to *bus stop* (location)
next to	links *you* to *someone* (location)
beside	links *you* to *someone* (location)
above	links *lamp* to *you* (location)
through	links the verb *is throwing* with the noun *doorway* (movement)
over	links the lamp which is throwing light – with the pronoun *there* – the place where your friend is leaning (location)
against	links *is leaning* with *the wall* (location)
down	links *to go* with *the road* (Here, think of *down* as meaning *along.*) (movement)
to	links *to go* with *the pub* (movement)

Well Done

Now, a final reminder – **nouns** name things, **adjectives** qualify nouns, **verbs** indicate the "action", the heart of a sentence, **adverbs** qualify verbs and adjectives, **pronouns** stand in for nouns, **prepositions** link nouns, or nouns and verbs, **conjunctions** join words and groups of words, and **articles** make clear the identity of things.

There are also **interjections** and **swear words**, and we will return to them later with **oaths** as well.

Next – words in groups – how words work together.

CHAPTER TWO

WORDS AND
THEIR WORK – 2

How words become phrases, clauses and sentences.
How we pick up words – learning from reading.

Before we look at the way phrases, clauses and sentences are formed we should look at the way words can connect themselves to each other. We know instinctively that some words go together: *Manchester United, fast food, best friend*. Others make no sense like this: *blue wide, bucket whistle, vanilla coal.*

When we assemble or construct a machine or a piece of equipment it helps to know how the components fit together. Words are not as easy to control. Sometimes they have a life of their own and one word or a phrase leads on to another.

Parsing – a job for every word.

Parsing is a way of checking that each word has a job to do and helps us to see how the components of language work together. Later, this will help us when we are writing.

Look at these examples:

1. My friend always smiles.

My – possessive adjective, qualifying *friend.*
friend – noun, subject of the verb *smiles* – tells us who is smiling.
always – adverb, modifying the verb, *smiles.*
smiles – verb, the action of the sentence.

2. Children play in the garden.

Children – noun – subject of the verb *play.*
play – verb, the action of the sentence.
in – preposition – links the action, *play,* with the location, *the garden.*
the – definite article, governing *garden* – it is a particular garden.
garden – noun, linked to the action, *play,* by *in.*

3. She sings well.

She – pronoun – stands for a female who is the subject of the verb *sings.*
sings – verb, the action of the sentence.
well – adverb, modifies the verb, *sings.*

EXERCISE EIGHT

Parse these sentences in the same way as the examples above.

1. They bribed a teacher.
2. The teacher was afraid.
3. The teacher's lawyer met them outside the classroom.

We started the first chapter with the question about how long a sentence can be. Now we need to ask what it is that makes up a sentence and why this is so very important. Once you have understood this section you will be well on the way to getting to grips with written English. The sentence is the key thing to master, even if you have to tackle this chapter more than once to do so.

> **Words become phrases, clauses and
> sentences and then mean something.**

You want to write a script, tell a story, provide a written statement for a court or describe something you have seen on television.

Look at this list of ideas which have just occurred to you:

1. *Doors*
2. *reinforced with large iron bolts*
3. *standing in the way*
4. *opened*

Look at this list of components which have just been delivered:

1. Noun – *Doors*
2. Phrase – *reinforced with large iron bolts*
3. Clause – *that stood in the way*
4. Verb – *opened*

Delivered, not in a white van, but by your imagination.

Somehow, they have arrived in your head and you want to assemble them, to compose a sentence so that you can show how these four ideas fit together, just like the components of a car, assembled so that the car will go. (One wheel at each corner for preference.)

Now look at what you have put together:

**Doors reinforced with large iron bolts,
that stood in the way, opened.** (Challenging you.)

Don't tell me, you're not very happy with this version. Would one of these be better?

**Doors that stood in the way, reinforced
with iron bolts, opened.** (Resisting you.)

or

**Doors standing in the way, that had been reinforced
with iron bolts, opened.** (Made to resist you.)

or

**Doors opened, doors that stood in the way reinforced
with iron bolts.** (Challenging and resisting you.)

or

**Doors opened, doors reinforced with iron bolts that
had been standing in the way.** (No longer obstructing you.)

We could go on. It would be interesting to see just how many different combinations of these words, phrases and clauses we could write, each with a slightly different emphasis or effect.

Suddenly then there is the screech of tyres outside; it's a special delivery, another word, an adverb this time.

There

And we're off again:

**There, doors that had stood in the way,
reinforced with iron bolts, opened.**

We were lucky to get out, weren't we? Just one extra word, *there*, and we can step back, like an artist, to see ourselves escape.

A sentence – two items joined by a verb.

THE BASIC SENTENCE

In a sense you have been bounced into discussing sentences without first deciding just what makes a basic sentence. Here is a simple demonstration.

If you have ever had to read to young children you will have noticed the simple, repetitive nature of sentences such as:

Noddy saw Big Ears.

There is a simple pattern; what is the sentence about? **Noddy**.

What are we told about Noddy? **He saw Big Ears.**

Whatever you add to a sentence it is assembled around this basic pattern: and we know which bit is which because of the order in which we meet the words. We cannot change the order of the words in this sentence – go on then, you try it. The best you will get is **Big Ears saw Noddy**, which is not the same.

> On the sat porch the dog.
>
> The porch sat on the dog.
>
> The dog sat on the porch.

In English we can add as much or as little information to a sentence as we want, so long as we place it carefully:

Big Ears saw Noddy clearly, or *Clearly, Big Ears saw Noddy,* or *Big Ears clearly saw Noddy.*

We can add to this growing sentence:

Big Ears, who had been busy all morning, clearly saw his best friend Noddy coming towards him with two enormous ice creams.

Five additional pieces of information, all built around the verb *saw*.

Now you try it. Take these short sentences and add more ideas to them. See how long a sentence you can build up.

She held him tight. (Where? How? Why? When?)
She dropped him.
He held her tight.
He ran away.

And now, to squeeze even more out of this bit of learning.

In other languages, such as Latin and German, word endings provide important information. In Latin – another free lesson here – *Taurus puerum fugavit* means the same as *Puerum fugavit taurus* or *Fugavit puerum taurus*. It doesn't matter whereabouts in the sentence the words are found, the meaning of the sentence is unchanged; **the bull chased the boy**.

However, if we change the ends of the words, if *taurus* becomes *taurum* and *puerum* becomes *puer* then *taurum puer fugavit* will mean, **the boy chased the bull**, not **the bull chased the boy**.

These Latin words each has its place in modern English:

Taurus – the sign of the Zodiac, the bull.
fugitive – someone who runs away and
puerile – childish, like a small boy.

Two explanations before we continue
How we learn to use our language.
Don't panic about grammar.

LEARNING AND HABITS

You might be wondering how on earth we make these choices, choosing different words and phrases, putting words in a different order. Well, we have been doing it ever since we started to speak, usually between the ages of one and two. It occurs naturally, so long as we can hear others speak, and becomes automatic.

Reading and writing have to be cultivated – encouraged, explained and sometimes imposed. They have to be learnt and become automatic through repetition, so they become mental habits, so that we can choose our words while we are also doing other things.

Things like walking and talking. Watch a baby learning either one of these – they struggle and concentrate, just as we probably did when we learnt to ride a bike. Once we have learnt to do these routine things they become automatic and then we talk to the people walking alongside us without having to think about the words we need. Those of you who are old enough will remember those tense moments when you start learning to drive. Now you start the engine and drive off without a moment's thought.

PROGRESS AND REASSURANCE

Do you have any idea how much progress you are making?

We are touching on later work, even before we finish with words working together. We are looking at the construction of sentences and the effect of setting out our words in one way or another.

Just as we cannot fix a spark plug to a piston – you can see four pistons in the second picture in the introduction – so we cannot put words together randomly if we want to make sense.

Bolts doors had in iron opened reinforced stood that the way with

These are the twelve words that we have just been using, in various orders and with different effects. Listing them alphabetically like this is to ignore the rules of English grammar. There, I have used the word "grammar", that is supposed to frighten some people. Say it, **aloud**!

GRAMMAR GRAMMAR GRAMMAR GRAMMAR GRAMMAR.

Grammar is simply the way that we know which words can work together and which cannot. You know this already and that is why you cannot make sense of:

Bolts doors had in iron opened reinforced stood that the way with

But you can make sense of:

Doors that had stood in the way, reinforced with iron bolts, opened.

In Chapter Fourteen the idea of the rules behind all this will be explained but, for the moment, you can rest assured that you already have the programs installed and working in your head. Later we will open up your properties page so that you can understand these rules more fully.

Career moves – words that change their jobs.

As you have seen, engine components cannot change jobs. Words are more interesting because they do change, and phrases, clauses and sentences will also change in ways that engine components cannot.
Look at what happens to *that* and *fair*.

> *That teacher is a fair one who always listens to her students. This means that when they are in trouble she always judges them fairly.*
>
> *The students who she particularly wants to help are those who are fairly hopeless. That is why she is popular.*

That (demonstrative adjective) *teacher is a* **fair** (adjective) *one who always listens to her students.*

This means **that** (conjunction) *when they are in trouble she always judges them* **fairly** (adverb – modifying judges).

The students whom she particularly wants to help are those who are **fairly** (adverb – modifying hopeless) *hopeless.*

That (demonstrative pronoun referring back to all the information about her) *is why she is popular.*

Similarly, phrases, clauses and sentences change, just like the doors with iron bolts through which you escaped just now.

> Don't read these words in silence.
>
> # Read them aloud.
>
> Remember, we first learn our language by listening to it, not by reading it in silence.

Sometimes I would write long strings of words on the board to catch out my classes.

> *While it was still raining and the flood water was surrounding the police car, and the policemen were struggling to keep their socks dry.*

Is this a sentence? I would ask. If they answered yes, I would ask another question – typical teacher – you answer one question so they ask you another one. If this is a sentence, I would ask, which is **the main verb**?

> **Main verbs and subordinate verbs.**
> Action words – foundations for sentences.

I am sure that you can identify the three verbs here: *was (still) raining, was surrounding* and *were struggling.* But you will not be able to specify one verb that is more important than the others. If my students were unsure, I would allow them to alter this string of words if that helped them to understand this point.

Some of them would simply remove just one word – *and.* Then the sentence would be properly assembled and could work:

> *While it was still raining and the flood water was surrounding the police car, ~~and~~ the policemen were struggling to keep their socks dry.*

Then it becomes clear that the main verb, the most significant idea, is that the policemen were struggling to keep their socks dry. The key thing is that the actions of *raining* and *surrounding* are controlled by the word ***while***, which is a <u>subordinating conjunction</u> and joins verbs of lesser importance to the main one: *struggling to keep (their socks) dry.*

With the removal of *and*, the idea of struggling is no longer subordinated by *while*. Put it another way:

> *The policemen were struggling to keep their socks dry while it was still raining and while the water was surrounding the police car.*

Some students would remove *and*, then play around with *while*, and we would get sentences such as:

> *While the flood water was surrounding the police car and the policemen were struggling to keep their socks dry, it was still raining.*

Here the word *while* subordinates the ideas of surrounding and struggling, instead of raining, and this sentence has a different main verb, and our attention is drawn more strongly to the fact that it is still raining.
What about this response?

> *It was still raining and the flood water was surrounding the police car while the policemen were struggling to keep their socks dry.*

This answer is one of those delightful ones that can catch out teachers because it goes a bit further along the path of learning all in one go. Here we are faced with two main verbs in one sentence (*was raining* and *was surrounding*), and only one verb, *were struggling*, that is subordinated. Here the word *and* is a **coordinating conjunction** and links the main clauses of the sentence each of which has a main verb.

Other students might provide a version like this:

While it was still raining and the flood water was surrounding the police car and the policemen were struggling to keep their socks dry, Father Christmas arrived.

Please don't ask me why Father Christmas should turn up just now. I'm not interested in the possibility of his reindeer pulling the police car out of the river, or of his bringing the officers dry socks in his sack of presents. The important thing is that he arrived and *arrived* is not subordinated like the other verbs in the sentence. It is the main verb.

In the classroom I would now invite my students to write long and complicated sentences about policemen, or parents or neighbours or traffic wardens or anybody who annoys them, so that they could feel the pull and power of main verbs. Something like:

While [Insert a sentence here.] and [Insert a sentence here.] and although [Insert a sentence here.] the head teacher/magistrate/prime minister/ newsreader/pilot/our granny [Complete a sentence here.].

You might end up with something like this.

While it was snowing outside and his mobile continued to demand his attention, and although he could not find his boots, Father Christmas, who did not like his toes to get cold, set off.

And of course you will have spotted the main verb, the last one of five: *set off.*

Assembling words – longer sentences.

Now I would like you to look at two sentences that I expand from small simple sentences into something more complicated. This will help you focus on the main verbs which are the key to all this. The point is that, however complicated the sentence, it must have a main verb somewhere.

The cat sat on the mat.

While it was raining outside the cat sat on the mat.

Although it preferred to be out in the garden first thing, while it was raining outside the cat sat on the mat.

Although it preferred to be out in the garden first thing, while it was raining outside the cat sat on the mat, which needed cleaning.

Although it preferred to be out in the garden first thing, while it was raining outside the cat sat on the mat, which needed cleaning, and read the paper.

I could go on! At each stage the main verb, the grammatical action, remains unchanged. Whatever else we are told, the cat sat on the mat. As we progress, we learn about the weather, the cat's preference for being out of doors, the condition of the mat and then we are told what else the cat is doing, and of course we have a second main verb. What did the cat do? It **sat** on the mat and **read** the paper. **And,** you will remember, is a coordinating conjunction and simply joins two sentences: **The cat sat on the mat** and **(The cat) read the paper**. (Subordinating conjunctions such as **while** and **although** also join sentences but make one sentence more important than the other.)

Then, if you are really clever, you will have noticed that the information about the mat is added in a different way from the information about the weather and the cat's preference for the outdoors: **which needed cleaning**. There is no subordinating conjunction here.

The idea of the mat is already in the sentence, it's what the cat is sitting on. To add information that relates to the mat, the word **which** provides the link to the words, **needed cleaning**. Now ask yourself, what was it that needed cleaning? The mat. We could add this information, about the mat needing cleaning, in a separate sentence and we would end up with something like this:

Although it preferred to be out in the garden first thing, while it was raining outside the cat sat on the mat, and read the paper. The mat needed cleaning.

Now go back and read the last sentence **aloud**. That's right – you do remember. The ideas do not follow smoothly here and our attention has to be drawn back to the mat in a second sentence and the wretched mat seems far more important than it really is.

Although it preferred to be out in the garden first thing, while it was raining outside the cat sat on the mat, which needed cleaning, and read the paper.

In this second version, the information about the mat is tucked in neatly so that we know that something more important is still to come; what could be more important than the cat reading the paper. **Which** is a relative pronoun and replaces **the mat** in the first version of this sentence. In the second version, **which** allows us to relate the information, that it needed cleaning, to the mat without having to set up a separate sentence to do so.

Who also functions as a relative pronoun and we can use it in a similar way.

Although she had a pile of marking to finish, the teacher, who was very thirsty, found herself in her favourite bar.

Who introduces the additional information that the poor girl was thirsty, and inserts it neatly into the sentence so that we feel sorry for her and don't ask questions about just when she is going to get round to marking our homework.

And now some exercises so that you can feel confident that you have mastered this section, one of the most important in this book. For once I feel at a disadvantage here because I can't keep you behind after school until you understand all this completely. So, stick at these four pages until you know that you can identify the main verb(s) in any sentence you encounter.

EXERCISE NINE

A number of sentences follow, of increasing complexity. Identify the main verb(s) in each one. Check your answers to make sure that you really have understood this section before going on to the next one.

a. This is easy.
b. All the cows in this particular field eat grass.
c. Because this is the third question it must be answered.
d. Despite the fact that we use our language every day, we can find that it is difficult to analyse.

e.   We realised that the old man next door only took his dog out for a walk when it was sunny because he had lost his umbrella along with his false teeth and his memory.

f.   However much she glared at him and stamped her foot her uncle simply smiled at her, picked her up with an enormous hand and dropped her over the side of the pier.

Another way to look at sentences

In this next section we are going to look at sentences in a very different way, through the other end of the telescope if you like, so take a deep breath. So far we have been looking for main verbs because I have told you that every sentence has at least one. You might have sneaked a look at a dictionary and found definitions of the word *sentence*, and you might have discovered that some definitions of the word *sentence* say little or nothing about main verbs. Don't even say it, but I know what you are thinking – doesn't know what he's talking about. Well, just have faith, boys and girls, just for a little bit longer. A lone voice calls from the back of the class.

"Please, sir, my granny says that sentences begin with a capital letter and finish with a full stop. That's how you can tell whether it's a sentence."

What, I ask myself, is the penalty for grannicide?

The dreaded word, Punctuation

I have only mentioned it once so far in this book and I will delay using it as long as I can. You will realise possibly that I am actually using the stuff all the time. There, I'm using it again right here – fifteen times in three sentences.

I promise to deal with punctuation and grammar later when you have got a secure idea about sentences. Remember, we have to be able to use the language sensibly and manageably while at the same time we are taking it to pieces. It was easy with that old Ford car; while it was in bits I knew that I could not use it. For us things are different; we have to continue talking even while the phrases, clauses and sentences which we use to analyse our language lie scattered around us.

> **Phrases and clauses** – components of sentences.

So we are no longer looking for main verbs, but we can look again at the sentences in Exercise Nine:

a. This is easy.
b. All the cows in this particular field eat grass.
c. Because this is the third question it must be answered.
d. Despite the fact that we use our language every day, we can find that it is difficult to analyse.
e. We realised that the old man next door only took his dog out for a walk when it was sunny because he had lost his umbrella along with his false teeth and his memory.
f. However much she glared at him and stamped her foot her uncle simply smiled at her, picked her up with an enormous hand and dropped her over the side of the pier.

a. This is a very simple sentence; a demonstrative pronoun, a verb and an adjective. We are told what the sentence is about; it's about whatever *this* refers to, perhaps the exercise itself. Then the adjective *easy* conveys something about *this*. The verb, *is*, links the two.
b. Another fairly simple sentence – which cows eat grass? All the cows in this particular field, every one of them, that's what the adjective *all* tells us. What else do we learn about the cows? We are told where they are, not with one word, but with several, *in this particular field*. None of these words can function here alone.

However, a preposition, *in*, a demonstrative adjective, *this*, an adjective, *particular*, and a noun, *field*, together provide information. We speak of them as **a phrase, a group of words that does not contain a finite verb**. This particular phrase does the work of an adjective so it's called ***an adjectival phrase***. It qualifies the noun ***cows***, and tells where they are to be found.

And it's part of a longer phrase which forms the answer to the question, *which cows eat grass?* This **phrase**, *All the cows in this particular field*, is followed by a verb, which tells us what they are doing and a noun which tells us what it is they are eating.

What do these cows eat? *Grass*, a noun. Do we learn anything more about their eating? No. Nothing more.

A phrase – words working together without a finite verb.

Where? – **in the mud.**
What? – **grass, a cow's natural food.**
When? – **after five o'clock.**

---

c. *Because this is the third question it must be answered.*

Two finite verbs, *is* and *must be*, joined by *because*, a subordinating conjunction. You should also be able to find – not in this particular order because I don't want to make things too easy for you – a pronoun, the definite article, a numerical adjective, a noun, a demonstrative pronoun and a verbal adjective (an adjective formed from a verb).

Now, a very important, crucial step. Can we divide this sentence into sections that make sense on their own? Yes. *It must be answered* could stand alone as a separate sentence. So would *this is the third question*, but it is preceded by *because* which changes it, makes it less important, subordinate.

Because this is the third question; if this is not a sentence, what is it? It's like a phrase, a group of words that function together, but it contains a finite verb, *is*. It is a ***clause***, a group of words that contains a finite verb, but is not a sentence because it cannot make sense alone. It is **a *subordinate clause***. The ***subordinating conjunction***, *because*, joins it to the **main clause** *It must be answered*.

We are making progress. Now we are just going to look for clauses and phrases in the last three sentences from Exercise Nine.

d.   *Despite the fact that we use our language every day, we can find that it is difficult to analyse.*

This sentence is very similar to the previous one in c. There is **a subordinate clause**, *Despite the...*, **and a main clause**, *we can...* At the end of this sentence, however, there is not an adjective, *answered*, but **an adjectival phrase**, *difficult to analyse.*

e.   *We realised that the old man next door only took his dog out for a walk when it was sunny because he had lost his umbrella along with his false teeth and his memory.* Three clauses. No, it's your turn to do some work; identify **two subordinate clauses and one main clause**. Close your eyes now if you don't want to see any clues. (When did he go out? Why did he go out?)

Then answer the following questions: Who took his dog out? Why, for what purpose, did he take it out? What had he lost?

You have now discovered **a noun phrase**, *the old man...*, **an adverbial phrase**, *for a walk*, and **another noun phrase**, *his umbrella...* Well done!

f.   *However much she glared at him and stamped her foot, her uncle simply smiled at her, picked her up with an enormous hand and dropped her over the side of the pier.*

Don't tell me, you're getting the hang of this now; **three main verbs/two subordinate clauses**. But what makes the first two clauses the subordinate ones? The word *because* would have done it. So would *while*. Here we find **However much** which subordinates two verbs, *glared* and *stamped*.

Two more phrases and we've finished. How did her uncle pick her up? Where did he drop her? (Adverbial phrases that qualify *picked*, and *dropped*. These phrases tell us more about the manner in which he picked her up and where he dropped her.)

> ## A Clause
>
> Words working together with a finite verb but without forming a sentence.
>
> When did her uncle smile at her? – **once she had glared at him.**
>
> Why are you working so hard? – **because you want to improve your English.**

EXERCISE TEN

This is difficult. Try to identify phrases, subordinate clauses, main clauses and conjunctions in each of these sentences.

a. While it rained Charlie was looking for something to do.
b. On the other side of the road a girl appeared.
c. Before he could cross over to her a large 4x4 came round the corner.
d. With his eye on the girl over the road, Charlie, who always fancied his chances, challenged the 4x4 to a game of chicken by pretending to step into the road.
e. When he reached the girl she was staring past him so he turned round and saw the vehicle parked on top of a lamp-post which it had destroyed completely and utterly.
f. Charlie removed the earpieces of his iPod so that he could speak to the girl.
g. He was really eager to find out more about her, but, when he heard the voice of the driver of the 4x4, he looked round and noticed the man who waved at him in a manner that was very disturbing.
h. Tall, good-looking Charlie, who always showed off in front of girls and who enjoyed annoying adults, had got it wrong.

If this has not worked, send me an email: peter@peterinson.net, and tell me as best you can what you are finding difficult. If I can read your question like this I will have an idea of how I will need to reply.

This is as complicated as things will get in this section.

We are going to keep the sentence firmly in our sights for the rest of this chapter, but there should be a sense now that we are beginning to move along more easily. In front of us lie two other ways of looking at sentences which you will find easier because we have built your understanding on the words that we use and the way we group them together to say whatever needs to be said.

> **Every sentence has two components – a subject and a predicate.**

First, what is a sentence about, what is the **subject** of a sentence? Then we look at what is said about the subject. This is the **predicate**.
Let's stick with something familiar.

a. While it rained Charlie was looking for something to do.

b. On the other side of the road a girl appeared.

c. Before he could cross over to her a large 4x4 came round the corner.

d. With his eye on the girl over the road, Charlie, who always fancied his chances, challenged the 4x4 to a game of chicken by pretending to step into the road.

e. When he reached the girl she was staring past him so he turned round and saw the vehicle parked on top of a lamp-post which it had destroyed completely and utterly.

f. Charlie removed the earpieces of his iPod so that he could speak to the girl.

g. He was really eager to find out more about her, but, when he heard the voice of the driver of the 4x4, Charlie looked round and noticed the man who waved at him in a manner that was disturbing.

h. Tall, good-looking Charlie, who always showed off in front of girls and who enjoyed annoying adults, had got it wrong.

You remember. Who or what is sentence a. about? It's about Charlie. What does it tell us about him? It tells us that he was looking for something to do. *Charlie* is the subject of the sentence and *was looking for something to do while it rained* is the predicate.

A girl is the subject of sentence b. and the predicate is *appeared on the other side of the road.*

Every word in a sentence is either part of the subject or the predicate; it is either part of what the sentence is about, the subject, or is helping to tell us something about the subject. **Each sentence has one subject and one predicate.**

This way of examining a sentence simply divides it in two and this will prove of importance in a later chapter when we want to concentrate on what is being said, rather than the mechanics of the words that are used.

For the remaining six sentences you will find the subjects in **bold** and the predicates in *italics.*

c. *Before he could cross over to her* **a large 4x4** *came round the corner.*
d. *With his eye on the girl over the road,* **Charlie, who always fancied his chances,** *challenged the 4x4 to a game of chicken by pretending to step into the road.*
e. *When he reached the girl she was staring past him so* **he** *turned round and saw the vehicle parked on top of a lamp-post which it had destroyed completely and utterly.*
f. **Charlie** *removed the earpieces of his iPod so that he could speak to the girl.*
g. **He** *was really eager to find out more about her, but, when he heard the voice of the driver of the 4x4, Charlie looked round and noticed the man who waved at him in a manner that was disturbing.*
h. **Tall, good-looking Charlie, who always showed off in front of girls and who enjoyed annoying adults,** *had got it wrong.*

One more exercise and then you will be given a break – you have been working very hard.

EXERCISE ELEVEN

Simply divide each sentence into subject and predicate.

a. Every one of the kids from Year Seven who bunked off her lessons was punished.

b. "Every single one of you silly little Year Seven girls will be punished," said the teacher.

c. Having set fire to the school office and tied up the head teacher, the mob made its way to the fitness hall where one of the teachers was holding up a white flag.

d. Although the caretaker could not stand children he allowed them to borrow his Alsatian to help control the teachers while they waited for the kids from the school down the road.

e. Unfortunately some spoil-sport phoned the RSPCA, who objected that the poor dog might find the company of teachers stressful and took him away for psychological counselling.

Sentences – all have a main verb. Some contain additional information in the form of clauses, groups of words that include finite verbs, and phrases which do not. All sentences can be divided into a subject and a predicate. The subject tells us what the sentence is about, and the predicate is what is said about the subject. Understanding this is important if we want to use the language well.

Earlier, someone's granny was reported as saying that a sentence is a group of words that begins with a capital letter and ends with a full stop. The trouble with this is that we need to know which groups of words form sentences before we can insert capitals and full stops. This is what we will tackle in the next chapter.

Later still, in another chapter, we will return to the sentence and look more closely at the way its constituent parts are assembled and the differing effects that can be achieved; the art of writing.

Learning from reading – make it easy for yourself.

Anxious parents once asked me to suggest a textbook that would help their son improve his written English. I pointed out that, just as listening is the way we learn to speak, so reading is the way we learn to write. We need to encounter spoken words and expressions many times before we speak them confidently. In the same way it is important to read as much possible to improve our writing.

Enrichment – a car engine has far fewer components than the language, probably no more than a hundred or so, and they have very fixed ways of fitting together. On the other hand our language has something like two hundred thousand words, many of which exchange roles, so the number of potential combinations is simply unbelievable. Our simple car engine can do only one simple thing, rotate, powerfully maybe, but that is all.

With words, we can ask questions, give instructions, tell lies, inspire other people, try out ideas, conspire, plot, motivate, calculate, describe, suggest, discuss, argue and flirt. Think of all the different things you might want to say and the different ways there are to say them.

> Get out of my way – right now!
>
> **or**
>
> If you could turn around and give me your attention I could show you how to move your trolley to one side so that I could get past you with my shopping and get home before my favourite television programme starts.

Start to assemble words, just a handful, or the three hundred or so that we find on a page of a book, and think of all the possible functions they could fulfil. Just think of the variety of sentences involving the door with the iron bolts. Just think of all the hinting, suggesting, instructing, describing, arguing, persuading that can be done with just a few hundred words.

We can begin to realise now why it is so important to know as many words as possible if we are to set out a recipe, describe a landscape, explain the economy or make clear the right and wrong ways of wiring a plug.

And it is not only the words themselves, the need for a varied vocabulary, but an appreciation of the variety of ways in which they can be assembled, the patterns of words that we need to encounter. **Look at the box above.**

And it is in the written form of the language that we find so much more variety and subtlety, because when we write we do so deliberately. When someone treads on our toes we say something very quickly. Later we can sit down and write a note explaining how badly our toe hurts and how cross we are that someone could be so careless.

When we apply for a job or a place at college or university we are expected to take some time to think about the really important things that we want to say about ourselves. Similarly, if we are interviewed about an accident that we have witnessed it helps if we think carefully about what we are going to say before it is set out in a permanent, written form that can be used over and over again.

Just us we pick up the spoken language with our ears, so much about written English is learnt by reading it and by examining it and thinking about it. Then we can understand it better and use it more effectively.

Assembling the Components of Our Language

Listen to a deaf person speak and you will be aware that they cannot speak as easily as the rest of us; they cannot compare the sounds that they make with the sounds that the rest of us make. Babies hear words thousands and thousands of times, and understand them, long before they try to make the sounds themselves. Spoken English words have to be learnt by listening first, thousands and thousands of times.

This is how we assemble our language, the stock of words that each of us has taken in and can use, sometimes very individually. These words become our personal repertoires and sometimes they become very familiar in catch-phrases such as: *Nice to see you, to see you nice.*

Once we can read, our repertoire can grow faster as we have access to more words, phrases and expressions as well as more ways of arranging words. **So long as we continue to read.**

These days there are many distractions to lure us away from reading: television, social media and electronic games, for example. Those of us who are not habitual readers need to discipline ourselves to read regularly. We should simply force ourselves to read for ten minutes every day as a minimum. The aim should be to catch the habit and read more and more. The other important part of this is the quality of the material that we read.

There is little point in reading the simplistic language of parts of the popular press, for example. This requires only the reading ability of a young child; we should move on. Whether we read fiction or non-fiction we should look for some sort of assurance about its quality, a well-established title or a well-regarded author, a classic perhaps. One of my favourites is the opening of Charles Dickens' *Great Expectations;* try reading it aloud.

Any hobby or interest has its books, magazines, periodicals and journals, many online. You can find dozens of them especially in the larger newsagents. So long as the pages are not simply full of pictures and large headlines they can provide good reading material that will improve your English.

Not to read is to force on yourself a kind of blindness, cutting yourself off from the written language just as deafness cuts people off from what other people are saying. Not reading is self-harming.

Speaking and Listening

If you are going to take a speaking and listening test you should read this.

- Remember, we learn to listen before we learn to speak.
- Practise listening, to entertainers, comedians, newsreaders and politicians, especially on the radio. When you can hear other people's conversations on public transport, for example, try to work out what is really important for the speakers. If the speaker is using a mobile phone see if you can imagine the beginning of a short story.
- Listen to ordinary conversations and to speeches.
- Practise listening to work out just what someone is really saying; if you can, listen with a friend and discuss together what you hear.
- Spotting what someone is really saying is similar to identifying the main

point of a written sentence; look again at the section in Chapter Two about subjects and predicates.

- Try to list the verbs used in the sentences to which you listen.
- Listen to the conversations on BBC Radio 4's *Desert Island Discs* and try following Radio 4's *Just a Minute* in which well-known contestants pick holes in each other's speeches. I have used this format in schools, as "Just half a minute", and it was hugely successful. My students laughed more then than they did in any other lessons of mine.
- When you have to speak, more formally perhaps, as part of an exam assessment, make and use very brief notes as a reminder.
- Don't rush – take more time and allow your listener more time.
- Practise with a friend or tutor if you can.
- When we speak aloud we require more breath, so try to breathe more deeply. This, too, will help you not to rush.
- Look up at your listener(s) from time to time and speak louder if they are not paying attention.

ANSWERS TO THE QUESTIONS IN CHAPTER TWO

EXERCISE EIGHT

1. They bribed a teacher.
   They – pronoun – subject of the verb, *bribed.*
   bribed – verb, action of the sentence.
   a – indefinite article – governing *teacher* – it is not a particular teacher.
   teacher – noun – object of the verb, *bribed.*

2. The teacher was afraid.
   The – definite article – governing *teacher* – it is a particular teacher, the one they had bribed.
   teacher – noun – subject of the verb – *was.*
   was – verb, action of the sentence.
   afraid – adjective, complement of the verb, *was.*

3. The teacher's lawyer met them outside the classroom.
   The – definite article – governing *teacher* – a particular teacher.
   teacher's – noun in the possessive form – qualifies *lawyer.*
   lawyer – noun – subject of the verb, *met.*
   met – verb, action of the sentence.
   them – pronoun – object of the verb, *met.*
   outside – preposition – links the verb, *met*, with *the classroom.*
   the – definite article – governing *classroom* – it is a particular classroom.
   classroom – noun, subject of the preposition, *outside.*

EXERCISE NINE

a. is.

b. eat.

c. must be answered. (Why must it be answered? Because it is the third question.)

d. can find. (*Can* is the auxiliary verb.)

e. realised. (What did we realise? That the old man next door only took his dog out for a walk when it was sunny because he had lost his umbrella along with his false teeth and his memory. Here the word *that* functions as a subordinating conjunction.)

f. smiled, picked (her) up, dropped her. Three main verbs here to emphasise the sense that, perhaps, she got what she deserved and that her uncle enjoyed providing her come-uppance.

EXERCISE TEN

Phrases <u>underlined</u>. Subordinate clauses in *italics*. Main clauses in **bold**. (Conjunctions in brackets.)

a. *While it rained* **Charlie was looking for** <u>something to do.</u>
Main verb – *was looking.*
Subordinate verb – *rained.*

b. <u>On the other side of the road</u> **a girl appeared.**
Main verb – *appeared.*

c. *Before he could cross over to her* <u>a large 4x4</u> **came round the corner.**
Main verb – *came.*
Subordinate verb – *could cross.*

d. <u>With his eye on the girl over the road</u> **Charlie,** *who always fancied his chances,* **challenged the 4x4 to a game of chicken** <u>by pretending to step into the road.</u>
Main verb – *challenged.*
Subordinate verb – *fancied.*

e. *(When) he reached the girl she was staring past him* **(so) he turned round (and) saw the vehicle parked** <u>on top of a lamp-post</u> *(which) it had destroyed* <u>completely and utterly.</u>
Main verbs – turned, saw.

Subordinate verbs – reached, was staring, had destroyed.

N.B. *parked* is a verbal adjective, an adjective formed from a verb.

f. **Charlie removed** <u>the earpieces of his iPod (</u>so that*) he could speak to the girl.*
Main verb – *removed.*
Subordinate verb – *could speak.*

g. **Charlie was really** <u>eager to find out more about her</u> **(but),** *(when) he heard*
<u>the voice of the driver of the 4x4,</u> **he looked round and noticed the man**
(who) waved at him <u>in a manner that was very disturbing.</u>
Main verbs – *was, looked, noticed.*
Subordinate verbs – *heard, waved, was.*

h. **Tall,** <u>good-looking</u> **Charlie,** *who always showed off* <u>in front of girls *(and)*</u>
who enjoyed <u>annoying adults,</u> **had got it wrong.**
Main verb – *had got.*
Subordinate verbs – *showed, enjoyed.*

EXERCISE ELEVEN

a. **Every one of the kids from Year Seven who bunked off her lessons** was
punished.

b. *"Every single one of you silly little Year Seven girls will be punished,"* said **the**
teacher.

c. *Having set fire to the school office and tied up the head teacher,* **the mob** *made
its way to the fitness hall where one of the teachers was holding up a white flag.*

d. *Although the caretaker could not stand children* **he** *allowed them to borrow
his Alsatian to help control the teachers while they waited for the kids from the
school down the road.*

e. *Unfortunately* **some spoil-sport** *phoned the RSPCA, who objected that the
poor dog might find the company of teachers stressful and took him away for
psychological counselling.*

Well done

Words working together.

Next – Punctuation

The signs that guide us when we read, made clear.

CHAPTER THREE

PUNCTUATION – 1

Capital letters, full stops, question marks, exclamation marks, dashes, hyphens, colons, semi-colons, brackets and apostrophes. Commas will come later.

First, a quick punctuation check.

Try this first exercise. If you get it right, you could move straight on to Chapter Five where you will return to the sentence.

EXERCISE TWELVE

Write out the following passage with complete punctuation.

the party had started well but then the boat struck something there was a loud crash and a jolt and a number of people fell to the deck the boat is sinking a man said its time to get off what shall I do said the woman who had boasted about the cost of her outfit swim said the man another boat from the shore approached them help called the man theres someone here who cant swim

Here you needed to use capital letters, full stops, question marks, exclamation marks, commas, apostrophes and speech marks.

Capital letters mark the start of sentences.

Full stops, question marks and exclamation marks indicate the end of a sentence.

You must use them accurately.

To help my classes I used to read something aloud to them. Before I started I told them to clap as loudly as they could every time I reached the end of a sentence. Naturally, they tried to make as much noise as possible and soon found themselves clapping at the same time as everyone else, at the end of each sentence.

What I didn't tell them was that I simply getting them to listen attentively so that they responded accurately to words and sentences. Teaching can sometimes be fun.

Ah – the dreaded comma. I'm saving that for the next chapter.

Right now, but before we move on, it is worth reminding you **why controlling written sentences is so important**.

When we speak we usually have little trouble making ourselves understood. When we write we have to try harder to do this so that our readers feel confident about what we have written. We need to show that we are in control so that other people can understand us. When other people cannot speak to us, to ask us to explain ourselves, we must write carefully. When examiners and others find writing that is uncontrolled they naturally ask how well the writer understands whatever it is that they are writing about. This is why I ask you to try reading things **aloud**, especially things that you have written, because **it is the sound of the human voice that reveals most quickly the shortcomings in a piece of writing**.

Another way of looking at punctuation is to see it as good manners, or consideration for other people. If we are carrying something that is heavy or awkward and we meet somebody in a doorway who insists on coming through first we find it frustrating. We have to stand to one side, with a heavy load, while someone else squeezes past. These people rarely say thank you. On the other hand, if the other person stands to one side, we can continue to move forwards without any hesitation and the way is soon cleared for the other person. Like good manners, punctuation requires us to make an effort to make life easier for other people. Then they can read easily what we want to say to them which, surely, is to our own advantage.

An introduction to punctuation – try this.

Read the following passage **aloud**, as loudly as you can, as if hundreds of deaf people are sitting in front of you and are trying hard to hear what you are saying.

> *The party had started well but then the boat struck something. There was a loud crash and a jolt, and a number of people fell to the deck.*
> *"The boat is sinking," a man said. "It's time to get off."*
> *"What shall I do?" said the woman who had boasted about the cost of her outfit.*
> *"Swim," said the man. Another boat from the shore approached them.*
> *"Help!" called the man. "There's someone here who can't swim."*

Now let's try the original, unpunctuated version, from Exercise Twelve, and try to read it aloud.

> *the party had started well but then the boat struck something there was a loud crash and a jolt and a number of people fell to the deck the boat is sinking a man said its time to get off what shall I do said the woman who had boasted about the cost of her outfit swim said the man another boat from the shore approached them help called the man theres someone here who cant swim*

It's not easy but you can get a sense of how important it is to have punctuation guide us along the lines of words. Punctuation functions like signs and markings on the road. In my old Ford car it was difficult to break speed limits – there was no national limit then and, in any case, a very noisy sixty was the best of which she was capable. However, chevrons on sweeping bends were particularly helpful as the rear spring stretched from one side of the rear axle to the other and the car wallowed at times like a small boat in a rough sea. When I heeded these road signs my journey was much easier and more comfortable. Punctuation provides road signs for readers.

> **Punctuation – like road signs –**
> **guides to keep you on the road.**

Punctuation tells us how the writer intended us to stop, to pause, or to alter our voice somehow to convey the meaning. Remember that writing is something we leave behind, to convey something to someone else once we have gone. Because we will not be there when our message is received the other person will not be able to ask us to explain ourselves so we must set things down as clearly as possible.

Let's start with *capital letters*; Clear and Bold.

1. At the start of a sentence they proclaim another point that is being made, another idea that is being introduced.
2. In direct speech the first word that is spoken takes a capital letter: All he said was, "Try to remember this."
3. Proper nouns, the names of particular people and things, are capitalised: James Clark, Euston Station. Hang on, you will probably say, *station* is a common noun. You are quite right, but when common nouns become part of a title or proper noun, they are capitalised. Even the definite article, *the*, is capitalised: The Beatles.

That's it. Easy, wasn't it; no tests, no exercises. Just remember.

Now, *full stops*.

Their most important job is to tell us that we have reached the end of a sentence, that a particular piece of information, or an opinion, or an instruction is complete. Here we can pause, very briefly perhaps, to make sure that we have understood before we move on.

Stop. Stop at once. Stop or there'll be trouble. Stop here if you want an ice cream.

Question marks

Used to indicate the end of a direct question:
Do you like ice cream?
At the end of a question in direct speech:
"Do you like ice cream?" he asked. (Here one sentence, the question, is located inside another sentence.)
But not in reported speech:
He asked whether they liked ice cream. (Full stop.)

Exclamation marks!

Use sparingly. Used too often they lose their effect – like excessive swearing. When there is a real shock or surprise, when someone's breath has been taken away, then try one.
We were paid to eat ice cream!
"Go home!" said the teacher. "I've had enough of you."

EXERCISE THIRTEEN

Punctuate this passage.

at the gate he waited he was late and very impatient at last a man who was weighed down with chains approached him with a large and rusty key he smiled the man who had been waiting did not he watched the new arrival try to insert the key in the lock it would not turn the man tried a second and third time but without success from his pocket the man who had been waiting drew out a small can of lubricating oil and inserted it into the lock he squeezed the can firmly and the other man tried once again to turn the key this time there was the sound of grinding metal and soon the gate was open and both men could go on their way

A student once asked me how we manage to speak without punctuation when it's so difficult to read and write without it. It was one of the most intelligent questions I was ever been asked in a lesson. This was my answer.

We have already realised that speaking is the natural form of the language which we use to communicate without much thought, rather like breathing. We just do it as small babies, listening only at first and then trying out some words around the age of one year.

> **Voice** – changes naturally.
> **Writing** – visual clues needed.

Now then. Think of the different ways you can say the words, ***Look out***. Read out these lines **aloud**.

I want you to keep a good look out.
You want me to be the lookout? Not the driver? The lookout?
Look out! It's that crazy grandad on a mobility scooter.

You probably read the first example in a level way, without emphasising particular words, without putting any stress on them. The words simply inform you that that is what you are to do, to keep a good look out.

In the second example your voice might have risen as you said ***look out***, especially the second time you say the words, and especially if you had wanted to convey your surprise that you were expected to be the lookout. This idea is conveyed by your not using the usual form of a question, ***Do you want me to be the lookout?*** which would indicate that you really did not know whether you were to be the lookout. Here you turn a simple statement into a challenging question because you want to make it very clear that you are surprised to be the lookout. Another form for a challenging question would be, ***Do you <u>really</u> want me to be the lookout?***

In the third example, both words would be spoken more strongly, but without emphasis on either of them. The raised voice would indicate some sort of urgency as an old man sweeps down the high street towards you with his coloured pennant fluttering brightly as he picks up speed.

Now try writing your own mini-dialogues, just three or four lines each, using each of these words several times.

1. What
2. Completely
3. Really
4. Brother

Punctuation – visual clues.

So, much can be done with the voice when we are actually speaking. When we are reading, however, we need visual clues. This is what punctuation provides. Now I will set out again these three lines about look outs, but this time in some sort of conversation which we can read. It would go something like this:

> *(Charlie speaks first.)*
> *"I want you to keep a good look out." Mark looked up.*
> *"You want me to be the lookout? Not the driver? The lookout?"*
> *Clare looked round and called out to them.*
> *"Look out! It's John's grandad, on a mobility scooter."*

To do this I have spread the original words over two additional lines, added thirteen words to the original thirty-three and inserted another fourteen items of punctuation among the original fourteen.

We can go further. If I set out the three lines containing *look out* as a script to be read out by actors there would be even more clues. And a lot more work to set all this out in the written form. *Punctuation helps, that's all.*

CHARLIE *(He is very clear about this.)*
I want you to keep a good look out.

MARK *(He really can't believe all this.)*
You want me to be the lookout? Not the driver? The lookout?

CLARE *(She's been looking in the other direction.)*
Look out! It's John's grandad, on a mobility scooter.

Script writing is a more extreme form of writing – it's an attempt to leave nothing to chance so that an actor knows just how the words are to be spoken. In this short piece of script I have now used **three additional lines**, more widely separated and set in from the edge of the page, and **twenty-two additional words**. I have used **italics** in order to get rid of the speech marks and brackets, and **emboldened** the character's names which are now written **in capitals**. All this makes it much easier for an actor – only the words that are actually to be spoken have been left unchanged, just like the first three lines above where I introduced those two words, **look out.**

It may be easier for an actor but what a lot of work for us.

I have to ask you at this point if anyone has ever pointed out to you how much hard work is involved in being lazy? If we don't bother with things which we could get done they tend to catch up with us; if we don't prepare ourselves for a test or an exam and we fail, then we may well have to repeat the process. Sometimes it is easier to make an effort first time around even though this goes against our natural inclination to avoid work. Writing is an excellent case in point here; we have to escape the natural easiness that most of us find when speaking to make things easy for whoever has to read what we have written.

> **Being lazy is such hard work.**

This is why I have asked you to read some things aloud. Reading a piece of your own writing **aloud** is the best way of checking it. Reading **aloud** puts you in the place of the person who is to understand what you have written. Like you, your reader is lazy and in a hurry, but if you, the writer, do not discipline yourself to set out your words carefully, a real effort will be required by anyone trying to make sense of your words. They could easily give up. You have a choice.

> **Are you going to be lazy, or will you be considerate and make things easier for your reader?**

So far we have learnt when to use capital letters: *at the start of a sentence, at the start of direct speech and for proper nouns*. We have learnt that the end of a sentence must be clearly marked, with *a full stop, a question mark* or an *exclamation mark*. These last three items tell the reader to stop at the point where a unit of meaning is completed. If you have got the hang of this, if you know now just where a sentence ends, then you are well on the way to controlling and using English effectively. **Congratulations!**

When you are ready we can move on. Just remember that question marks and exclamation marks can also indicate the way words are to be spoken and we have seen that words that are actually spoken are marked with speech marks. (We call this **direct speech**.)

Although we have been using commas, we will leave them with apostrophes until last. Commas can get themselves involved in all sorts of complications and lawyers like to avoid them if they can. For the moment we are going to look quickly at the rest of the list.

The remaining five items are not surrounded by hard and fast rules. Some writers rarely use them and it is more important to use them clearly, when they can be helpful, than to worry ourselves about rules for their use. Such rules as we can find are often ignored or dismissed by other writers. Practical common sense is important here. Hyphens are easily dealt with.

Hyphens

Hyphens join words and ideas. In the Middle Ages, when it involved whole village populations struggling to carry a ball into their neighbours' territory, England's national game was known as **foot ball.** As there grew the idea that foot and ball were essential components of this game, it was for a time written as **foot-ball**, to indicate the close connection between the two words, **foot** and **ball**. Nowadays the idea of the game and all that goes with it has resulted in one word that refers to a lot more than simply a foot and a ball, the whole business of a world-wide sport, **football**.

We should try to use hyphens where they help clarify meaning and not otherwise. Read these examples **aloud**.

The two-year-old was encouraged by his mother to talk.
The two two-year-olds were encouraged to talk by their mothers.

In the first sentence the hyphens make it clear that only one child is involved. In the second sentence there are two children involved, both two-year-olds.

The hyphen is used to show words that need to stay together to make sense. *Two* and *year* and *old* together make sense here. Think of words that are joined by a hyphen as one word standing for one idea.

> **Apostrophe –** a simple mark for a missing letter.

Look again. The word ***apostrophes*** can be written without an apostrophe.

We make easy jokes about greengrocers and their signs, *cauliflower's, grape's, etc.*, all with unnecessary apostrophes. It is easy to say that these tiny, stray marks don't do any harm, but if you expect them to help us on our way as we read, then using them for no reason is a pain, like those fog signs that are sometimes left switched on above motorways, even when the fog is long gone.

Apostrophes are inserted *where letters are* **omitted**, *a* **contraction** *of two words into one*:

It's impossible. *(It is impossible.)*
You can't. *(You can not.)*

Or *to show* **possession**, *or* **ownership**:

Kevin's *ice cream,* **the children's** *party,* **the players'** *girlfriends.*

Like road signs, apostrophes can help us on our way.

Apostrophes show an **ellipsis**, a contraction where it is clear just what has been omitted. Look at these three sentences.

Their mother's walked off.
Their mothers walked off.
Their mothers've walked off.

Decide which are plural, with more than one mother involved, and which are singular, with only one mother. Not easy, is it, especially with the first two sentences sounding identical. Now look at them again.

Their mother's walked off. She's furious.
Their mothers walked off. They were furious.
Their mothers've walked off. They are furious.

In the first sentence ***mother's*** is a contraction of ***mother has*** – one mother.

In the second sentence mothers is simply plural: ***they*** were furious.

In the third sentence, ***mothers've*** is clearly a contraction of ***mothers have***, a plural.

Apostrophes that show possession: four simple rules.

1. An elephant's tail is hardly noticeable. One tail – one elephant. *Elephant* is singular so the apostrophe is placed <u>before</u> the *s*.
2. Elephants' tails are hardly noticeable. *Elephants* is plural so the apostrophe <u>follows</u> the *s*.
3. The children's mother. *Children* is plural, without the need for an *s,* so the apostrophe <u>precedes</u> the *s*.
4. Jess's mother. Singular words that end in *s* or *z* are followed by *'s*. (James's bosses were good to him. Liz's boss's favourite ice cream was strawberry.)

> **It's** – always used as a contraction, never as a possessive.
> <u>It's</u> *easy to see that the elephant has lost* <u>its</u> *tail.*

A reminder that uncertainty in a conversation should be cleared up easily.

"Their mothers walked off." (or, "Their mother's walked off.")
"What, all of them?"
"No. Just Shirley and Dean's mother."

Just by listening we cannot tell whether the first line refers to one or more mothers whereas when we leave information in writing we avoid this sort of uncertainty with the most simple of marks, the apostrophe.

EXERCISE FOURTEEN

Which of the following would you consider correct?

a. It's a good day to talk to an elephant.
b. The elephant opens it's mouth to speak.
c. The mothers' boy sat down.
d. The boys' mothers sat down.
e. The childrens' father was angry.
f. The children's mother had hidden his cigarettes.
g. Chris's mother says that Chris is troublesome.
h. Chris' father banned him from ice cream shops.

Now you can sort out the following:

The boy's mother's handbag contained a large ice cream. (Both singular possessives: one boy and one mother.)

The boys' mother's handbag contained several large ice creams. (The boys, plural, are brothers as they have the one mother.)

The boys' mothers' handbags contained an enormous number of ice creams. (Some of the boys at least are not brothers as there are at least two mothers involved.)

The boy's mother's handbagged his father; the handbag had contained a small tub of raspberry ripple ice cream. His father sat on it and now there's a mess everywhere! (Mother's is now a contraction of mother has; *there's* is a contraction of *there is.)*

Somewhere in the back of an imaginary classroom there is the scraping of a chair. Samantha gets noisily to her feet just as we are trying to concentrate on all this.

> *"Samantha, what are you standing up for?"*
> *"I can't take any more." The girl's arms are raised in frustration. "Don't ever talk to me about ice cream again." She glares angrily at all of us. "Dunno how you can stand all this – it's driving me nuts," and the door slams behind her. From out in the corridor her voice troubles us still. "Not bloody vanilla again…" And then her voice fades and she's gone.*

Where were we? Apostrophes. We are back to laziness.

In speech, Samantha could have said, **I cannot take any more**, and, **Do not ever**… and **I do not know how you can stand**… and **it is driving me nuts**. The final words could have been, **she has gone**.

This would have surprised us because we are used to hearing one another contract phrases that are used frequently. It is natural to take short cuts like this, to say *can't* and *don't* and *won't* to save effort and to say what we want to say as quickly as possible. These routine, familiar, contracted phrases make for comfortable speaking. In writing, apostrophes remind us of the bits that are left out.

> **Apostrophes – some words of explanation – a bit of history.**

When writing and printing really were hard work writers and printers took short cuts. Words were carved or chiselled in wood or stone or written laboriously with ink using pens that had to be dipped about every six words or so. Making curved shapes was particularly difficult – try painting a mixture of curved letters, *a, e* and *o*, for example and then try *v, w* and *x*. (Why do you think there are more straight lines in capital letters?)

Tell me then; how much easier would it be to carve an apostrophe, especially a rather straight one ', rather than a small **e**?

Here are the opening words of the Christmas story written about one thousand five hundred years ago in **Old English.**

Joseph, Cristes foster-faeder, ferde mid Marian…

(*Ferde* is related to modern German, *fahren* – to travel, and to our *Farewell*, and *mid* (modern German *mit*) – with – survives in *midwife*.)

In Old English there was a common possessive ending, es, which we can see here in *Cristes*. Now we can read:

Joseph, **Christ's** foster-father, went with Mary… And there is our modern apostrophe replacing that awkward **e** shape.

At ze back you vill now shut up and listen carefully to vat I am tellink you! It is time for a free Cherman lesson.

Das Buch des Mannes – the man's book, literally the book of the man.
Der Freund des Kindes – the child's friend, the friend of the child.

(In case you were wondering, all German nouns take capital letters.)
This Germanic system of indicating that one thing belongs to another arrived in England around fifteen hundred years ago with the people we call Anglo-Saxons, from Saxony in modern Germany. Now, of course the apostrophe also indicates the omission of a letter when in speech we take short cuts and leave out letters as in:

We've – we have.
She'll – she will.
It's – it has or it is.

Remember that the possessive form of *its* does not require an apostrophe: *the elephant lost **its** pencil sharpener.*

> **All together now, brackets, dashes, colons and semicolons.**

Consider two ways of writing down something that is said:

Go on – it's delicious, or Go on; it's delicious.

Both versions are correct and, yes, we are of course talking about **ice cream** again. The difference is not that one version is right and the other wrong. The difference is more a matter of style, the manner in which you want to convey the idea that, in the first version, someone is being encouraged to try something – you can almost imagine someone nudging you with an elbow. In the second version the idea is that the speaker is concerned to provide a reason to try the ice cream – the ice cream really is delicious. This time the speaker's hands are turned towards you, palms up.

In the first version I used a dash, to indicate with a pause that you are expected to do something and this emphasises the idea that follows – the ice cream really *is* delicious. In the second version, the semicolon connects the two ideas, joins two sentences more closely, as if to say, *You don't think I'd get you to try something that was not delicious.*

The first version makes me think of words that are actually spoken, direct speech, and has something of the energy and enthusiasm of speech. While we are "reading" the dash there are no sounds to make and we can control the delay between the words, *on* and *it's*. In the second version it seems that the speaker is rather more thoughtful and is trying to justify the encouragement of *Go on.* Both versions are correct. The difference is a subtle one, of style, of emphasis.

Now you try this. Extend each of the following sentences twice, once using a dash and once using a semicolon.

Let go.
It's too late.

That is great news.
Where have you been?
That's too much homework.

Next, what do you make of this sentence and the use of a colon?

The list of candidates was much longer than usual: Conservative, Labour
and Liberal Democrat, the usual suspects, then UKIP, BNP, the Greens
and, thank goodness, the Raving Monster Loony Party which does for
elections what Terry Wogan used to do for the Eurovision Song Contest.

(Should you not understand this last observation, you can find an
explanation in the answer section.)

I have used the colon simply to indicate that what follows, the names of the
parties, is evidence that the list of candidates was longer than usual. The brackets
here contain information which is significant only if you do not understand
the observation about Terry Wogan. If there is no misunderstanding, the words
in the brackets can be ignored.

There is a frequent and delightful bus service between the two places: every
ten minutes on weekdays (fifteen minutes on bank holidays) and every half
an hour at the weekends.

Again the colon introduces evidence – a comma would be confusing because it
could be indicating a pause at the start of a clause like the one in the sentence
which follows this one. The brackets contain information, which we may
want to run over quickly and forget, but which is important here following
immediately the information about normal weekday services.

Sometimes, in order to both use and analyse our language simultaneously,
we can jot down notes somewhere – just to keep hold of our ideas.

But try changing a wheel on your car while you are driving.

We can play around with different versions of this sentence:

> *There is a frequent and delightful bus service between the two places: every ten minutes on weekdays and every half an hour at the weekends. On bank holidays services run every fifteen minutes.*

This version is equally correct, it uses an additional three words and involves starting a second, separate sentence to complete the information. You might well prefer this version and the way that information about bank holiday services is kept separate.

Finally three versions of one piece of nonsense.

1. *There is a delightful bus service, with ice cream served in hot weather, which runs between the station and the public toilets in the high street.*
2. *There is a delightful bus service (ice cream served in hot weather) which runs between the station and the public toilets in the high street.*
3. *There is a delightful bus service: ice cream served in hot weather – between the station and the public toilets in the high street.*

EXERCISE FIFTEEN

One of these three versions has a weakness. Can you explain what this weakness is?

Now, if you have stuck with this so far you can be confident that you are making very good progress, for you are beginning to appreciate the benefits of taking care with your words and the way you punctuate them.

Very soon you will do another exercise with brackets, dashes, colons and semicolons. Here is an example, just to get you started.

> *My favourite band with its standard four-man set-up sank without trace years ago when vinyl discs were still the norm and when new groups were dropping like flies.*

Here are my variations.

My favourite band – with its standard four-man set-up – sank without trace years ago when vinyl discs were still the norm and when new groups were dropping like flies.

(Dashes – a hurried reminder about the line-up before the sad, sad part: they sank.)

Or

My favourite band (standard four-man set-up) sank without trace years ago when vinyl discs were still the norm and when new groups were dropping like flies.

(Brackets – like sticking a label on a parcel. We quickly put the band into a category, onto a particular shelf, or section of the mind, then move on. In brackets we use as few words as possible.)

Or

My favourite band with its standard four-man set-up sank without trace years ago; vinyl discs were still the norm and new groups were dropping like flies.

(A semicolon links two sentences and two ideas as closely as possible – without a conjunction – and suggests a link, the idea that it really was a very long time ago. Not a peep out of them for the last forty years.)

Or

My favourite band with its standard four-man set-up sank without trace years ago when new groups were dropping like flies and vinyl discs were still the norm: shellac then vinyl, tape then CDs.

(Here the colon introduces additional information about an idea that has just been mentioned, the changes in the technology for recording sound, starting with the reference to shellac. Take note, CDs. No apostrophe here. The small, lower case s alone is sufficient to indicate that there was more than one CD.)

Or

My favourite band sank, without trace, years ago, when vinyl discs were still the norm and when new groups were dropping like flies.

(Two brief pauses and two incidental pieces of information which we pass over quickly so that you are not reminded of just how long ago it was that I was a teenager.

No, there is nothing more to say. With commas, rather than dashes or brackets, punctuation is far more subdued.

The commas allow me to drop in all sorts of additional, (here's another comma) depressing information: all those *years ago* and they were older than me then, *without trace* – I can no longer play their 78s (note – <u>no</u> apostrophe here for the plural, 78s), shock horror – *vinyl discs were still the norm* and new groups were dropping *like flies.*

Notice, by the way, the number of times that I use brackets and dashes in my explanations, the very features of the language that we are working on.

Now see what you can do.

There are no "correct" answers. To check what you have written, read it **aloud** a few times and try it out on friends. This is your chance to insist on the version you prefer. Just be confident that you provide an answer to anyone who asks you to explain any of the decisions you make. So long as you can do this, confidently, there is no point in my even trying to list "correct" answers. Good luck.

Work on variations of these sentences until you are confident that you can control the changes. Don't forget to read out your changes **aloud** as a check.

EXERCISE SIXTEEN

Rewrite the following sentences with minimal changes to the words, using brackets, dashes, colons and semicolons.

a. Below the cliffs in exactly the same place they could see that someone had parked an old Ford Prefect just like the one for which they had been searching.

b. Once there had been John Smith then there had been Samantha the girl with a mouth and a taste for ice cream and now they were sitting next to each other at the back of the class.

c. It happened last Saturday a miserable wet day at the end of a miserable wet week towards the end of the holiday when the car clamper found that while he was busy clamping an illegally parked car someone had clamped his white van which he had parked out of sight round the corner.

So, just to remind ourselves, in this chapter we have learnt about:

Brackets which allow us to dump additional words (like the words in these brackets) back onto the page as we rush along. It is information that is easy to leave behind. Brackets (even with fancy letters) tend to be rather official and a little boring.

Dashes which allow us to insert additional ideas with a sense of immediacy – they can't possibly be left until we get to the end of the sentence – and they are not easily forgotten. They make me think of a lot of excited students all waving their arms in the air and calling out: *Please, sir – we'll do anything, sir – just for an ice cream, sir.*

Semicolons which allow us to join closely linked sentences; properly used they are said to impress examiners.

They are also used to separate items in a list when commas would not be suitable.

> *They arrived early: Charlie, all five foot nothing of him, who could empty a can faster than he could open the next one; Mary, the nurse, who was always complaining about him; Michelle, who was jealous and, so she said, had once gone out with him on a date; and finally, Harriett, the security agent, who was expected to arrest all three of them before they reached the pub.*

Here the use of commas in dealing with each item on the list, the four characters, would make it difficult to keep clear each of these characters and what is said about them.

Colons which introduce evidence immediately to support what has just been written: examples, lists of names, something to add to what has been stated. Look again at the example we used for colons: *The ice cream was especially good: blackcurrant and beetroot.* Here the colon after *good* tells us that we are going to learn something about the ice cream.

But before we relax there is the little matter of the **comma**, which does several jobs. It's doing one of those jobs here, providing a pause for emphasis.

The comma involves itself in the following: pauses, the separation of direct speech; the separation of items on a list, like this one; the start and finish of phrases and clauses used in apposition, and the business of distinguishing non-defining clauses from defining clauses.

ANSWERS TO THE QUESTIONS
IN CHAPTER THREE

EXERCISE TWELVE

The party had started well but then the boat struck something. There was a loud crash and a jolt, and a number of people fell to the deck.

"The boat is sinking," a man said. "It's time to get off."

"What shall I do?" said the woman who had boasted about the cost of her outfit.

"Swim," said the man. Another boat from the shore approached them. "Help!" called the man. "There's someone here who can't swim."

Compare your version with the version in the answer section. If you separated all nine sentences and enclosed the words that were actually spoken inside speech marks, and you are in a bit of a hurry, then you can go straight on to the next chapter. What you have established is that you can recognise and control written sentences, something that identifies an educated writer. We ask ourselves, *does the writer recognise the sentence, the basic unit of meaning?* You do, so you can move on. **See you later.**

EXERCISE THIRTEEN

At the gate he waited. He was late and very impatient. At last a man who was weighed down with chains approached him with a large and rusty key. He smiled. The man who had been waiting did not. He watched the new arrival try to insert the key in the lock. It would not turn. The man tried a second and third time but without success. From his pocket the man who had been waiting drew out a small can of lubricating oil and inserted it into the lock. He squeezed the can firmly and the other man tried once again to turn the key. This time there was the sound of grinding metal and soon the gate was open and both men could go on their way.

EXERCISE FOURTEEN

Correct: a, d, f, g. Incorrect: b, c, e, h.

Listing the answers is easy, easier probably than explaining them. These are difficult questions and, more important than getting the right answers it is understanding why some are wrong and others are right that matters. Remember, apostrophes are simply components of our written language which we must insert properly if we are to use the language accurately.

Now we must try to explain the use of the apostrophe in all of these sentences.

a. It's – *It is*. The apostrophe replaces the letter *i*.
b. *The elephant opens* it's *mouth to speak* **is wrong**. *Its*, without an apostrophe, is required here. *Its* is the possessive pronoun – the mouth belongs to the elephant. *It's*, with an apostrophe, represents a contraction of *it is* or *it has* from which the *i* or the *a* has been left out. This rule is simply a matter of convention; this is the way it is done and the way that the distinction is recognised.
c. *Mothers'* is plural so there cannot be one son alone.
d. *The boys' mothers*. Placed after the *s* the apostrophe indicates plurality, that there is more than one boy. If there is more than one mother there must be more than one boy. In the same way we could find, *the girl's right arm* or *the girls' right arms*.
e. and f. the word *children* indicates plurality without a final *s* so there is no possibility of confusion and we simply insert the apostrophe in its (did you notice – another possessive *its* – no apostrophe) usual place, before the *s*. We avoid confusion with *boys* and *girls* by inserting the apostrophe after the *s*. So with e. we put the apostrophe before the *s*, although *children* is plural. The *children's* father was angry.
g. and h. In *Chris's mother*, we can hear the extra *s* sound. This is correct. On the other hand, in h. we cannot see, or hear the extra *s* so this is incorrect.

EXERCISE FIFTEEN

In the third sentence the phrase, **between the station and the public toilets in the high street**, is joined by the dash to the information about the serving of ice cream and so the impression is given that it is the ice cream that is served between the station and the toilets, rather than the bus service which is run between the two places.

Another weakness is that the more important information about the bus service, that it runs between the station and the public toilets, is placed after the information about the ice cream. Here we must not forget that it is a transport service, not a catering service that is the subject of the sentence.

EXERCISE SIXTEEN

For this question you are to provide your own answers.

> **This is getting serious so why don't we take a break??**
> **Then we will be ready for the next chapter and the comma.**

CHAPTER FOUR

PUNCTUATION – 2

Commas

Pauses: parts of a sentence to be emphasised, direct speech (and reported speech), lists, words used in apposition, defining and non-defining constructions.

Some people will try to tell you that commas are difficult, but they are not. Just stand still – do not run away – you will cope.

We have simply to break down the task of understanding and using commas into manageable pieces.

THREE USEFUL THOUGHTS

First. Many people worry about the rules of spelling, punctuation and grammar. You must not do this. It makes much more sense to think of conventions, of agreements about how things are to be done. They are rather like the conventional signs on video equipment: a single arrow to move on and a double arrow – fast forward. You don't have to use them but life can be troublesome if you don't.

Second. If you find yourself in doubt, you should aim to write clearly rather than concern yourself about "rules". There is, supposedly, a rule about not separating prepositions from words to which they are linked. Winston Churchill is believed to have said of such a rule:

This is something up with which I will not put.

He said this to show how foolish it can be simply to worry about rules without making sure that we express ourselves clearly. He could have ignored the rule and said, more naturally:

This is something which I will not put up with.

Up and *with*, of course, are the prepositions concerned here.

Another example of this "rule" being broken appeared in *The Times* earlier on the day this was written (Monday, February 6, 2011). A piece by the Chief Rabbi at the time, Jonathan Sacks, about the protection of cultures, was presented with a subtitle:

Despite good intentions, multiculturalism has created a void that fascists could march into.

I would have written:

Despite good intentions, multiculturalism has created a void into which fascists could march.

My concern would have been less about separating *march* and *into* and much more with placing the word *march* at the very end of the sentence. There its strength would lend itself even more to the warning contained in the sentence; it is a verb and refers to an action that suggests energy and purpose.

Third. You should be prepared to rewrite sentences to avoid complication, ambiguity or long-windedness (verbosity – excessive words from *verbum*, Latin for *word*). At the end of this chapter you will find some examples to work on. **Now, what exactly do commas do?**

It's time to eat Grandad.

Of course, you've noticed; here we need a comma to save Grandad.

It's time to eat, Grandad.

Often it is as simple as this to use commas to make clear our intention.

Simple pauses, while you take a breath.

Read **aloud** the sentence that follows.

It is natural to pause when we are speaking, isn't it?

The slight hesitation caused by the comma makes us take a little more notice of the last two words which emphasise the writer's confidence that the pause is a natural feature of speech.

Erica, can you give me a hand?

Here we need to indicate the speaker's pause which is designed to attract Erica's attention.

This is one job that is done by a comma, to mark these pauses when the language is written down.

Now try the next sentence; start by reading it **aloud**.

Finally after years of anxiety uncertain and too scared to discuss the matter John and Samantha those irritating classmates discovered that they both adored ice cream.

Here there are a number of places where we might want to pause, to separate items of information so that they are clear. Pauses are not obligatory but without some at least the meaning is less clear and this will show itself as uncertainty as you read the sentence **aloud**, certainly the first time.

As you read it a second time you will be able to anticipate the places where you are going to pause. Once you have decided just how much you need to punctuate the sentence, write it out then read it **aloud**, as rapidly as you can. This should be much easier. You might end up with something like this:

Finally, after years of anxiety, uncertain, and too scared to discuss the matter, John and Samantha, those irritating classmates, discovered that they both adored ice cream.

Six pauses before we get to the end of the sentence, before we get to the point, **that they discovered that they both like ice cream.**
First, remove the essentials of the sentence:

John and Samantha discovered that they both adored ice cream.

We are left with:

Finally,
after years of anxiety,
uncertain,
(and) too scared to discuss the matter,
those irritating classmates

Here are five additional pieces of information, four if you put together *uncertain* and, ***and too scared to discuss the matter***. I separated them to emphasise that the uncertainty was additional to their fear of discussing the matter and not part of it.

Each of these pieces of information can be incorporated alone into the main part of the sentence, but none of them is essential. The pauses should alert us to all this as we read or listen to the words.

We will return to this sentence later in this chapter but for now you can move on quickly.

EXERCISE SEVENTEEN

Complete the punctuation of the sentences that follow. Where possible provide more than one answer.

1. Despite the darkness he did not bother with a torch
2. All cows eat grass unless they are on a diet
3. So help me I'll sue that English teacher
4. Where have all the flowers gone Mohammed
5. Excuse me can I help
6. Carlo will you pass the pasta please
7. Unless you finish your homework you will be in detention

> **Direct speech – words actually spoken.**

Earlier we dealt with some direct speech – we looked at different ways of speaking the words *look out* and the punctuation that we would need. This is what we ended up with:

> *Charlie spoke first.*
> *"I want you to keep a good lookout." Mark looked up.*
> *"You want me to be the lookout? Not the driver? The lookout?"*
> *Clare looked round and called out to them.*
> *"Look out! It's John's grandad, on a mobility scooter."*

Before we go on, try extending this narrative for another four to six lines, including some dialogue.

The thing to remember is that the words that are actually spoken are enclosed in **speech marks** or **inverted commas**. We also need to remember that when a new speaker starts, this is made clear by our starting a new line.

Here we are going to deal with speech marks and commas together, two jobs for the price of one. Read this **aloud**.

> *Come any closer and I'll scream John approached Samantha brandishing an ice cream put that down she shouted you don't know where it's been so what said John opening his mouth wider and wider look there it's gone.*

First of all let's embolden the words that are actually spoken then try again to read it **aloud**.

> **Come any closer and I'll scream** *John approached Samantha brandishing an ice cream* **put that down** *she shouted* **you don't know where it's been so what** *said John opening his mouth wider and wider* **look there it's gone**.

Easier, perhaps, but lacking something still.

Now enclose the words that are spoken in speech marks and try to read it **aloud**, again.

> *"Come any closer and I'll scream" John approached Samantha brandishing an ice cream "put that down" she shouted "you don't know where it's been" "so what" said John opening his mouth wider and wider "look there it's gone."*

It's a little better, but basic punctuation is still required, to mark pauses, and the ends of sentences. First let's separate and punctuate the sentences.

> *Come any closer and I'll scream.*
> *John approached Samantha, brandishing an ice cream.*
> *Put that down, she shouted.*
> *You don't know where it's been.*
> *So what, said John, opening his mouth wider and wider.*
> *Look.*
> *There, it's gone.*

Now we combine speech marks and ordinary punctuation and make full use of the lines; go on, read it again, **aloud**.

> *"Come any closer and I'll scream." John approached Samantha, brandishing an ice cream. "Put that down," she shouted. "You don't know where it's been." "So what," said John, opening his mouth wider and wider. "Look. There, it's gone."*

Some clarity has been lost. This is what we must do.

Come any closer and ***So what***, <u>must</u> start on new lines because new speakers are starting. We could leave on its own the first line of speech, Samantha's reaction to John's approach, for its dramatic effect and *Look…* on a new line would signal the change in John's voice, from the dismissive comment, ***So what***, to the instruction, ***Look***.

Yes, read it again, **aloud**.

> *"Come any closer and I'll scream."*
> *John approached Samantha, brandishing an ice cream.*
> *"Put that down," she shouted. "You don't know where it's been."*
> *"So what," said John, opening his mouth wider and wider.*
> *"Look. There, it's gone."*

I also chose to start a new line with ***Put that down*** to make clearer that it is not John, the subject of the previous sentence, who is speaking.

This second final version above uses more lines, but makes clearer what is happening, and what the characters are saying, while allowing the reader's eye to pick up clues to help the mouth form the words appropriately.

We have looked at speech marks, basic punctuation and line spacing, and the need to combine these elements to enable our readers to take in what we have written, as quickly and as easily as possible. It's what we want to be able to do when we are reading something, **a sort of transferable laziness. Remember?**

One final, technical detail and I will let you loose on some simple exercises.

I have tweaked the first of the sentences we were working on. Look at the two versions and see if you can pick out a mistake in the punctuation.

> *"Come any closer," she snarled, "and I'll scream."*
> *"Come any closer," she watched him then snarled. "I'll scream."*

Yes, it's the punctuation which follows the verb ***snarled***, a comma in the first version and a full stop in the second. It looks as though a mistake has been made in the second sentence, but there is an explanation.

The first version forms one sentence which is interrupted for dramatic effect by ***she snarled***. The comma following ***snarled***, indicates a pause. In the second version the full stop brings the sentence to a halt and suggests that

Samantha pauses before finishing with a threat: *"I'll scream."*

Look at the two versions in script form.

SAMANTHA *(Very, very frightened.)* *Come any closer, and I'll scream.*

or

SAMANTHA (Measured, weighing him up.) *Come any closer.*
(She pauses and watches him. He says nothing.) *I'll scream.*

My final note here: *Come any closer* is part of a clause, a contraction where we more easily take short cuts and don't say, *If you come any closer…*

Now I want you to tackle a couple of exercises on your own, so that you feel really confident with all this. You might find this sort of exercise easier with a pencil and paper so that you can play around with the words. Remember to decide first which words are actually spoken and then mark out the sentences.

EXERCISE EIGHTEEN

Punctuate the following sentences.

a. I think ill wait he said its raining outside
b. I think ill wait he said and hope that it will stop soon
c. Credit cards are an everyday necessity she called out you must let me have one
d. Credit cards are an everyday necessity she whispered so you must let me have one (Two possibilities here.)
e. Come back at once he shouted brandishing a stick and waving it angrily
f. Come back at once he shouted brandishing a stick and waving it angrily wont help

> Reported speech – conveying what was said
> without repeating the words that were spoken.

Linked to the business of direct speech, which you have now conquered, there is the matter of indirect or reported speech with which we can deal, here, very quickly. Imagine that you are at a meeting and that other people, who are not present, will want to hear from you something of what the chairman has to say. You hear the following:

We must get off our backsides and do something about global warming.

You could convey this by simply writing his words directly:

*The chairman **said**, "We must get off our backsides and do something about global warming."*

Or you could modify his words in order to report them:

*The chairman **urged** us to get off our backsides and do something about global warming.*

Or you could report this in your adaptation of his words:

*The chairman **encouraged** us to get off our backsides and tackle global warming.*

Yet another variation would be:

*We **were strongly encouraged** by the chairman to become active and do something about global warming.*

Sometimes we have to modify some of the speaker's words to convey matters accurately. Someone says, "Look at the state of them – he only got home yesterday."

What you can report is something like: *She drew their attention to the couple's appearance, only the day after his return.*

The essential thing here is to use an appropriate verb: here the verbal phrase, *drew their attention*, suggests that she spoke. (She might have pointed to the couple.)

In direct speech we use verbs such as *speak, cry, shout, called.* In reported speech we can use a wider range of verbs.

> *She **outlined** the difficulties facing them.*
> *In court he **claimed** that he was looking the other way at the time.*
> *The students **maintained** that the previous teacher had never set homework on Fridays.*
> *His doctor **begged** him to stop smoking.*

From these examples of reported speech it is not difficult to imagine the sort of thing that was said and, possibly, the manner in which it was said.

Try the next exercise then move on.

EXERCISE NINETEEN

Rewrite the following sentences as reported or indirect speech.

a. The man called out, "Where on earth has she gone? I haven't seen her for ages."
b. "We will do anything it takes," said the Prime Minister at his weekly press conference, "to prevent an increase in the price of ice cream."
c. "Tomorrow we will celebrate. Then, the day after, you will have to pay," she said.
d. "It's getting late," she said, "so you should be getting home."
e. "Our elephants," he explained, "only eat ice cream in the rainy season."
f. "If you don't believe that," I said, "then you should have been with me in Kyoto when I gave a green tea-flavoured ice cream to a deer which dropped it as soon as it had tasted it."

Lists – Precise Information

Read this growing sentence **aloud**.

> *Even in simple lists commas are a great help.*

Even in simple lists, commas are a great help. (One comma.)

Even in simple lists, **such as those we use every day**, *commas are a great help. (Two commas.)*

Even in simple lists, such as those we use every day, **shopping lists, list of things to do, lists of people to phone, lists of groceries** *and* **presents for your friends**, *commas are a great help. (Six commas.)*

Before we go on, just make a list of the things you can see around you: a light switch, poster, door handle, perhaps, or the people with you in the room. Make it a list of imagined items if that's more fun.

Then imagine a busy street scene where we can watch cars, buses, delivery vans, cyclists and pedestrians making their way along without damaging one another. The convention is that the **first comma** follows the **first item** on the list to indicate that there are more items to follow and that the use of the word *and* before the final item signals the end of the list. As usual reading **aloud** will help to make things clear.

There is a simple modification of this convention which you can see here:

Imagine a busy street scene where we can watch cars, buses, delivery vans, cyclists, pedestrians, *and elderly men and women mounted on mobility scooters making their way along without damaging one another.*

The final item on our list is now ***elderly men and women mounted on mobility scooters*** which is more involved, especially because it contains another ***and***. It is the additional, final comma before ***and*** that alerts us to the more complicated final item.

> **With these commas, the items here are clearly identified.**

We are due in court again and someone is calling out charges, names of witnesses, cases to be heard and lists of jurors. Inside there is a buzz as people settle into their seats; outside there is the noise of people calling out to one another.

Now, try reading this list as quickly as you can – **aloud**. (Come on, you don't really need to be reminded again, do you?)

Henry Alexander Fleming you are charged with truancy from school theft of an ice cream assaulting a traffic cone failing to complete a tax return and parking on a double yellow line refusing to smile at your teachers.

And of course the insertion of commas makes the task much more manageable.

Henry Alexander Fleming, you are charged with truancy from school, theft of an ice cream, assaulting a traffic cone, failing to complete a tax return, parking on a double yellow line and refusing to smile at your teachers.

The first comma attracts Fleming's attention.

EXERCISE TWENTY

Punctuate the following sentences without altering the words.

1. the baker used to call with his trays of vienna slices cream buns walnut whirls and danish pastries
2. she was beautiful charming witty and very wealthy he was dead lucky
3. with his string of hits with rap hip-hop poetry and short stories he could afford to take a break (There is more than one answer here.)
4. she remembered the naughty boys in her first class Glen Harry Sean and Bryn and Gareth who had set fire to the curtains during an assembly
5. all winter long they had maintained their daily intake of ice cream
6. as a matter of fact they had eaten more ice cream than ever
7. Henry Alexander Fleming Floriel Braithwaite John Henry Newman Hyong Lee Aziz Khan Lee David Paul White Charles Edward Smith Mary-Anne du Pres Walter Williams William Potter Peter Higginbottom William Williams Montague Algenon Arbuthnot Upraj Singh were discharged

> ## Phrases and words used in apposition –
> ## slipping additional information into a sentence.

Spanners at the ready, folks, we are going to dismantle again a sentence which we first looked at earlier in this chapter.

> *Finally, after years of anxiety, uncertain, and too scared to discuss the matter, John and Samantha, those irritating classmates, discovered ice cream.*

Last time we identified the items of **additional information** which could be removed from the sentence. (This is rather like removing the spare wheel from a car – you can still drive it.)

1. Finally – an adverb qualifying *discovered*.
2. after years of anxiety – adverbial phrase qualifying *discovered*.
3. uncertain – an adjective qualifying *John and Samantha*.
4. (and) too scared to discuss the matter – adjectival phrase qualifying *John and Samantha*.

These first four items can only add to the information that we have. The fifth item is different.

5. This phrase, *those irritating classmates*, not only adds information, but can replace an essential item in the sentence, in this case the subject, the words *John and Samantha*, become an inessential item and we could write:

> *Finally, after years of anxiety, uncertain, and too scared to discuss the matter, those irritating classmates, John and Samantha, discovered ice cream.*

Here we have interchanged the two phrases: *John and Samantha* and *those irritating classmates*. **The first word or phrase is followed by an additional phrase or word which conveys further information about its contents.** This is what defines a phrase or word used in apposition. Each word or phrase can stand in for the other word or phrase.

The important, practical thing about phrases in apposition is that they allow us to incorporate additional information into a sentence with scarcely an interruption to the flow of words.

Here are two more examples of words and phrases used in apposition; read them **aloud**.

Welsh collies, those dogs that round up sheep, are a delight to train.
Appenzeller, that rather dry Swiss cheese, is one of my favourites.

These can become:

Those dogs that round up sheep, Welsh collies, are a delight to train.
That rather dry Swiss cheese, Appenzeller, is one of my favourites.

Now it's over to you. You are going to write a couple of sentences using words or phrases in apposition. In the first sentence find two ways of referring to someone and in the second find two ways of referring to an object. When you have finished, read your sentences **aloud**.

So far you have had an easy and enjoyable time with commas.

Now, for a short, final section, that will challenge us.

We could be back in court.

If you find this next section really difficult go on to the next chapter then return later and try again until you are confident that you really understand.

Do not give up.

**Commas that separate and redirect items –
defining and non-defining phrases and clauses.**

In the previous section we looked at sentences containing additional but inessential information: Welsh collies round up sheep and Appenzeller is a dry, Swiss cheese. Sometimes **essential** information is slipped into sentences, rather like the information provided by a noun in apposition.

Imagine a band competition and consider the next two sentences.

The drummer who was wearing a green scarf was brilliant.

(It was the drummer who was wearing a green scarf, not any of the others. The word <u>who</u> introduces the **defining clause**, <u>who was wearing a green scarf</u>, which tells us which particular drummer was brilliant. Without these additional words we would not know which drummer was being referred to.)

The drummer, who was wearing a green scarf, was brilliant.

(This brilliant drummer just happened to be wearing a green scarf. The additional information is rendered inessential by the two commas and becomes a **non-defining clause or phrase**, just like the information about the sheep dog and the cheese.)

EXERCISE TWENTY-ONE

Which of the following sentences contain a defining clause and which a non-defining clause?

1. The boy who threw an ice cream at his English teacher was permanently excluded.
2. The boy, who loved ice cream, was excluded.
3. The ice cream which was made by Rossi's had been specially purchased.
4. The ice cream, which was made by Rossi's, had been specially purchased.
5. Throwing ice cream at teachers who don't like ice cream is wasteful.
6. Throwing ice cream at teachers, who don't like ice cream, is wasteful.

Now read this very carefully.

The most costly piece of failed punctuation in Canada.

A blunder cost a Canadian company millions of dollars after the placement of a comma in a contract permitted the cancellation of a deal.

The company thought it had a five-year contract with another company but the punctuation of a single sentence allowed the entire deal to be scrapped with only one year's notice. The sentence at issue stated:

The agreement shall continue in force for a period of five years from the date it is made, and thereafter for successive five-year terms, unless and until terminated by one year's prior notice in writing by either party.

The validity of the contract and the millions of dollars at stake all came down to one point – the second comma in the sentence. This second comma separates the requirement to give one year's notice from the successive five-year terms and leaves it applying to the main part of the sentence.

What is this all about?

We are faced with some very careful dismantling here to see how this part of the language works.

First of all let's identify the main verb of the sentence: ***shall continue***.

Now the subject: ***The agreement*** – the thing that ***shall continue***.

Now **the main clause**, which could stand as an independent sentence:

The agreement shall continue for a period of five years from the date it is made.

Here we have simple, straightforward information.

So far, so good. I am sure that you will have followed all this.

To this basic sentence two pieces of additional information are added. First:

and thereafter for successive five-year terms

This adverbial phrase clearly belongs to the main clause and together they form a longer sentence.

The agreement shall continue in force for a period of five years from the date it is made, and thereafter for successive five-year terms.

Here we have a five-year agreement that can be renewed for a further five years. However, there was a need to specify just how the contract could be cancelled so a second piece of information, an adverbial clause, was added:

unless and until terminated by one year's prior notice in writing by either party.

The final result should have been:

The agreement shall continue in force for a period of five years from the date it is made, and thereafter for successive five-year terms unless and until terminated by one year's prior notice in writing by either party.

Here the two additions to the basic sentence work together: <u>after the first five years</u> the contract will continue unless it is cancelled.

However, that second, deadly comma separates the matter of giving a year's notice from the five-year terms. We can link it directly to the main clause and we read this:

The agreement shall continue in force for a period of five years from the date it is made unless and until terminated by one year's prior notice in writing by either party.

In other words, the contract may be cancelled at any time. This is the problem caused by the second comma. The second company did decide to cancel the contract after just one year and this caused the first company the loss of millions of dollars.

Enough.

If you really want to continue with this topic you might like to look ahead at the chapter concerning the way that the components of a sentence can be assembled.

If the meantime you have a...

Special Exercise

Try to write a simplified version of material in the original contract sentence. Incorporate each of the seven additional terms in a separate sentence. Then count the words in the original sentence and the number of words in your version and you will see why legal contracts are so tightly written and are so dependent on accurate writing.

All that remains now is a final punctuation exercise.

EXERCISE TWENTY-TWO

Write out the passage that follows with full punctuation.

there were two people in the room shelley and her man there was a pause he drummed his fingers on the table toby i asked him i dont suppose hell bother to say anything shelleys words seemed very calm toby was usually much more relaxed than this suddenly his fist crashed onto the table damn shelley looked directly into tobys eyes and spoke softly you dont really want to fall out with me do you he stared straight back at her clearly awaiting a response she shook her head as if wondering whether he would take the hint his patience was wearing thin and he continued to glare at her he was so unlike other men she knew those previous employers who had always spoken well of him she remembered the others those employers who had had no time for him she had already dismissed the waiter who had just come into the room waited for the right moment then stepped across to them with a menu

ANSWERS TO THE QUESTIONS
IN CHAPTER FOUR

EXERCISE SEVENTEEN

1. Despite the darkness he did not bother with a torch.
    (A simple statement of fact.)
    Despite the darkness, he did not bother with a torch.
    (Emphasis on the adverbial phrase – *Despite the darkness.*)

2. All cows eat grass unless they are on a diet.
    (A simple statement of fact.)
    All cows eat grass, unless they are on a diet.
    (Emphasis on the adverbial phrase – *unless they are on a diet.*)

3. "So help me, I'll sue that English teacher."
    (A dramatic pause – you can't be matter-of-fact about suing a teacher and,
    in any case, you would probably want your classmates to know what you
    are up to.)
    (A longer pause, "So help me – I'll sue that English teacher," would give
    you time to wave your arms or cry. If you had a lot more to say you might
    not bother with any pause at all: "So help me I'll sue that English teacher
    and then I'm going after that fool who supplied him with that vile ice
    cream he gave us last week.")

4. "Where have all the flowers gone Mohammed?"
    (Mohammed is already listening or paying attention.)
    "Where have all the flowers gone, Mohammed?"
    (A nursery class perhaps, where the identity of the child who is to answer
    the question is made clear at the last possible moment.)
    "Mohammed, where have all the flowers gone?"
    (This way the teacher takes the pressure off the rest of you by using
    Mohammed's name at the start, but also puts extra pressure on Mohammed.
    Perhaps he was inattentive earlier on.)

5. "Excuse me. Can I help?"
    (There are two sentences here where the full stop suggests a pause while the person addressed signals their readiness to listen.)
    "Excuse me; can I help?"
    (Less of a pause here; the speaker attracts the other person's attention and starts the question immediately.)
    "Excuse me – can I help?"
    (Treated as a piece of dialogue – a longer pause.)
    "Excuse me, can I help?"
    (The first two words are used simply to get attention, as we would with someone's name: "Excuse me Charlie, can I help?" Or "Excuse me. Charlie, can I help?" The second example here emphasises Charlie's identity.)

6. "Carlo, will you pass the pasta please."
    (No, not a question mark. It's an instruction, a polite one.)

7. "Unless you finish your homework you will be in detention."
    (A statement of fact, possibly accompanied by a cold, withering look.)
    "Unless you finish your homework, you will be in detention."
    (A dramatic pause, a warning, perhaps – you know what to expect.)

EXERCISE EIGHTEEN

a. "I think I'll wait," he said. "It's raining outside."
b. "I think I'll wait," he said, "and hope that it will stop soon."
c. "Credit cards are an everyday necessity," she whispered. "You must let me have one."
d. "Credit cards are an everyday necessity," she called out, "so you must let me have one."
e. "Come back at once," he shouted, brandishing a stick and waving it angrily.
f. "Come back at once," he shouted. "Brandishing a stick and waving it angrily won't help."

EXERCISE NINETEEN

No answers for you here, so you must provide your own.

Your answers will need to include information or points made in the original, direct speech, or at least hint at what was said.

They will have to satisfy your ear when you read them **aloud**.

EXERCISE TWENTY

1. The baker used to call with his trays of Vienna slices, cream buns, walnut whirls and Danish pastries.
2. She was beautiful, charming, witty and very wealthy; he was dead lucky. (Did you remember how to join two sentences without an additional word?)
3. With his string of hits with rap, hip-hop poetry and short stories he could afford to take a break.

With his string of hits with rap, hip-hop, poetry and short stories he could afford to take a break.

With his string of hits, with rap, hip-hop poetry and short stories he could afford to take a break.

4. She remembered the naughty boys in her first class: Glen, Harry, Sean and Bryn, and Gareth who had set fire to the curtains during an assembly.
5. All winter long they had maintained their daily intake of ice cream.
6. As a matter of fact, they had eaten more ice cream than ever.
7. Henry Alexander Fleming, Floriel Braithwaite, John Henry Newman, Hyong Lee, Aziz Khan, Lee David, Paul White, Charles Edward Smith, Mary-Anne du Pres, Walter Williams, William Potter, Peter Higginbottom, William Williams, Montague Algenon Arbuthnot and Upraj Singh were discharged.

EXERCISE TWENTY-ONE

Defining clauses – 1, 3, 5.
Non-defining clauses – 2, 4, 6.

EXERCISE TWENTY-TWO

There were two people in the room, Shelley and her man.

"Toby?" I asked him.

There was a pause. Toby drummed his fingers on the table.

"I don't suppose he'll bother to say anything." Shelley's words seemed very calm; Toby was usually much more relaxed than this. Suddenly his fist crashed onto the table.

"Damn!"

Shelley looked directly into Toby's eyes and spoke softly.

"You don't really want to fall out with me, do you?"

He stared straight back at her, clearly awaiting a response.

She shook her head as if wondering whether he would take the hint. His patience was wearing thin and he continued to glare at her. He was so unlike other men she knew. Those previous employers who had always spoken well of him, she remembered. The others, those employers who had had no time for him, she had already dismissed.

The waiter, who had just come into the room, waited for the right moment then stepped across to them with a menu.

You might be pleased to learn that writing this chapter has proved to be one of the most demanding pieces of writing that I have ever undertaken.

I hope you have enjoyed it.

By now you will be more aware of what can be done with the language. Now we are going to find out how much more you can do yourself.

PART TWO

Now we are going to move away from dismantling the language and move on to finding out how it works. In Part Two we will find ways of reassembling the components of language, the actual words we use.

CHAPTER FIVE

DIFFERENT KINDS
OF SENTENCE

Is the sentence simple, compound or complex?

Is it balanced, loose or periodic?

Now let's go back to consider this **sentence**.

But, why?

Well, it's the smallest independent unit of meaning we can deal with in written language.

Do you remember this sentence?

It's a one-word sentence.

Of course you remember! A sentence is formed by a **verb**; this sentence could not be formed by any other kind of word.

Every sentence must have a main verb. It is around this main verb that everything else is put together.

You are going to look at the various ways this can be done and then you can start trying out the different kinds of sentence for yourself. This will extend your writing skills and your confidence.

Sentences – Assembling the Components
The machinery – is the sentence simple, compound or complex?

Last time we saw this dog he was on the phone.

The dog is sitting on the chair.
He is still using his owner's mobile.
His owner will be home soon.
His owner has received enormous phone bills recently.
His owner cannot stand getting dog hairs on her clothes.
"Doggie" is in serious trouble.

Look at the first sentence.

Subject:
What it's about.

Predicate:
What's said about the subject.

Identify the **subject** – *The dog* – and the **predicate** – *is sitting on the chair.*
We can extend this analysis slightly to see that the sentence follows the pattern:

Subject: *The dog*
    Verb: *is sitting*
        Adverbial phrase: *on the chair.*

Another way to help us to analyse this sentence would be to consider the three questions that it answers, a sort of reverse engineering. So, we have:

Q. *What is sitting on the chair?* **Answer:** *The dog.*
Q. *What is the dog doing?* **Answer:** *It is sitting.*

Q. *Where is the dog sitting?* **Answer:** *On the chair.*

Now it's over to you. All the sentences about the dog follow the same pattern so you should be able to analyse them all in the same way.

EXERCISE TWENTY-THREE

1. He is still using his owner's mobile.
2. His owner will be home soon.
3. His owner has received enormous phone bills recently.
4. His owner cannot stand getting dog hairs on her clothes.
5. "Doggie" is in serious trouble.

Now instead of using **simple sentences** to tell the dog's story we will do things differently – rather like the business of Billy and his mother and the ice cream in **Chapter One** – remember we were dealing with pronouns at that time.

The first two sentences can be combined as:

*The dog is **sitting** on the chair and is still **using** his owner's mobile.*

In this case we have combined two simple sentences, two simple pieces of information – *sitting* and *using* – to form a **compound sentence**.

We can make a similar compound sentence with sentences 3 and 4.

His owner will be home soon and has received enormous phone bills recently.

And again with sentences 5 and 6, the two pairs of sentences that follow.

His owner cannot stand getting dog hairs on her clothes and "Doggie" is in serious trouble.

These pairings form **compound sentences** in which two or more simple sentences are joined together. Reading the passage now is easier because we have only two intermediate full stops, rather than five.

We can go further than this.

Think about the worrying or dramatic items of information that the dog ought to be aware of. What are they?

You would probably say the approach of his owner, the large phone bills and the owner's dislike of dog hair.

> *The dog is sitting on the chair and is still using his owner's mobile.* **His owner, who has received enormous phone bills recently, will be home soon.** *His owner cannot stand getting dog hairs on her clothes so "Doggie" is in serious trouble.*

How many compound sentences do we have here now? Also, ask yourself if the second sentence is simply the result of joining two sentences, or is it something else now?

The original **compound** sentence 2. that we created ran like this with two main clauses:

> *His owner will be home soon* **and** *has received enormous phone bills recently.*

Look at the way a new **complex** sentence has been formed to include one of these main clauses, in **bold**.

> **His owner**, *who has received enormous phone bills recently,* **will be home soon.**

Making the sentence a **complex** one enables two things to happen.

> **First**, the sequence of information is changed to increase the sense of drama; so we learn about the enormous phone bills and then of the owner's approach.

> **Second**, the information about the phone bills is presented in a **subordinate clause** so that we can move on easily to the end of the sentence and the approaching threat to the dog.

Here are the same sentences "dismantled" in a different way. I am only going to analyse the main clauses.

His owner will be home soon and has received enormous phone bills recently.

1. Subject – *His owner* **2. verb** – *will be* **3. complement** – *home* **4. adverb** – *soon* **5. conjunction** – *and* **6. verb** – *has received* **7. object** – *enormous phone bills* **8. adverb** – *recently.*

Notice that here there are eight items to consider.

His owner, who has received enormous phone bills recently, will be home soon.

1. Subject – *His owner,* **2. subordinate clause** – *who has received enormous phone bills recently,* **3. main verb** – *will be* **4. complement** – *home* **5. adverb** – *soon.*

In this second case there are only five items to consider. The first comma, followed by '*who*', tells us that we have something additional to consider before we get to the main verb, which is the main point of the sentence.

This additional something is a **subordinate clause**, which provides a background to the owner's arrival, leads us to wonder what will happen to the dog when he is caught with the phone.

EXERCISE TWENTY-FOUR

The ten sentences below formed part of the complaints against King George III in the American colonies' Declaration of Independence in 1776.

Which of these ten sentences are simple, which compound and which complex?

1. He has refused his assent to laws, the most wholesome and necessary thing for the public good.
2. A Prince, whose character is thus marked by every act which may define a tyrant, is unfit to be the ruler of a free people.
3. He has erected a multitude of new offices, and sent hither swarms of officers to harass our people and eat out their substance.
4. He has refused to pass other laws for the accommodation of large districts of people, unless those people would relinquish the right of representation in the legislature, a right inestimable to them and formidable to tyrants only.
5. He has dissolved representative houses repeatedly, for opposing with manly firmness his invasions on the rights of the people.
6. He has endeavoured to prevent the population of these states, for that purpose obstructing the laws for naturalization of foreigners, refusing to pass others to encourage their migrations hither, and raising the conditions of new appropriations of lands.
7. He has obstructed the administration of justice by refusing his assent to laws for establishing judiciary powers.
8. He has plundered our seas, ravaged our coasts, burnt our towns, and destroyed the lives of our people.
9. He has excited domestic insurrections amongst us, and has endeavoured to bring on the inhabitants of our frontiers, the merciless Indian savages whose known rule of warfare is an undistinguished destruction of all ages, sexes and conditions.
10. He has abdicated government here, by declaring us out of his protection and waging war against us.

And to finish this section:

Here is the final sentence of the United States' Declaration of Independence which rings with gallant determination. Read it and tell me whether this is a simple sentence, a compound sentence or a complex one?

11. And for the support of this declaration, with a firm reliance on the protection of divine providence, we mutually pledge to each other our lives, our fortunes, and our sacred honor.

What? You don't really expect me to tell you the answer, do you?

Here are some questions.

Remember the old teacher's trick; just keep on asking them questions.

EXERCISE TWENTY-FIVE

In this last sentence of the American Declaration of Independence identify the following:

1. The main verb.
2. The subject.
3. The direct object of that verb.
4. The indirect object of that verb.
5. Any other finite verbs ("complete" verbs that have an agent and are set in the past, present or the future). In other words, identify any other clauses in the sentence.
6. Indicate the function of the rest of the words in the sentence.

I am going to make a suggestion for you to consider.

Why not simply take sentence 11. to bits like this, and ask yourself about the job done by each group of words?

So, it would go like this:

And for the support of this declaration, – tells us the reason for the action.

with a firm reliance on the protection of divine providence, – tells us how the action is being done.

we – tells us who or what is doing the action.

mutually – tells us how the following action is carried out.

pledge – tells us what the action is.

to each other – tells us to whom the action is directed.

our lives, – tells us to what the action is done.

our fortunes, – tells us something else to which the action is done.

and our sacred honor. – tells us something else to which the action is done.

I rather like this sentence. You might have been surprised to realise that it was a **simple** sentence. Perhaps it tricked you because the verb does not appear until halfway through what is a really long sentence. We have to read through *seventeen* words before we encounter the verb, the grammatical *action* of the sentence.

Do you feel that you are beginning to get the hang of this?

Soon we are going to consider another way of categorising sentences.

However, before we do this, you are going to try using the three types of sentence that you can now identify and understand.

The object here is to increase your confidence in handling the language for your own purposes. By using the patterns of the sentences that you have dismantled you will find the confidence to express yourself more effectively.

EXERCISE TWENTY-SIX

Turn each of the following groups of simple sentences into a short narrative. Combine and modify the sentences as you wish. You may not need to change every sentence. This should feel like fun.

Are you ready?

Group One: The traffic lights changed. There was a roar as the vehicles surged forwards. On the kerb there was panic. One woman dropped an ice cream into a pram. The child in the pram cried out in alarm. Then the child refused to hand back the ice cream. The lights changed. Other pedestrians hurried across the road. The woman struggled to retrieve the ice cream. The lights had changed again.

Group Two: He stared into her eyes. They were deep blue in colour. There were no veins visible around the iris. He could hear her breathe. He continued what he was doing. She kept very still. Had she got a boyfriend? It was an interesting notion. His task was complete now. He stood up. He switched on the light. To one side he picked up his notes and a pen. He spoke to the woman. The woman stood up. The receptionist knocked at the door. The receptionist came in.

Group Three: The man left the kitchen. There was still a lot of fat in the sink. Outside smoke could be seen coming from the ventilator. A car door slammed. The engine was started. She came back across the road. She saw that the door was open. It took her only seconds to see what had been going on. Upstairs she opened the wardrobe. She remembered something. Downstairs she found her scissors. She could not wait to get back upstairs. She remembered him buying the first suit that she selected from the wardrobe. There was a mirror inside the wardrobe door. She caught a glimpse of herself.

> **I hope it is not a shock, but of course
> you will read your answers ALOUD!**
>
> **Read out them aloud even though nobody else is there.**

Try to understand why I want you to do this; it is your ears that provide the best guide to the quality of what you have written. You will judge it better if you read it **aloud**.

If you are not in a position to read aloud, on the tube perhaps, then try to imagine the sound of someone reading your work back to you.

Imagine what *my* voice would sound like – you can find my voice on my website, in the *'dunno'* section.

But I have no answers for you this time.

This time you will have to become your own judge and jury. You will have to decide whether or not you have made a good job of rewriting these sentences because this is what you have to do with your own writing.

You have to ask yourself whether or not you have done a reasonable job. If you think that further improvements are required you need to ask yourself the sort of questions that I would ask you if I could, about the choice of words and the ordering of the words.

Experiment: Try out words, phrases and sentences on a piece of scrap paper if that helps. Don't be afraid to experiment with words until you get things right. There is nothing wrong with tearing up something that you have written once you can produce something better.

Progress with sentences

Handling the language like this now is not intended to make you do this for the rest of your life. It's to help you develop a feel for the language, so that you do these things automatically, whether you are writing or reading.

So far we have looked at the way the components of a sentence are assembled. Now we are going to use a very similar technique to see how the meaning of a sentence is revealed, how the ideas count.

Locating the force – is the sentence loose, balanced or periodic?

If you take one step away from a concern with simple, compound and complex sentences there is a parallel exercise that brings you closer to the way the meaning of a sentence is built up.

Let me explain. Look at the following sentence.

> ### The centre forward struck the ball which slammed into the corner of the net.

It's a complex sentence. The **main clause**, *The centre forward struck the ball,* is followed by a **subordinate clause**, *which slammed into the corner of the net.* This form of analysis, the fact that it is a complex sentence rather than a simple sentence or a compound one, simply tells us how the sentence was put together, mechanically, how the components were assembled, if you like.

Had you been **watching** your favourite team and the score was still drawn in the final seconds of the game, and it was your team's centre forward who had just received a pass in front of their opponents' goal, where would you have been looking as he struck the ball?

Had you been **listening** to a live commentary, trying to imagine every move out on the pitch, hearing the commentator describe a high, looping pass to the centre forward, which part of the pitch would have been in your mind's eye as the voice of the commentator rose excitedly?

The answer is the same in both cases – the goal, of course!

This categorising of sentences, into **loose**, **balanced** and **periodic** groups, is similar to the listing of them as simple, compound or complex, but is aimed at discovering what it is about a sentence that will get you to your feet, like the example of the centre forward and the welcome goal. Instead of being about the mechanical business of identifying finite verbs, it has more to do with the sense of where the main point of the sentence is to be found.

The sentence:

> ### The centre forward struck the ball which slammed into the corner of the net.

is a **periodic** one.

This is because its main point – the reference to the corner of the net, where the ball has come to rest – comes at the very end of the sentence, immediately preceding the full stop; remember that the full stop is called the **period** by Americans.

News of the goal could have been reported differently:

> **The ball arrived in the corner of the net,**
> **having been slammed there by the centre forward.**

This is a **loose** sentence.

The order of events has changed – we are told first about the ball's arrival in the net – and there is only one clear action, one finite verb, *arrived*. In this sentence the slamming of the ball seems to carry as much weight as its arrival in the net; there is no one, clear event to get us to our feet.

Now consider the sentence:

> **The centre forward received the ball**
> **and slammed it into the corner of the net.**

This is a **balanced** sentence.

Compare it with the first version.

Instead of a main verb – *struck* – and a subordinate verb – *slammed* – we have two main verbs, *received* and *slammed*.

Here the dramatic effect of the first part of the sentence leads us towards a second main verb which follows and competes for our attention.

If we try separating this into two short sentences:

> **The centre forward received the ball.**
> **He slammed it into the corner of the net.**

– there is very little sense of rising drama and we would probably remain in our seats.

Look again at the original version.

> **The centre forward struck the ball**
> **which slammed into the corner of the net.**

Here the main verb's action, **the striking of the ball**, is linked smoothly by the relative pronoun *which*, to the drama of *slammed* and the final phrase, *into the corner of the net*, where the end of the sentence coincides with the end of the action it describes.

This is what makes it **a periodic sentence**.

EXERCISE TWENTY-SEVEN

Decide which of the sentences that follow are loose, balanced or periodic.

Try to decide how you make your decisions. We have got to the stage where having a good reason for your decisions is more important than getting a "*correct*" answer.

1. The traffic lights changed.
2. Beyond the ice cream shop the traffic lights changed.
3. In school the last lesson dragged on and the children waited impatiently for the bell.
4. Red, red and amber, green, amber and back to red, all day long the lights changed and, when they arrived on their way home from school, the children waited impatiently to cross over to the shop.
5. Finally, they would be going home.
6. If you had been at the match would you have cheered?
7. Had boys never taken an interest in girls none of us would be here now.
8. Go home.
9. Home you go.

10. It is high time that you took yourself home.
11. It was boring and they could not wait to get to the end of Exercise Twenty-seven.
12. Now it was complete, finished and done with, whether they had answered correctly or not, and they could put the book away and relax.

Now write forty to sixty words for yourself.

You could try writing about a simple event, a door opening, perhaps, or a voice calling out, in different ways, using **loose**, **balanced** and **periodic** sentences.

ANSWERS TO THE QUESTIONS IN CHAPTER FIVE

EXERCISE TWENTY-THREE

1. **Subject** – He, **verb** – is, **adverb** – (still) using, **object** – his owner's mobile.
2. **Subject** – His owner, **verb** – will be **complement** home soon.
3. **Subject** – His owner, **verb** – has received, **object** – enormous phone bills, **adverbial phrase** – recently.
4. **Subject** – His owner, **verb** – cannot stand, **object** – getting dog hairs on her clothes.
5. **Subject** – "Doggie", **verb** – is **complement** in serious trouble.

EXERCISE TWENTY-FOUR

Simple (a single main verb and no subordinate verbs or clauses) – numbers **1, 5, 6, 7** and **10**
Compound (more than one main verb) – numbers **3, 8, 9**
Complex (with one or more subordinate clauses) – numbers **2** and **4**
A Commentary on the Answers to Exercise Twenty-four

1. He has refused his assent to laws, the most wholesome and necessary thing for the public good. **Simple**
(One verb – *has refused*. The comma introduces a phrase in apposition.)

2. A Prince, whose character is thus marked by every act which may define a tyrant, is unfit to be the ruler of a free people. **Complex**
(A subordinate clause: *whose*.)

3. He has erected a multitude of new offices, and sent hither swarms of officers to harass our people and eat out their substance. **Compound**
(*sent* – a second main verb.)

4. He has refused to pass other laws for the accommodation of large districts of people, unless those people would relinquish the right of representation in the legislature, a right inestimable to them and formidable to tyrants only. **Complex**
    (*unless* – a subordinate clause. *A right inestimable* – A phrase in apposition which tells us more about the *other laws.*)

5. He has dissolved representative houses repeatedly, for opposing with manly firmness his invasions on the rights of the people. **Simple**
    (One main verb – *has dissolved.*)

6. He has endeavoured to prevent the population of these states, for that purpose obstructing the laws for naturalization of foreigners, refusing to pass others to encourage their migrations hither, and raising the conditions of new appropriations of lands. **Simple**
    (One main verb – *has endeavoured* – and three adverbial phrases.)

7. He has obstructed the administration of justice by refusing his assent to laws for establishing judiciary powers. **Simple**
    (One main verb – *has obstructed* – and one adverbial phrase – *by refusing.*)

8. He has plundered our seas, ravaged our coasts, burnt our towns, and destroyed the lives of our people. **Compound**
    (Four main verbs – *has plundered, ravaged, burnt* and *destroyed.*)

9. He has excited domestic insurrections amongst us, and has endeavoured to bring on the inhabitants of our frontiers, the merciless Indian savages whose known rule of warfare is an undistinguished destruction of all ages, sexes and conditions. **Complex**
    (Two main verbs – *has excited* and *has endeavoured.* A subordinating conjunction – *whose* – introduces additional information including *is*, a subordinate verb.)

10. He has abdicated government here, by declaring us out of his protection and waging war against us. **Simple**
    (Main verb – *abdicated* – followed by an adverbial phrase – *by declaring.*)

EXERCISE TWENTY-FIVE

The sentence is a simple one – one main verb and no subordinate clause.

1. The main verb – *pledge.*
2. The subject – *we.*
3. The direct objects of that verb – *our lives, our fortunes, and our sacred honor.*
4. The indirect object of that verb – *to each other.*
5. Any other finite verbs ("complete" verbs that have an agent and are set in the past, present or the future). In other words, identify any other clauses in the sentence. *This was a trick question – there are none.*
6. Indicate the function of the rest of the words in the sentence. *Two adverbial phrases – And for the support of this declaration, with a firm reliance on the protection of divine providence, which qualify the verb, pledge.*

EXERCISE TWENTY-SIX

No specific answers were required.

EXERCISE TWENTY-SEVEN

1. The traffic lights changed. **Loose**
   (One simple idea so there is no emphasis in one part of the sentence rather than another.)

2. Beyond the ice cream shop the traffic lights changed. **Periodic**
   (Additional information at the start leaves the action to the end of the sentence.)

3. In school the last lesson dragged on and the children waited impatiently for the bell. **Balanced**
   (Two main verbs, two important actions.)

4. Red, red and amber, green, amber and back to red, all day long the lights changed and, when they arrived on their way home from school, the children waited impatiently to cross over to the shop. **Loose**
(Three main verbs and ideas that are not ordered significantly.)

5. Finally, they would be going home. **Periodic**
(The main verb is followed with a powerful word, *home.*)

6. If you had been at the match would you have cheered? **Balanced**
(The condition – *If you had been at the match* – is as important as the main clause that follows.)

7. Had boys never taken an interest in girls none of us would be here now. **Balanced**
(The first part of the sentence is simply another condition.)

8. Go home. **Loose**
(The verb, the action, is the first thing referred to.)

9. Home you go. **Periodic**
(The main verb completes the sentence.)

10. It is high time that you took yourself home. **Loose**
(There is no single focal point.)

11. It was boring and they could not wait to get to the end of Exercise Twenty-seven. **Balanced**
(Two main verbs of equal weighting.)

12. Now it was complete, finished and done with, whether they had answered correctly or not, and they could put the book away and relax. **Periodic**
(Two main verbs separated by a subordinate clause, *whether they had…* but, the second action, putting the book away and relaxing, is possible only once something is complete, finished and done with.)

You could argue that sentence 12 is **balanced**; two main clauses find themselves separated by the subordinate clause *whether they had...*

However, the sequence of verbs leads up to the final verb and creates a sense of completeness which coincides with the full stop.

A similar argument is possible with questions 8–10, all of which involve an instruction to go home.

Here you are stepping into a world where you are beginning to understand better how meaning is developed, how words are put together so that they mean one thing rather than another. Here you will combine understanding what groups of words mean with appreciating the subtleties of their effects on one another.

Remember

These exercises are intended to help you to understand and appreciate effective English and to express yourself more effectively in speech and writing. This will help you if you happen to take examinations.

Next, in Chapter Six, we will take a final look at the way sentences are put together before we get you writing.

CHAPTER SIX

ASSEMBLING THE COMPONENTS

Fitting groups of words together.

First of all you are going to look again at clause analysis which we touched on in Part One. Then we will return to the matter of subject and predicate.

First we will examine all the words in a written passage.

Later we will consider the two sections into which every sentence can be divided. This will ensure that you are ready to deal with groups of sentences, with paragraphs.

Clause Analysis

Looking at groups of words which contain a finite (complete) verb.

EXERCISE TWENTY-EIGHT

The passage that follows has 116 words, divided into six sentences. For each sentence identify the main and subordinate clauses then analyse the sentence into subject, verb, objects, etc.

It was wet. It was a wet Friday when they would all be finishing the week's work and hoping to get outside over the weekend. This weekend was the last long weekend of the summer and already a touch of autumn had greeted them on their way to work. It chilled their bare arms and legs and forced some of them into light coats or jackets. There might be something on the television or a DVD somewhere, although sitting in front of a screen would be no substitute for going out and hanging about with their friends. Later, a strong gust of wind greeted them when they got off the bus, and the decision was made.

> **Last time that you enjoyed a bottle of good German wine did you find these words on the label?**

Loosely translated *mit predikät* means *special quality*. From the picture we can assume that the man is saying that it is a good wine. Simplify this last sentence and we have:

The man is saying that it is a good wine.

It is a simple, periodic sentence. If we remove part of the sentence we can begin another way of looking at sentences.

…is saying that it is a good wine.

Consider what is missing here. Think of some words that you could use to complete the sentence. (The dog? Your aunt's favourite cat? Alexander the Great?)

We know which words are missing but the interest here is in what those words, *The man*, tell us. Without them, of course, we don't know who or what is talking about the wine; we don't know what **the subject of the sentence** is. We don't know what the sentence concerns.

What is conveyed to us then by the rest of the words in the sentence? If we have the subject, *The man*, what else do we need? To complete the sentence we need something to be said about the subject. This is **the predicate**. Together they form a sort of verbal arithmetic:

Subject + predicate = a sentence

The man plus *is saying that it is a good wine* forms a complete sentence.

Even when there is only one word in the sentence it will have both a subject and predicate.

Does this word tell us who or what the sentence is about or does it tell us what is said about it? Is this word the subject or the predicate? The word *stop* is the main verb and the main verb of a sentence must be in the predicate. The subject of the sentence is *you*, which is implied or understood, not stated. Put another way, the subject of a command is the person who reads it or the person who is expected to respond to it. The subject is the person to whom the instruction is directed, who is expected to carry it out.

> **Why is it so important to distinguish subject and predicate?**
>
> They represent the two aspects common to any communication.
>
> We must be absolutely clear about what it is that we are talking or writing about, not only when we are dealing with simple sentences such as *stop*, but also when things are far more complicated.
>
> If we are not clear about these two matters then we are in danger of talking or writing a great deal and yet saying absolutely nothing at all.

Here are some examples; read them aloud.

For each one ask two questions:

What is the subject of the sentence?
What are we told about the subject?

1. Fleetingly, not quite shyly, but glancing quickly over her shoulder, the girl smiled at him.

The **subject** is *the girl*.

We are told that the girl, *fleetingly, not quite shyly, but glancing quickly over her shoulder, smiled at him.*

So, the **predicate** is *fleetingly, not quite shyly, but glancing quickly over her shoulder, smiled at him.*

2. The shy girl, the one who would normally glance quickly over her shoulder, smiled at him.

The **subject** is *The shy girl, the one who would normally glance quickly over her shoulder*
The **predicate** is *smiled at him.*

3. She smiled at him, the shy girl who would normally glance quickly over her shoulder.

The **subject** is *She... the shy girl who would normally glance quickly over her shoulder.*

The **predicate** is *smiled at him.*

4. She smiled at him, shyly, glancing fleetingly over her shoulder.

The **subject** is *She.*

The **predicate** is *smiled at him, shyly, glancing fleetingly over her shoulder.*

5. The shy girl, the one who would normally glance quickly over her shoulder and who had just caught his eye, smiled at him.

The **subject** is *The shy girl, the one who would normally glance quickly over her shoulder and who had just caught his eye.*

The **predicate** is *smiled at him.*

Now count the number of words used in each section of each sentence. The subject of each sentence is in bold type.

1. Fleetingly, not quite shyly, but glancing quickly over her shoulder, **the girl** smiled at him. (Subject – two words, predicate – thirteen words.)
2. **The shy girl, the one who would normally glance quickly over her shoulder**, smiled at him. (Subject – thirteen words, predicate – three words.)
3. **She** smiled at him, **the shy girl who would normally glance quickly over her shoulder**. (Subject – twelve words, predicate – three words.)
4. **She** smiled at him, shyly, glancing fleetingly over her shoulder. (Subject – one word, predicate – nine words.)
5. **The shy girl, the one who would normally glance quickly over her shoulder and who had just caught his eye**, smiled. (Subject – twenty words, predicate – one word.)

Essentially, each of these five sentences has to do with the girl smiling at him, but there is additional information. This additional information tells us more about the girl, about her shyness and, in sentence number five, tells us that she was also the girl who had just caught his eye. Note the different lengths of subject and predicate which provide much flexibility.

For our purposes, to understand how the language works, it is helpful to see here that information can be set out in different ways for different effects. In sentences 1 and 4 the emphasis is on the way the action of the sentence was carried out, the **predicate**, and in 2, 3 and 5 the emphasis is on the girl, the **subject** of the sentence, rather than on the way she smiled at him.

Understanding this will help a great deal in the next chapter where we start to look at the meaning of longer passages. Before we go on, try the following exercise.

EXERCISE TWENTY-NINE

Identify the subject in the sentences that follow.

1. He is still using his owner's mobile.
2. Which team won?
3. Wait there.
4. He is still using his owner's mobile although he has a better one at the back of his kennel.
5. The helicopter which had just thrilled the crowds, landed right next to the ice-cream van.
6. Flecks of ice cream, wooden spoons, plastic tubs, paper serviettes and several large dollops of tomato sauce fell out of the sky.
7. Fortunately it began to rain so that the spectators were soon washed clean.
8. Once upon a time a wild mob invaded the city, took over the public houses and attempted to give away their stocks of food and drink.
9. Try not to sing out of tune.
10. Never in the field of human conflict have so many owed so much to so few.

Here are some more examples for you to consider. What is the subject of these sentences?

a. It is fine.
b. What is this?
c. There is a hut.

It's very easy really. *It* and ***What*** are pronouns. Each stands for something that can form the subject of a sentence.

a. It is fine. ***It*** could stand for anything that could be fine, probably the weather – *The weather is fine.*
b. What is this? ***What*** is an interrogative pronoun and stands for whatever it is that requires identification. Of course, were the subject known there would be no need to ask this question.
c. There is a hut. **There** is an adverb, of location. The subject of the sentence is *a hut.* We could have said, *A hut is there,* but it would be misleading to draw attention to the hut before we pointed out the location.

ANSWERS TO THE QUESTIONS IN CHAPTER SIX

EXERCISE TWENTY-EIGHT

Only subordinate clauses are highlighted.

1. It was wet.

One clause.

> Subject – **It** (A neutral pronoun which provides a grammatical agent, something or someone to do the action.)
> Verb – **was**
> Complement – **wet** (An adjective which complements the verb to be.)

2. It was a wet Friday when they would all be finishing the week's work and hoping to get outside over the weekend.

Three clauses, a main clause and two subordinate, adjectival clauses.

a. Subject – **It**
   Verb – **was**
   Complement – **a wet Friday**

b. Subordinating conjunction – **when** – links the main and subordinate clauses
   Subject – **they all** – pronoun and adjective
   Verb – **would be finishing** – auxiliary verbs plus participle
   Direct object – **the week's work**

c. Coordinating conjunction – **and** – links the two subordinate clauses
   Subject – **(they)**
   Verb – **(would be) hoping to get outside**
   Adverbial phrase – **over the weekend**

> **Adjectival clauses answer questions such as –**
> **What sort of wet Friday?**
>
> One when they would all be finishing the week's work.
> One when they would be hoping to get outside over the weekend.

3. This weekend was the last long weekend of the summer and already a touch of autumn had greeted them on their way to work.

Two main clauses, joined by a coordinating conjunction, **and**.

a. Subject – **This weekend**
    Verb – **was**
    Complement – **the last long weekend of the summer**

b. Adverb – **already**
    Subject – **a touch of autumn**
    Verb – **had greeted**
    Direct object – **them**
    Adjectival phrase – **on their way to work**

> **Main clauses can stand alone. Remove the *and*:**
>
> This weekend was the last long weekend of the summer.
> Already a touch of autumn had greeted them on their way to work.

4. It chilled their bare arms and legs and forced some of them into light coats or jackets.

Two main clauses, joined by a coordinating conjunction, **and**.

a. Subject – **It**

Verb – **chilled**

Direct object – **their bare arms and legs**

b. Subject – (**it**)

Verb – **forced**

Direct object – **some of them**

Indirect object – **into light coats**

5. There might be something on the television or a DVD somewhere, although sitting in front of a screen would be no substitute for going out and hanging about with their friends.

Two clauses, a main clause and a subordinate clause linked by a subordinating conjunction, **although**.

a. Subject – **There**

Verb – **might be**

Complement – **something**

Adverbial phrase – **on the television or a DVD somewhere**

b. Subject – **sitting in front of a screen**

Verb – **would be**

Complement – **no substitute for going out and hanging about with their friends**

A Killer Sentence

...*but* leads to a subordinate clause with a negative comparison – *no substitute for...*

However, this sentence is periodic and the strong ending provides a dramatic contrast with the first main clause.

---

6. Later, a strong gust of wind greeted them when they got off the bus, and the decision was made.

Two main clauses, linked by the coordinating conjunction **and**, and a **subordinate clause of time** which is linked by the subordinating conjunction, **when**. The comma is an important one which separates the subordinate clause from the second main one.

a. Adverb – **Later**
    Subject – **a strong gust of wind**
    Verb – **greeted**
    Direct object – **them**

b. Subject – **they**
    Verb – **got off**
    Direct object – **the bus**

c. Subject – **the decision**
    Verb – **was made**

(This last verb is rather different. We could have been told that *they made the decision* and we would have known who or what the agent was. Here we are simply told that the action occurred. More about the ***passive voice*** later.)

> **What happened as they got off the bus?**
>
> A strong gust of wind greeted them.
> *What happened next?*
> The decision was made.

EXERCISE TWENTY-NINE

1. He is still using his owner's mobile.

2. <u>Which team</u> won?
3. <u>(You)</u> Wait there.
4. <u>He</u> is still using his owner's mobile although <u>he</u> has a better one at the back of his kennel.
5. <u>The helicopter which had just thrilled the crowds</u>, landed right next to the ice cream van.
6. <u>Flecks of ice cream, wooden spoons, plastic tubs, paper serviettes and several large dollops of tomato sauce</u> fell out of the sky.
7. Fortunately <u>it</u> began to rain so that the spectators were soon washed clean.
8. Once upon a time <u>a wild mob</u> invaded the city, took over the public houses and attempted to give away their stocks of food and drink.
9. <u>(You)</u> try not to sing out of tune.
10. Never in the field of human conflict have <u>so many</u> owed so much to so few.

You have now dealt with a very great deal of information about the way words are put together and about the way they work together.

All these technical terms are useful when you want to consider the way the language is used or think about the way a piece of writing is put together.

You might find them helpful in an exam or a test.

Here they are important to help us to appreciate English and use it well.

Now it is time to look at the meanings that we can convey with words.

CHAPTER SEVEN

IN SO MANY WORDS – PRECIS AND SUMMARY

Clarifying and communicating our understanding.
Be prepared to take your time with this chapter.

A reminder. We are now going to make sure that you can pinpoint the main points expressed in a written passage, or in a speech, and then communicate them, clearly and economically. This is a key skill which provides a very demanding test of English. Here, we will examine other people's ideas; in a later chapter we will look at ways to develop and communicate your ideas.

> **Precis and Summary**
> **Identifying ideas and conveying them economically.**

Precis and summary: these are the words common to British use, but, along with Americans, we also use the term *abstract*, often in academic contexts. Each of these three words can help us to grasp what is involved here.

Put simply, *précis*, a French word meaning related to **condense**, reminds us that we need to reduce the length of a piece of writing. *Summary* reminds us of sums, of adding up, an effort to get to **the bottom line**, a concern to find what is really important in a passage. *Abstract* comes from Latin – *ab*, meaning **from**, and *traho*, meaning **I drag**.

Put these three words together and you will get the idea. The ideas that you express must come from the passage, must be clearly identified as the really important ones and the whole thing that you present, whatever you call it, will be shorter than the original by about two thirds.

To keep things simple I am going to use the term *summary*, to include all these ideas. Sometimes you will feel that you really are having to drag ideas from a passage.

Let's get started. Read this paragraph at least twice. Read it quickly the first time, to get an impression, then read it through again, more slowly, so that you can give some thought to its purpose.

> *This is where we start to summarise passages of writing. One purpose of this kind of exercise is to encourage you to read intelligently. Then, when you have read a passage of writing, you will be expected to set out the main ideas of the passage, briefly but accurately and in your own words. The ability to do this is important, not just to help you pass exams in many different subjects, but also to help you to understand more clearly what other people have to say. It will also help you to communicate more effectively. These skills are important in commerce and industry as well as in academic work and were once regarded as an effective means of identifying good candidates in English examinations. (125 words)*

Essentially, there are two phases to this task: identifying the main ideas, and then communicating them clearly. Here our aim should be to write a summary of between thirty-five and fifty words.

Finding the Main Ideas

Sometimes it helps to give a provisional title to the piece that we are summarising, a few words that seem to catch the essentials of the words in front of you. For this piece I would suggest *The Importance of Summary Skills*.

Next, identify the finite verbs in each sentence of the passage above that begins, *This is where…*

Now we need to look closer at each sentence to identify the important words that accompany each verb. Here is the passage again, this time with the verbs emboldened.

*This **is** where we **start** to summarise passages of writing. One purpose of this kind of exercise **is** to encourage you to read intelligently. Then, when you **have read** a passage of writing, you **will be expected** to set out the main ideas of the passage, briefly but accurately and in your own words. The ability to do this **is** important, not just to help you **pass** exams in many different subjects, but also to help you to understand more clearly what other people **have** to say. It **will** also **help** you to communicate more effectively. These skills **are** important in commerce and industry as well as in academic work and **were** once **regarded** as an effective means of identifying good candidates in English examinations.*

The significant words could be in the subject of each sentence or in the predicate, so:

Identify the subject of each sentence.

Now we can highlight **the subjects** as well as the verbs in the passage.

This <u>*is*</u> *where* **we** <u>*start*</u> *to summarise passages of writing.* **One purpose of this kind of exercise** <u>*is*</u> *to encourage you to read intelligently. Then, when* **you** <u>*have read*</u> *a passage of writing,* **you** <u>*will be expected*</u> *to set out the main ideas of the passage, briefly but accurately and in your own words.* **The ability to all do this** <u>*is*</u> *important, not just to help you (to) pass exams in many different subjects, but also to help you to understand more clearly what other people* <u>*have*</u> *to say.* **It** <u>*will*</u> *also* <u>*help*</u> *you to communicate more effectively.* **These skills** <u>*are*</u> *important in commerce and industry as well as in academic work and* <u>*were*</u> *once* <u>*regarded*</u> *as an effective means of identifying good candidates in English examinations.*

This completes the mechanical work. Now we are going to make judgements about what is significant in each sentence. For this passage I am forcing you to look painstakingly closely at these six sentences, but later, with the next passage, we will move along much more rapidly.

In the first sentence something is starting; the verb is *start* and that is the main idea in the sentence. Next we should ask whether this sentence conveys an idea that is particularly important. Ask yourself, does it tell us anything very striking or obviously important?

No. All it seems to do is to introduce the topic, the idea of summarising sentences. Nothing more; something that a title could provide more effectively. All it does is establish the subject of the passage.

Does this make sense to you? If it does then you can move on to the next sentence.

If it does not then I'm afraid that you can't raise a puzzled arm and expect answers to your questions from me. What you could do is to look again at the sections on subject and predicate in Chapter Two then return to the battle.

Do Try Again

Just remember the scars on your knees that come from your determination to master the riding of a bike.

If you have tripped over these words just pick yourself up and try again, **immediately**.

The second sentence has a new idea, *purpose*, and at the end of the sentence the words *read intelligently* are linked by the verb to this idea. This is how we summarise writing. The significant idea here, that must appear in your written summary, is that one aim of summary writing is intelligent reading.

The third sentence continues the idea of *purpose*. The first word, *Then*, links this idea to a further expectation, that you will write – *set out the main ideas of the passage* – *briefly*, *accurately* and *in your own words*.

(Did you spot here my summarising of **set out the main ideas of the passage** as **write**?)

The fourth sentence tells us that doing all this, reading and writing accurately, is important and gives us two reasons why this is so. One is to pass exams and the other is to improve your understanding of other people's ideas. These two reasons are introduced with the words *not just*, which indicate that it is the second of these two reasons which is the really important one, *to understand more clearly*.

In the fifth sentence the word *also* indicates that the idea of the ability to understand ideas and express them effectively remains the focus. This time it concerns communicating more effectively.

Finally, in the sixth sentence, another idea is introduced: the importance of these skills, in various settings (I'm summarising again – three words here to represent twenty-five in the passage – *in commerce and industry as well as in academic work and were once regarded as an effective means of identifying good candidates in English examinations*. An alternative would be *at work or when studying* – just five words this time. This would retain detail which is more convincing.) *Commerce* and *industry* both suggest *work* and the words *academic* and *exams* both suggest studying.

Now I have **capitalised** the words that I think contain the main ideas, the ones that we need to pass on, in our own words.

> **This** *is* where **we** *start* to summarize passages of writing. **One PURPOSE of this kind of exercise** *is* to encourage you to **READ INTELLIGENTLY.** *Then, when* **you** *have read* a passage of writing, **you** *will be expected* to **SET OUT THE MAIN IDEAS** of the passage, **BRIEFLY** but **ACCURATELY** and **in your own words**. *The ability to* **do all this** *is* important, not just to help you pass exams in many different subjects, but also to help you to **UNDERSTAND MORE CLEARLY** what other people *have* to say. It *will* also *help* you to **COMMUNICATE MORE EFFECTIVELY.** These skills *are* important in **COMMERCE AND INDUSTRY** as well as in academic work and *were* once *regarded* as an effective means of **IDENTIFYING GOOD CANDIDATES** in English examinations.

Note that I have **capitalised** twenty-two key words, about one word in five. With one exception, the key ideas are to be found, not in the subjects or the verbs, but in the information that accompanies them. You might think of the subject and verb, essential components of any sentence, as providing a framework into which clues about the important points can fit.

The passage is now marked to reveal the steps we have taken; the verbs and subjects are revealed along with the words that I think are really important.

Another Way to Identify the Main Points

Try this, especially when your confidence has grown. Simply strike out words that are less important. This is what we will be able to do once the more mechanical work has been done. Then we are left with clear ideas to be written up as the summary.

Here is the passage again. This time I have struck out the words of lesser importance in order to leave the important ones. Your attempt at this is likely to differ from mine, at least to a limited extent. This matters less than identifying the main points which you will write up as your summary.

> ~~This is where we~~ start to summarise passages of writing. The purpose ~~of this kind of exercise is to encourage you~~ to read intelligently. ~~Then, when you have read a passage of writing,~~ you will be expected to set out the main ideas ~~of the passage,~~ briefly but accurately and in your own words. ~~The ability to do~~ this is important, ~~not just to help you pass exams in many different subjects, but also~~ to help you to understand more clearly what other people have to say. ~~It will also help you~~ to communicate more effectively. ~~These skills are~~ important in commerce and industry ~~as well~~ as in academic work ~~and were once regarded as~~ an effective means of identifying good candidates ~~in English examinations.~~

We should now be able to draw up a list of key points, the main ideas of the passage, usually one from each sentence.

1. Title – The Importance of Summary Skills
2. To read intelligently
3. Expressing own ideas
4. Develops understanding
5. Effective communication
6. Importance in various settings

At this stage the order of the key points can be changed if this will help you to present them more effectively.

A Checklist

Before we continue it would be useful to remind ourselves of the various techniques that we have used in order to identify these key points.

---

1. Reading the passage at least twice.
2. Finding a provisional title.
3. Finding the finite verbs.
4. Identifying the subjects of those verbs.
5. Deleting or striking out words that are of little or no importance.
6. Looking for one or more significant ideas in the sentence.
7. Deciding whether each idea is a new one or the development of an idea that is already established.
8. Deciding how each point relates to the provisional title.
9. Using words from the passage, or words of your own, chosen to form a reminder of the main points to be listed.

Now, writing the summary.

Let's start by looking at the nineteen words in our list of main points.

The Importance of Summary Skills – To read intelligently – Expressing ideas succinctly – Develops understanding – Effective communication – Importance in various settings.

Like this we have a series of disjointed reminders of what was in each of the original sentences. The words do not flow because they are not linked as they would be in complete sentences. Our job now is to join these main points in sentences so that they can be read quickly and easily.

How Many Sentences?

Points 2 and 3 concern what we have to do when we summarise a passage, while points 4, 5 and 6 indicate the importance of being able to do this well. Two sentences then, that is what we will aim to write.

Write a draft summary of these two sentences, check them as instructed below – in the box below – then modify them if necessary.

> **Checking Our Written Summary**
>
> 1. First identify the words in your draft that convey the main points of the original passage.
> 2. Where you can, remove or replace more economically words and phrases from your first draft.
> 3. Read through your drafts, **aloud**. Better still, get **someone else** to read aloud through your first draft.

You can see here the changes I made between my first draft and my third, final draft.

Second Draft

The importance of learning summary skills is that you learn to read intelligently and become proficient at expressing ideas succinctly and clearly. From this you will develop a better understanding of what others write and say and an enhanced ability to communicate, something that matters in education, at work and in so many aspects of our lives. (57 words)

Final Draft

The importance of learning summary skills is that you learn to read intelligently and express ideas succinctly. You will develop a better understanding of what others write and say and an enhanced ability to communicate, something that matters in education, at work and in so many aspects of our lives. (50 words)

You may well find that you could have made other changes or worded things better. This is fine, especially if it means that you are thinking things out for yourself.

> **Now here are two passages for us to summarise, one from South Africa and the other from Hong Kong.**

We are going to summarise the two passages that follow, reducing them to about one third of their original length.

1. Mongi Zulu, AfricaNews reporter in Mbabane, Swaziland, reports on preparations for the 2010 football World Cup.

Swaziland teachers are mooting for the close down of schools in the country throughout the World Cup period in neighbouring South Africa. The teachers contend that their pupils would lose concentration during the football fiesta as well and they would like to give them an opportunity to watch the games.

A teacher in the Mbabane city told AfricaNews: "The World Cup fever is already affecting us. I personally think the pupils should be given a break in order for them to watch the soccer tournament."

"This year is different. The soccer mood is affecting us as teachers already. I strongly believe that the Swaziland National Association of Teachers (SNAT) has to do something as the focus of teachers and pupils will shift as they will not give themselves for school work but watch the World Cup soccer games," another teacher from one of the top schools who pleaded anonymity said.

Most of them concurred with their colleagues and argued that it would be a waste of time to keep them in class as Africa as a whole celebrates the World Cup on home soil.

However, the General Secretary of SNAT, Muzi Mhlanga, said they are aware of the concerns but are yet to discuss them with the Ministry of Education. "The issue of taking a break in June is among issues that would be discussed. We will be informing the ministry about the break," he said.

Minister of Education and Training Wilson Ntshangase said there is no way that classes can be suspended for teachers and pupils to watch the 2010 Soccer World Cup.

"We can't afford to make the pupils fail just because of the World Cup. I love soccer too, but I can't leave work just to watch the tournament. I think even teachers should look at it the same way," the minister said.

"But South African schools will enjoy an extended holiday break for the 2010 World Cup. The winter holidays which normally last 15 days

will now be adjusted to 22 days to accommodate the global event in order to avoid pupil and teacher absenteeism."

348 words

Identify the main idea in each sentence. *(On paper you could cross out unwanted words.)*

Swaziland teachers *are* **mooting for the close down of schools** *in the country* **throughout the World Cup period** *in neighbouring South Africa.* **The teachers contend that their pupils would lose concentration during the football fiesta** *and* **would like them to have an opportunity to watch the games.**
(Same subject in both sentences. They want something and they claim something, a. and b.)

A teacher in the Mbabane city told AfricaNews: "The **World Cup fever** *is already* **affecting us.** *I personally think the* **pupils should be given a break** *in order for them* **to watch** *the soccer tournament."*
(Another claim, about the effect of the competition, c., and a repetition of the very first idea – allowing time off during the competition.)

"This year is different. The soccer mood is **affecting us** *as teachers* **already.** *I strongly believe that the Swaziland National Association of Teachers (SNAT) has to do something as the focus of teachers and* **pupils** *will shift as they* **will not give themselves for school work but watch the World Cup** *soccer games,"* *another teacher from one of the top schools who pleaded anonymity said.*
(Mostly repetition here – schools are already affected, and pupils will not concentrate. One new idea – the pupils will watch anyway, d.)

Most of them *concurred with their colleagues and* **argued that it would be a waste of time to keep them in class** *as Africa as a whole celebrates the World Cup on home soil.*
(More repetition – pupils will not concentrate.)

However, the **General Secretary of SNAT,** *Muzi Mhlanga, said they are aware of the concerns but are* **yet to discuss them with the Ministry** *of*

Education. "The issue of taking a break in June is among issues that would be discussed. We will be informing the ministry about the break," he said. (One new idea – e. – no discussion yet with the minister.)

Minister *of Education and Training Wilson Ntshangase* **said there is no way that classes can be suspended** *for teachers and pupils to watch the 2010 Soccer World Cup.*

"We can't afford to make the pupils fail just because of the World Cup. I love soccer too, but I can't leave work just to watch the tournament. I think even teachers should look at it the same way," the minister said. (A new idea – f. – the minister's refusal to suspend classes.)

"But South African schools will enjoy an extended holiday break *for the 2010 World Cup. The winter holidays which normally last* **15 days will now be adjusted to 22** *days to accommodate the global event in order to avoid pupil and teacher absenteeism."*

(Another new idea – g. – that in neighbouring South Africa additional holidays will be granted.)

There are 125 words highlighted out of 348.

List each point just once:

a. Swaziland teachers want schools closed during the soccer World Cup in South Africa.
b. Teachers claim that pupils will be unable to concentrate.
c. They claim that the World Cup is already affecting their work.
d. They claim that pupils will watch matches in any case.
e. No discussion yet with the minister.
f. The minister says that classes cannot be suspended.
g. In South Africa school holidays extended from 15 to 22 days during the competition.

78 words

Decide whether the main points are in the best order:

a. Swaziland teachers want schools closed during the soccer World Cup in South Africa.
b. They claim that the World Cup is already affecting their work.
c. No discussion yet with the minister.
d. The minister says that classes cannot be suspended.
e. Teachers claim that pupils will be unable to concentrate.
f. They claim that pupils will watch matches in any case.
g. In South Africa school holidays will be extended from 15 to 22 days during the competition.

Write a first draft, linking points to save words:

Swaziland teachers want schools closed during the soccer World Cup in South Africa which, they claim, is already disrupting classes. They have yet to discuss the matter with the minister, who says that classes cannot be suspended. Teachers claim that pupils will be unable to concentrate and will watch the matches in any case. In South Africa school holidays will be extended from 15 to 22 days during the competition.

70 words

Now read aloud your draft and check that all the main points are included. Your ears should tell you whether further modification is required to make it even easier to follow.

2. Humour me. Adapted from the *South China Morning Post*, November 4, 2009.

A determined group of comedians want Chinese stand-up to tickle more funny bones.

As comedy impresario Jami Gong sees it, diversity is a sign that Chinese-language improv is starting to take off. For the first time since he began organising an international comedy festival three years ago, the Chinese section drew contestants from outside Hong Kong – four mainlanders and an American, in addition to five Hongkongers.

Chinese-language stand-up isn't a novel concept in Hong Kong: local funnymen such as Dayo Wong Chi-wah have been entertaining fans for years with their brand of humour. But although their performances are called dung duk siu – an almost literal Cantonese translation of stand-up comedy, they're typically held in concert halls and stadiums. The experience is very different from the intimate shows that form the backbone of stand-up circuits in the West.

Stand-up comedy is new to many people in Hong Kong, Gong says.

"I still get calls from people asking if there are seats at the venue because they think stand-up comedy means they have to stand to watch the show."

But the scene has developed since the New Yorker relocated to Hong Kong and opened his club in 2006. Gong's workshops have already produced some popular comedians, most notably Vivek Mahbubani, who won in the English section in 2007 and the Chinese section last year.

Cultural differences between English and Chinese-speaking crowds, however, mean comedians need to tailor their material differently. While Leung's routine focuses on her life as a single woman in Hong Kong, Mellen, another contestant and Mahbubani play on the contrast between their foreign looks and fluency in Cantonese.

"Ultimately, everyone wants to laugh at a gweilo (foreign devil) who speaks broken Cantonese," says Mellen, who likens himself to an egg because he's "white on the outside but yellow on the inside".

For banker Hu Yebi, who took the first prize in the Chinese section at this year's comedy festival, doing stand-up is primarily a form of stress relief.

"It feels good to make people laugh, even if they're laughing at me," says the 46-year-old Beijing native.

Much of Hu's set centres on his day job: he compares banking to robbery, although most of the work is mundane and tedious. He even looks the part, appearing in a sober business suit and maintaining a stern expression even when delivering the punchline. His routine draws on two distinct cultures: he combines the deadpan delivery of his idol, David Letterman, with the quick patter reminiscent of cross-talk, or xiang sheng, a traditional Chinese comedy format involving rapid-fire repartee between two performers.

416 words

This time you are going to rely more on yourself.
A first list of points:

a. As Jami Gong sees it, diversity is a sign that Chinese-language improv is starting to take off.
b. For the first time in an international comedy festival the Chinese section drew contestants from outside Hong Kong.
c. Chinese stand-up isn't novel.
d. Typically held in concert halls and stadiums, very different from the West.
e. Stand-up is novel in Hong Kong but it has produced popular comedians.
f. Cultural differences require a different approach with Chinese speakers.
g. Everyone wants to laugh at foreigners with "broken" Cantonese.
h. Hu Yebi, banker and winner of the Chinese section, finds that stand-up provides a relief from stress.
i. He uses material from two different cultures: deadpan delivery and rapid-fire repartee.

119 words

> **White on the outside but yellow on the inside.**
>
> An important detail because it forms a striking,
> or easily remembered, description.

Now compare your list with this one. Don't expect them to be identical.

When you have written your first draft and read it aloud, try to reduce the number of words and ensure that one idea leads easily to the next.

Just before we move on – the CV – a summary of our education and our work. An introduction of ourselves to potential employers and others.

Here is a practical use to which we can put our summary skills. There are times when it is very useful to be able to present someone with a clear and carefully organised summary of our background, our education and our relevant experience, both paid and unpaid.

Our aim should be to present or send one or two pages from which essential information about us can be quickly read, in note form, rather than in complete sentences. The information can be presented in chronological order or arranged thematically. Instead of writing this out in continuous sentences, select and list important points, much as you have been doing for summaries, and set them out generously spaced in tabular form with sub-headings.

For example:

Personal
Born 1995. Unmarried.

Education
2000–2006 The Oaks Primary School, Chelmsford.
2006–2011 Wanstead HS – 6 GCSEs. English, Maths, Geography, Combined Science, IT, Art.

Employment
2008–2010 Paper round – daily, early morning deliveries.
2010–2011 Saturday job – retail – hardware shop.
2012–Present, full-time, shelf stacking at Sainsburys.

Interests
Rugby – play for local club.
Internet games.

Further Information
I'm learning to weld – my grandad's teaching me.
Travel – camping abroad with my family.

In this chapter I have led you through a very detailed approach to writing a summary. It is important to ensure that you understand the commentaries and model answers. Next – further comprehension and better understanding.

CHAPTER EIGHT

COMPREHENSION – PLUS

Demonstrating what you can really do.
Beyond the simplicities of multiple-choice.
Questions with clues and guesswork.
Questions without clues or guesswork.

Another joint exercise. Read the passage that follows and answer the three questions in Section A.

Official records state that the Pueblo Indians lived in New Mexico and Arizona. The word "pueblo" is the Spanish for town or village. The Spaniards found these American Indians living in apartment houses, some of them on the side of a cliff in order that they could be reached only by ladders. Whenever they were attacked by Apaches, the Pueblos would pull up the ladders. They grew corn, which they watered with water flowing in ditches. They wove cloth, made wonderful baskets, and created jars and pots out of clay proving how skilful they were at handcraft.

A. Use information from the passage to complete the following sentences.
(Your answers do not need to match these answers word for word.)

1. From the passage we understand that the Pueblo Indians were afraid of…

2. The Spaniards called these American Indians "Pueblos" because...
3. Some Pueblo Indians lived on the side of a cliff...

Reponses to Section A

1. From the passage we understand that the Pueblo Indians were afraid of attack.
2. The Spaniards called these American Indians "Pueblos" because they lived in settlements.
3. Some Pueblo Indians lived on the side of a cliff to be more secure.

Commentary on the responses to Section A

1. From the passage we understand that the Pueblo Indians were afraid **of attack**.

   In the fourth sentence we find the word **attack**, the only source of fear. Your answer might be a little longer: "of attack by Indians", identifying the Apaches as the cause of their fear. It must be made clear that it is some sort of violence or invasion which these Pueblo Indians fear. This is the key idea.

2. The Spaniards called these American Indians "Pueblos" **because they lived in settlements**.

   The Spaniards simply used their own word for town or village to describe these Indians who lived in settlements. The meaning of the word "pueblo" is explained before it is used to describe these native Americans and this indicates the importance of understanding this.

   Your answer must include the link between the meaning of "pueblo" and the communal living of these people. In this answer the word **because** provides that link. Another acceptable answer might be **"because they lived in towns or villages"** or **"because they lived in settled groups"**.

3. Some Pueblo Indians lived on the side of a cliff **to be more secure**.

   In the third sentence of the passage the information that some of the Pueblos lived on the cliffs is followed by words of explanation, "**in order that they could be reached only by ladders**". In the next sentence we learn that the ladders could be pulled up during an attack, which suggests that the Pueblos found this a way of thwarting such attacks. This is their means of security, the reason why they lived on the cliffs.

You might have answered something along the lines of: **to protect themselves** or **to prevent the Apaches from getting into their homes**. (Not **preventing the attacks** because the very act of arriving in a village and menacing the population is itself an attack.) The point of living up in the cliffs is to survive an attack, not prevent one.

Assembling an Answer

With this type of question you are expected to understand the passage sufficiently to be able to complete statements about the material it contains. By completing these statements you reveal your understanding.

Finding the answer partly written for you provides clues about the material you need to add, which is suggested by the words that start the sentence. Then you need to find something with which you can complete the sentence.

This technique would help introduce the idea of reading and answering questions, but it is not a form of questioning that is found outside school.

The next questions, multiple-choice questions, are very easy to mark and were in use thirty years ago. Candidates indicated their choice of answers on card with a pencil and card readers were used to mark them, very quickly and very cheaply.

Now try a different type of question.

B. Tick the answers that you have chosen:

3. What were the Pueblo Indians afraid of?

    a.   A lack of water.

    b.   Attacks by Apaches.

    c.   Falling off ladders.

2. Why did the Spaniards call the Indians "Pueblos"?

    a.   They had always been known by that name.

    b.   They lived apart.

    c.   "Pueblo" is Spanish for "town" or "village".

3. Why did the Pueblo Indians live on the side of a cliff?

    a.   To be near the mountains.

    b.   To protect themselves from attacks.

    c.   To keep an eye on their vegetables.

Answers to Section B

1. b.

2. c.

3. b.

Commentary on Responses to Section B

1. b. – attacks by Apaches.

      Both watering the corn and pulling up ladders are mentioned but there is nothing in the passage to associate them with fear. There is a reference to attacks by Apaches and it is clear that these American Indians feared these attacks sufficiently to take steps to thwart them.

2. c. – "Pueblo" is Spanish for "town" or "village".

      We are not told for how long these people had been known as "Pueblo Indians". It is likely that they did live apart in a village occupied only by their own kind, but the passage makes it clear that the Spaniards adapted one of their words to describe these people.

3. b. – To protect themselves from attacks.

Although cliffs can be associated with mountains, there is no mention of mountains in the passage. It is possible that these villagers could keep watch over their vegetable patches from their cliff apartments, but living on the cliffs enabled the Indians to pull up their ladders to protect themselves from attack.

C. Answer the following questions with complete sentences; consider carefully the verbs in these questions.

4. Explain what it was that the Pueblo Indians feared.
e. How did they come to be called "Pueblo Indians"?
f. Explain why some of these people lived on cliffs.

Responses and Commentary for Section C

1. The Pueblo Indians feared attacks by Apaches and lived up on cliffs where they were safer.

An answer such as, "The Pueblo Indians feared attacks by Apaches," would be accurate, as a piece of information, as in **Sections A** and **B**. However, it explains nothing. The fact that some of the Indians at least, live up on the cliffs in order to escape the attacks is evidence of their fear and needs to be included in a complete answer.

2. They were given this name to describe them by Spaniards who use the word "pueblo", to mean town or village in their own language.

How did the Indians come to be named Pueblos? Another answer would be something like, "The Spaniards chose an appropriate word from their own language to describe them." The two essential elements to this answer are the **Spaniards**, who gave them the name and did so by **adapting a word** from Spanish.

3. The Pueblo Indians were attacked by Apaches from time to time. By living up on the cliffs the Indians could protect their homes by pulling up the ladders to prevent the Apaches gaining access.

By living on the cliffs, where ladders were needed to provide access, the Indians could repel any attackers, such as the Apaches. An answer that concentrated on the ability to defend homes on the cliffs would be a reasonable one, but including **the likelihood of attack** makes for a stronger answer. There is no doubt then that there is a good reason for the Indians to do this.

You Have Been Very Patient

In ordinary conversation receiving a number of varied answers to the same question would be most annoying. Why, we would ask, why doesn't this stupid person listen first time? In these exercises, however, we needed to explore the best ways of providing answers to questions.

You have probably worked out by now that the essential thing when answering this type of question is to add information or an explanation to simple facts. In this way you show your understanding in addition to your ability to pick out simple facts or make intelligent guesses.

Tourists Flock to Serengeti Park for Wildebeest Calving Spectacle
An article from Kenya's *Daily Nation*

A similar exercise here will reinforce what you have learnt about answering questions and then, in the next chapter, you will be left to your own devices. *(If you are feeling really confident now you may choose to go to the next chapter.)*

Tourists from around the world are flocking into Tanzania's Serengeti National Park. *Monday, March 4, 2013*

Tourists from around the world are flocking into Tanzania's Serengeti National Park to witness a unique experience of the wildebeest's annual birthing season. It is estimated that wildebeests will deliver new calves in the wilderness of the Serengeti plains at the rate of 8,000 newborns a day this season. Last month, more than 16,500 tourists, among them 5,800 domestic visitors, visited the national park to view the wonders of the wildebeests' calving event. The event also attracted wildlife researchers and zoologists. Last week park conservator William Mwakilema described the event as fantastic as it brings people to see miracles in the World Heritage

Site of Serengeti. "It is a spectacular sight. This is the only place on earth where nearly two million herbivores – eaters of grass – are giving birth at the same time in what is known as synchronised calving," he said.

"What I am seeing here is amazing and despite the pictures taken, many people back home may not believe it when I tell them about this important story," Belgian tourist Robert Joseph said.

The wildebeests' calving season is expected to last for the next five weeks at the end of which nearly 500,000 calves will be born into Tanzania's second largest national park. More enthralling, according to other tourists who are witnessing the event, the animals do not have to lie down but can deliver their babies as they move about. What is more, once the calves drop from the wombs, they start hopping about after two or three minutes.

"Normally, February is a low tourism season but we are recording nearly 17,000 visitors in just one month. It goes to show how the world's one and only synchronised calving event is creating great interest," said Mr Paschal Shelutete, public relations manager of Tanzania's national parks.

According to Serengeti park senior warden, Mr Godson Kimaro, the plains attract over 350,000 tourists every year. The peak tourism season is usually between the months of June and September when the north-bound great migration of the ungulates – animals with cloven or split hooves – takes place.

But most of the half a million newborn wildebeest calves may not survive the jungle – which is full of hyenas, lions and leopards, not to mention wolves, all of which should be happy to chew the soft and tender bones of the young herbivores. Mr Weth Mihayo, the tourism conservator at the park said half of the newborn wildebeests are likely to die from predator attacks, drowning in the giant Mara River or succumbing to the hostile elements that accompany the ungulates' 1,000 kilometer annual migration. (Predator – a creature that hunts other creatures.)

"But it is the way of Mother Nature, balancing the ecosystem because the 2010 animals' census indicated that there were 1.5 million wildebeests. This means an increase of 500,000 ungulates every year could overwhelm the park, therefore natural selection trims them to a manageable size," said Mr Mihayo.

493 words

Reread the passage then respond to the three groups of questions that follow. Remember to match up key words in the questions to key references in the passage.

Section A. Complete the three sentences below in the light of what you have learnt from the passage.

1. Large numbers of tourists are attracted to the Serengeti to…
2. Robert Joseph's words, "What I am seeing here is amazing", refer to…
3. The words of Mr Seth Mihayo, "balancing the ecosystem", are a way of explaining…

Suggested Responses with Commentaries

1. Large numbers of tourists are attracted to the Serengeti to watch the birth of large numbers of wildebeests.

   Two phrases in the opening paragraphs tell us that the visitors come, "to witness a unique experience" and "to view the wonders of the wildebeests' calving event".

2. Robert Joseph's words, "What I am seeing here is amazing", refer to his amazement at seeing vast numbers of herbivores giving birth at the same time.

   We are not told that he is amazed by the animals giving birth on the move, nor by the ability of the calves to get up and move about immediately they are born.

3. The words of Mr Seth Mihayo, "balancing the ecosystem", are a way of explaining the death of most of the calves that are born in such numbers that they would otherwise overwhelm the park. (Ecosystem – the interaction of climate, soil, plants and living creatures.)

   The phrase "balancing the ecosystem" is found in the penultimate paragraph which begins with the word "But". This links it back to the previous sentence, where we are told that half the calves will soon die. In the sentence which follows there are important ideas: the potential overwhelming of the park by wildebeests and the fact that natural selection, which leads to the death of many calves, prevents this.

In this specimen answer all the information has been included in one sentence and the advantage of this is not only the complying with the direction "complete the sentence" but keeping pieces of information together as they should be.

EXERCISE THIRTY

Choose an answer for each question and tick it to indicate your choice.

1. What brings large numbers of tourists to the Serengeti?

   a. The drama of natural selection.
   b. The opportunity to take lots of photographs.
   c. The birth of vast numbers of wildebeests.

2. What is it that amazes Robert Joseph?

   a. The large number of visitors.
   b. The arrival of thousands of wildebeest calves every day.
   c. The death of so many calves.

3. To what do the words "balancing the ecosystem" refer?

   a. The natural forces that prevent the number of wildebeests becoming a threat to the park.
   b. Drowning in the River Mara.
   c. Predators and hostile elements.

Go on, you can check Exercise Thirty for yourself.

1. Look for just the information required by the question.

2. Find the relevant part of the passage to check that you have considered anything that might be required.
3. Make sure that your choice of answer contains all that is required.

In the next section there will be specimen answers which you will have to compare with your own answers. This is to encourage you to think things out for yourself and save me half an hour's hard work, marking.

EXERCISE THIRTY-ONE

Answer the following questions about the passage with complete sentences.

1. What do you think brings tourists to the Serengeti?
2. Overwhelmed by numbers. What part do large numbers play in this account of the Serengeti?
3. What is, "the way of Mother Nature"?

ANSWERS TO THE QUESTIONS IN CHAPTER EIGHT

EXERCISE THIRTY

1. c.
2. b.
3. a.

EXERCISE THIRTY-ONE

Compare your responses with these suggestions.

1. The principle attraction is the sheer number of wildebeests giving birth, but there is also the amazing ability of the calves to move on immediately after birth and the drama of the natural hazards they face.
2. Firstly, there is the huge number of tourists who come to the park, then the vast herds of wildebeests giving birth and finally the array of predators and other threats to the newborn calves. Together these three things all contribute to the impression of the enormous scale of the park.
3. "Mother Nature's way" is to check an imbalance in one area by means of another natural agency or force; here predators and other natural forces keep the number of wildebeests in check which prevents damage to the park.

What Next?

In this chapter I have presented you with questions in different guises to help you find ways of answering questions confidently.

By this stage you should be able to ask yourself questions about the contents of your answers as well as check the way you put them into words, by reading them **aloud**.

Got your passport? The next chapter introduces more material from around the world.

CHAPTER NINE

STRENGTHEN YOUR COMPREHENSION SKILLS

*by understanding the world; look at some of the things
that the English-speaking world is telling us about itself.*

Discover journo-tourism – here we bring you:

*Health, politics, earthquake-proofing buildings,
sport, family trauma and music.*

Apply your skills to anything written in English.

Six newspaper or web articles for you to work on.
Answer the questions in complete sentences then check them yourself.
Specimen answers are not provided, but for each question there is an indication
of the essential feature(s) of an answer.

Each section finishes with one or two questions about the writing of the
article.

| 171

Canwest News Service
Canada Will Ice Younger Hockey Club in 2010
By Wayne Scanlan, October 27, 2009 11:31am

Since his rookie season, Roberto Luongo has been the league's most consistent goalie and proved he can compete at an elite level with the likes of other Team Canada potentials Martin Brodeur, Cam Ward and Marc-André Fleury.

Now that the Olympic torch is on the move, expect the hockey hype to build until Canada names its men's roster for Vancouver sometime in December.

Fans and media are already all over this one, with weekly dissertations on which Olympic candidates are hot or not, who is healthy and who is hurt.

Did Marc Savard of the Boston Bruins lose his chance to make Team Canada when he broke his foot during the pre-season (he started the season before re-injuring it)? Or did he have a shot to begin with? Savard, a crafty centre and power-play specialist, was not invited to the Olympic orientation camp in Calgary last summer.

Savard's teammate, Milan Lucic, built like a real bruin roaming the woods, was at the camp in his role as a bruiser, but is also sidelined, with a broken finger.

Even if official Canadian selectors don't get as caught up as the media are in the ebbs and flows of individual players in the early weeks of the NHL season, they are scouring these games to watch prospective candidates in live action. As one selector told Canwest on Friday, the time to shine is now and over the next month or so, especially for position players.

Goaltenders will be given an extended audition, through November and into December. Given the number of injuries to hit big-name international players already, all bets are off on a final roster until the Olympics approach.

278 words

EXERCISE THIRTY-TWO

1. What event in the world of ice hockey is the centre of attention here?
2. Explain the difficulties for some players as they hope to be included.
3. What advice is given to ambitious players?
4. Explain the difficulties for the selectors.
5. With what creature is Milan Lucic compared?
6. Which word is used to describe the intensity of the selectors' search for talent?

THE AUSTRALIAN
Coalition Yet To Sign Off On Asylum Plan: *Ben Packham*
March 5, 2013 1:34pm

SENIOR opposition figures have failed to endorse colleague Scott Morrison's plan for new behaviour rules for asylum-seekers, while confirming the proposal has not been signed off by shadow cabinet.

Amid government claims the Coalition is demonising asylum-seekers, opposition legal affairs spokesman George Brandis said he was unable to explain the policy.

"I don't think it's for me to do that. It's for Mr Morrison, as the shadow immigration minister, to specify the details of such protocols," Senator Brandis told Sky News.

"I haven't had a discussion with Mr Morrison about this particular matter. When the shadow cabinet next meets, no doubt that matter will be addressed."

Opposition treasury spokesman Joe Hockey also appeared to distance himself from the proposal, which would impose new "behaviour protocols" on asylum-seekers and require neighbours to be notified when bridging visa-holders were living in the vicinity.

"That's an issue for debate," Mr Hockey said. "My personal view of this doesn't matter."

On the ABC's Q&A program last night, deputy Liberal leader Julie Bishop suggested the policy had been announced on the run.

"We were responding to a circumstance that we hadn't realised had got so bad," she said.

"We are responding to the circumstances as they unfold."

Julia Gillard accused the opposition of demonising asylum-seekers for political gain.

"Mr Abbott and his team have been out there in the community trying to stoke fear and trying to profit from that fear."

Mr Morrison announced the proposed new protocols following the indecent assault of a student in her dormitory at Macquarie University in Sydney, allegedly by an asylum-seeker.

He said asylum-seekers released into the community would normally be kept in detention and had only had "light-touch assessments" by security agencies.

After Mr Morrison was accused by Labor and the Greens of dog-whistle politics, he said his comments had been met with overreaction and hysteria.

"They are in a special class because they would otherwise be in detention and the Minister for Immigration is otherwise responsible," Mr Morrison told the ABC's Insiders program on Sunday.

338 words

Questions

1. What is the basis for the Australian government's accusation against the opposition?
2. What do we learn about the opposition's proposals?
3. How would you describe the announcements made by opposition spokesmen?
4. Why do you think the author quotes four politicians?

Suggestions

1. The demonising of asylum seekers for political gain.
2. The imposition of new "behaviour protocols" on asylum seekers and requirement that neighbours be notified when temporary visa-holders are living in the vicinity.
3. Uncoordinated, chaotic, in disarray.
4. To leave the reader to judge their words for him or herself and to bring the account to life, as if we were actually present during an argument.

Trinidad Express
TALENTED: Xavier Strings, a band that explores the versatility of the violin and viola with modern electronic instruments – keyboard, guitars and drum and bass – is among the acts headlining Jazz Artistes on the Greens 2013.

'The premier jazz event on the local social calendar'
By Verdel Bishop
Story Created: February 28, 2013 at 11:05pm ECT

A number of local, regional and international jazz musicians will be featured in the Jazz Artistes on the Greens concert (JAOTG), on Saturday March 16, 2013 at The Greens, Farm Road, St Joseph (WASA Sports Grounds) from 4pm. The 11th edition of the concert will feature Latin Jazz Sextet, Alexis Baro, Jesse Ryan 6TET, Xavier Strings, and pannist Andy Narell and other artistes. (Pans, originally made from scrap oil drums and played to produce the distinctive sound of a steel band.)

Staged by Production One Limited, the event is being billed as one of the premier jazz events on the local social calendar. Concert organiser Rolf Doyle said patrons can expect great music and a festival atmosphere. He described the jazz concert as a contemporary blend of Latin and Caribbean flavours. "Over the years what we have found is that more and more non-traditional jazz lovers are coming to experience the event. We have seen an increase of a younger audience who are appreciative of the music. The whole atmosphere is relaxed and laid back and very festive. You can walk with your mats, pillows, blankets or beach chairs and lull off. There will be a well-stocked bar, food and a lot of giveaways," Doyle said.

Doyle said patrons are more appreciative of the new open air St Joseph venue. The concert was previously held at the Centre for Creative Arts, UWI St Augustine. "People are a lot more comfortable in the new location. It's open air, well-lit and secure; there is secured parking. Patrons loved the old venue but they are also appreciative of the new venue," Doyle said.

Alexis Baro (trumpeter, flugelhornist) was born into a musical family in Havana, Cuba. Classically trained, he took up the trumpet as a youngster, pursuing his music studies until ultimately receiving a teaching certification from Havana's Amadeo Roldan Music Institute.

Best known as a Latin jazz specialist, Baro began exploring a multiplicity of other musical styles after moving to Toronto in 2001, embracing not only the jazz genre but adding R&B, funk, and calypso, working with a diverse list of artists that included Ruben Vazquez, Evaristo Machado, Cassava, David Rudder, The Clash, Son Ache, and Kollage. His artistic abilities led to more high-profile engagements, too, backing touring entertainment names including The Temptations, Donny Osmond, Sheena Easton, and Jon Secada.

In early 2008, Baro released his debut CD, 'Havana Banana', featuring a sextet of some of the most accomplished players on Toronto's jazz roster. He has been nominated for Best Trumpet Player at the National Jazz Awards for 2005, 2006 and 2007 and is co-winner of a Juno as well as a Gemini for best live performance with Kollage.

Andy Narell, with his first solo album in 1979 took the steelpan out of the steelband and brought it into the jazz band, and with every recording and concert since, he has explored the possibilities and expanded the role of the pan in contemporary music. 2011 marked the release of Narell's DVD package 'Alive', which includes two full length documentaries about his work. 'Andy and the Jumbies' takes us from the panyards of Trinidad to the streets of New York, and follows his projects with Trinidad All Stars Steel Orchestra and the great calypsonian Relator, also featuring interviews with David Rudder, Ray Holman, Peter Minshall, and Kim Johnson. 'Calypso Fever' documents Andy's collaboration with the WDR Big Band, merging the Andy Narell Steelband with the WDR to create a new 40 piece orchestra.

Narell has made more than a dozen albums as leader, one as co-leader with Relator (University of Calypso), two as co-leader of the Caribbean Jazz Project (with Paquito D'Rivera and Dave Samuels), and two as co-leader of Sakésho (with Mario Canonge, Michel Alibo, and Jean Philippe Fanfant). Along the way he has worked with artists as diverse as Chucho Valdes, Bela Fleck, Marcus Miller, Maraca y Otro Vision, Willie Colon, Bebo Valdes, Flora Purim and Airto, Vince Mendoza, The WDR Big Band (Köln), The Metropole Orchestra (Holland), Andre Ceccarelli, Spyro Gyra, Dr Billy Taylor, Nancy Wilson, Irakere, Tito Puente, Orquestra Aragon, David Rudder, Black Stalin, Andre Tanker, Angelique Kidjo, Etienne Mbappé, Mokhtar Samba, Karim Ziad, Ray Lema, Kora Jazz Trio, Kassav, Vusi

Mahlasela, Philippe Lavil, Toto, Aretha Franklin, and the Kronos String Quartet. He has performed on movie scores by James Horner, Maurice Jarre, Elmer Bernstein, Hans Zimmer, Michel Colombier, and Thomas Newman, and his compositions have been featured in the film The Firm, and on TV shows such as Designing Women and Going to Extremes, as well as commercials for Apple Computers, Sony, Porsche, and Southwest Bell.

Xavier Strings is a band that explores the versatility of the violin and viola with modern electronic instruments – keyboard, guitars and drum and bass. At its core are sisters Janine and Janelle Xavier – two experienced and versatile violinists, violists and vocalists. These improvisational specialists have performed in Europe and across the Caribbean, in a range of jazz, classical, Caribbean and fusion musical ensembles and as soloists. They created and performed original work for the BBC and have also worked alongside a host of acts including local artists like the late Ras Shorty I, and the Love Circle, Black Stalin, Sean Daniel, Rikki Jai and Ravi B. Between them, they have graced the stages of Jazz, Music Festivals and Carnivals in Trinidad and Tobago and the UK.

893 words

EXERCISE THIRTY-THREE

1. Explain the musical essence of this concert.
2. What are we told about the new venue?
3. Explain Andy Narell's musical innovation.
4. What is distinctive about Xavier Strings?
5. Identify the most important common characteristic of all the artistes mentioned.
6. What do you think the writer is trying to suggest with the words, "from the panyards of Trinidad to the streets of New York"?

The New Zealand Herald
Shock In Store For Building Owners With At-risk Assets
By Anne Gibson
Monday, March 4, 2013, 10:52am

The Government wants 193,000 major structures assessed within five years for earthquake safety. This week – before the deadline for submissions on the plan – Anne Gibson examines the big shake-up.
Heritage buildings will be assessed for earthquake safety. Photo / John Anderson

(In February 2011 an earthquake caused severe damage in Christchurch, New Zealand's second-largest city, killing 185 people.)

The Government is proposing building owners strengthen earthquake-prone buildings within the next 15 years so that by 2028, we will be much safer if another major quake strikes.

Building and Construction Minister Maurice Williamson is fronting a national campaign for all non-residential and multi-unit, multi-storey residential buildings – of which there are about 193,000 – to be seismically assessed within five years.

Information about whether a building is above or below the earthquake-prone building threshold would be made publicly available on a register.

An earthquake-prone building is defined as being below 33 per cent of the standard required of a new building, and those built before 1976 are being targeted for assessment. Buildings with unreinforced masonry are also classed as at-risk.

It is expected that 15,000 to 25,000 buildings will be assessed as earthquake-prone – a figure that could rise – and all will have to be strengthened or demolished within 15 years of the legislation taking effect.

At present, owners have about 28 years on average to bring their buildings up to code or demolish, Mr Williamson said.

Opposition leaders are critical of the plan, saying there is not enough information to put forward a realistic strategy.

Labour's building and housing spokesman, Raymond Huo, said the Ministry of Business, Innovation and Employment's consultation document did not contain enough data to be able to accurately gauge how much the changes could cost or the true number of earthquake-prone buildings in New Zealand.

"If the Government's own ministry has insufficient data at present to give a clear indication, it's not good enough," Mr Huo said.

The ministry points the finger at councils, citing "poor information on the number and specific location of earthquake-prone buildings across the country, due to inadequate data collection."

The ministry also points to failings by central government, for providing limited information and guidance to local authorities on stronger buildings.

The plan has also met with outrage from some civic leaders and landlords. Dunedin Mayor Dave Cull, Otorohanga Mayor Dale Williams and Hastings Mayor Lawrence Yule, who is also president of Local Government NZ, have spoken out against the proposals, claiming provincial towns and rural communities would be financially ruined.

Timaru Mayor Janie Annear has described the proposals as devastating.

But Mr Williamson said the Canterbury Earthquakes Royal Commission report showed the Government had to take the issue seriously.

The minister said assessments would initially be a desk-top exercise, examining materials, design and structure, and then if an owner objected, a more detailed analysis by an engineer would be needed.

"We must ensure the earthquake-prone buildings policy system strikes an acceptable balance between protecting people from serious harm, and managing the significant economic implications of strengthening or removing the most vulnerable buildings," he said.

The Government was mindful of the potential cost put on owners but the destructive Canterbury earthquakes highlighted the need to review and improve the system of dealing with unsafe buildings.

Labour's Mr Huo said he understood why mayors were so worried.

"It's not right for the minister to criticise the local mayors, because they are kept in darkness and of course are concerned about the possible loss of their heritage. If you talk to building owners in Christchurch, not many can afford to get their buildings strengthened to 33 per cent and insurance companies refuse to cover the costs associated with strengthening issues," Mr Huo said.

"Of course building owners, consumers and local mayors are concerned and are going to the minister for a solution. But when they do this, they're being told it's their problem," he said.

Mr Williamson has suggested building owners could be required to do as little as posting a sign saying the building was not up to earthquake strength.

But Mr Huo said this was plainly inadequate.

"I think that is a pretty flippant option… It's a hands-off approach, it's somebody else's problem."

He had talked to builders, engineers, designers and subcontractors and said the feedback was that the Government needed to balance various interests, including public safety, costs, heritage, the viability of businesses and the wider interests of small communities.

Asked what alternative Labour proposed to the Government's scheme, Mr Huo said its policy had not yet been formulated, nor had Labour released an official statement in response to Mr Williamson's stance or the ministry's consultation document.

Mr Williamson said the proposals were up for public comment. A consultation document was issued after the Canterbury Earthquakes Royal Commission report was released to the Government in October and to the public on December 7.

Meetings have been held in the past few weeks to get feedback about the issues and submissions on the document close this Friday.

Mr Williamson said the Government would release its decision around the middle of this year.

789 words

Most of us live free from the fear of earthquakes, but a friend on a visit to NZ was lucky to walk out of Christchurch Cathedral five minutes before it was destroyed by the quake.

As practical people, with lives to live, we often have to take notice of technical details and ask, how will all this affect me?

EXERCISE THIRTY-FOUR

1. Outline the main aspects of the government's proposals.
2. What are the current requirements of property owners?
3. What does the government propose to do with the information about assessments?

4. What seems to be the main objection to the proposals?
5. What is the government doing now?
6. How satisfied would you be with Mr Huo's response when asked what the Labour opposition proposed as an alternative policy?

AP Associated Press
Taken from:
Argentine stolen at birth, now 32, learns identity
AP foreign, Wednesday, February 24, 2010

MICHAEL WARREN – *Associated Press Writer* – *BUENOS AIRES, Argentina (AP)*
Abel and Francisco Madariaga
Father and son together for the first time

The search is finally over for Abel Madariaga, whose pregnant wife was kidnapped by Argentine security forces 32 years ago.

After decades of doubt and loneliness, of searching faces in the street in hopes they might be related, Madariaga has found his son.

"I never stopped thinking I would find him," the 59-year-old father said, squeezing his son's arm during a packed news conference Tuesday.

"For the first time, I know who I was. Who I am," the young man said, still marveling at his new identity: Francisco Madariaga Quintela, a name he only learned last week.

The Grandmothers of the Plaza de Mayo rights group believes about 400 children were stolen at birth from women who were kidnapped and killed as part of the 1976-1983 dictatorship's "dirty war" against political dissidents, which killed as many as 30,000 people.

Madariaga and his wife, Silvia Quintela, were members of the Montoneros, a leftist group targeted for elimination by government death squads. He last saw his wife – a 28-year-old surgeon who treated the poor in a Buenos Aires suburb – being pushed into a Ford Falcon by army officers dressed as civilians as she walked to a train on Jan. 17, 1977.

Madariaga managed to flee into exile to avoid the same fate. Ever since, he has made finding the children of those who disappeared his life's cause.

Returning to a democratic Argentina in 1983, he became the grandmothers group's secretary and first male member. He lobbied the government to create a DNA database and dedicate judicial resources to the effort, and developed strategies for persuading young people with doubts about their identities to come forward and get DNA tests.

All the while, his own son's fate remained a mystery.

As it turned out, Quintela gave birth to the son the couple had planned to name Francisco in July 1977 while imprisoned in Buenos Aires. Surviving prisoners later reported that the newborn was taken from her the next day, and she disappeared shortly thereafter.

A military intelligence officer brought the baby, his umbilical cord still attached, home to his wife and they named him Alejandro Ramiro and never told him he was adopted. The marriage didn't last – the husband was a violent man, Francisco Madariaga said – and he never felt as if he belonged, looking nothing like his brother and sister.

While this family fell apart, the younger Madariaga escaped in his own way, twice touring Europe as a professional juggler.

Meanwhile, the officer who had taken him home to his wife was convicted of murdering a couple and their child during a robbery in 1994 and served a 10-year prison term.

Francisco Madariaga's doubts increased, until finally he confronted his adoptive mother. "She broke down and was able to tell me the truth," he recalled, adding that he can't say he blames her. "There was so much violence – physical and mental – and she suffered. She also was a victim."

On Feb. 3, encouraged by his friends, the young man approached the grandmothers group to tell their story. Fearful of his adoptive father, he rushed to take a blood test the next day, and DNA results arrived last week. Father and son finally met on Friday – the same day the adoptive father was arrested on suspicion of illegal adoption.

Over the years, the grandmothers' group has succeeded in identifying 100 children of the disappeared. Madariaga has organized many news conferences announcing such victories. This time, his chest heaved as he presented his own son to the world.

"At times I wondered what the hell I was living for. I had to find a way to continue, thinking about everyday things, hoping for this moment of happiness," the elder Madariaga said. "Hugging him that first time, it was as if I filled a hole in my soul."

Trembling before the cameras, Abel Madariaga recalled his reunion with his son.

"When he came through the door that night, we recognized each other totally, and the hug that brought us together was spectacular," he said. Francisco Madariaga stopped smiling only at the mention of the name he was given by his adoptive family.

"Never again will I use this name," he said. "To have your identity is the most beautiful thing there is."

707 words

This is one of the most moving pieces of journalism I have ever encountered.

Many of us will find it hard to imagine living in a country where the forces of law and order turn on those they are bound to protect.

The bravery and determination of the Madariagas is breathtaking as well as humbling.

Sadly, Francisco Madariago died on September 20th 2020, aged only 43.

EXERCISE THIRTY-FIVE

1. What do we learn about the Montoneros?
2. What do we learn about the adoptive father?
3. Explain the fate of Francisco's natural mother.
4. Why would being reunited with his own son be so especially moving for Abel Madariaga?

5. Identify any words or phrases used to describe the emotions of the father and son.
6. The second sentence is a periodic one. (Remember?) What is the effect of the last five words?
7. Which words indicate Francisco Madariaga's understanding of his adoptive mother?

Isabelle Caro bravely challenges the power of the picture, to reveal truths rather than misleading images.

Health & Medical News
Anorexia Fashion Ads – Statement Controversy
September 29, 2007
Posted by: Dr Dobson

In the midst of Milan's all-important Fashion Week, the picture that is turning heads in Italy is a shocking one. An Italian advertising campaign featuring photos of an Italian label, Nolita and an emaciated girl is supposed to serve as a warning to young women, but medical experts fear it could encourage anorexia and other eating disorders. It's the latest work by controversial Italian photographer Oliviero Toscani.

It shows what anorexia looks like stripped bare. And, it is re-igniting the debate in the fashion industry over whether designers should make sure that the models who appear on their catwalks are really healthy. French actress Isabelle Caro, 27, who has suffered anorexia for 15 years and weighs just 31 kilograms appears in the adverts next to the slogan "No Anorexia".

"When I see myself now, I say, 'what a horror'", Caro told a French TV interviewer. "I'm trying to get out of it, and I want young women to know that is possible."

The campaign, for fashion label Nolita, Flash & Partners is intended to show the reality of anorexia – an illness the company says that "in most cases is caused by the stereotypes imposed on women by the fashion world."

Clothing designers and the government this week praised the ad for targeting anorexia, but endocrinologist Fabrizio Jacoangeli warned the campaign risked creating "competition" among anorexic people to be like the woman in the photograph.

"When you do something extreme, there are always people who oppose it," Toscani said. "It shouldn't be the photos that shock, but the reality."

The Italian photographer said he became aware of anorexia while working in the fashion world.

"It's this milieu that influences women to go on diets, to become thin. I studied the disease while making a short film about a 16-year-old girl suffering from anorexia that was shown at the Locarno (Italy) film festival in 2006," he said.

However, the campaign has already alienated some of the very people who champion the cause Nolita is trying to embrace. And it has also stirred up controversy over whether the brand is raising awareness about anorexia, or possibly profiting from it.

"This girl needs to be in a hospital, not at the forefront of an advertising campaign," said Fabiola De Clercq, founder and president of ABA, the Italian association against anorexia, bulimia and obesity.

Ms. De Clercq, who says she suffered from anorexia for more than 20 years, called the ads "useless and dangerous". She said the campaign "glorifies a woman who is sick and could lead others to be sickly thin because of all the attention."

432 words

EXERCISE THIRTY-SIX

1. What is the purpose behind the publication of this advertisement?
2. Explain the view of the woman who appears in the advertisement.
3. What contrary view is reported?
4. What is the view taken of this campaign by the second sufferer of anorexia mentioned in the article?
5. What is the effect of the sentence – "It shows what anorexia looks like stripped bare."?

ANSWERS TO THE QUESTIONS IN CHAPTER NINE

EXERCISE THIRTY-TWO

1. The selection of players for the national team.
2. Injury.
3. Show what you can do, now.
4. The number of injured players.
5. A bear.
6. Scoured.

EXERCISE THIRTY-THREE

1. Jazz with Caribbean and Latin influences.
2. Open air, well-lit and secure, secured parking.
3. Steel pan used in other types of music.
4. Traditional instruments used with electronic ones.
5. The large numbers of other artistes with whom they have worked.
6. Movement from a modest workshop on an island to one of the world's most important cities.

EXERCISE THIRTY-FOUR

1. Major buildings to be assessed for their ability to withstand earthquakes within five years and strengthened or demolished if necessary within fifteen years.
2. Improve property within twenty-eight years.
3. Publicise it.
4. The lack of data, or its poor quality.
5. Meetings, consultation.
6. No alternatives given, only three reasons (or excuses) why they offered none

– policy not yet formulated and no official statements yet in response, either to Mr Williamson's stance or to the ministry's consultation document.

EXERCISE THIRTY-FIVE

1. A left-wing group singled out for killing by the government of the dictatorship.
2. He was violent and was convicted of murder, robbery and finally arrested on suspicion of kidnapping.
3. Kidnapped, gave birth in prison then disappeared, presumed murdered.
4. He had worked for The Grandmothers of the Plaza de Mayo, an organisation that aimed to reunite child victims of the dictatorship with their parents. Now the organisation was able to reunite him with his own son.
5. Trembling before the cameras, his chest heaving, squeezing his son's arm, still marvelling at his new identity.
6. The last five words convey the central drama of the story and are preceded by references to elements of the father's struggle: decades of doubt, loneliness, searching and hopes.
7. She also was a victim.

EXERCISE THIRTY-SIX

1. To warn young women of the dangers of the stereotypes projected by the fashion industry which can lead to anorexia.
2. Appalled by her own state – keen to persuade other sufferers that they can escape.
3. A concern that the campaign will encourage other women to emulate the woman in the picture.
4. It glorifies a sufferer and the attention might encourage others to copy her.
5. It suggests that the campaign to save young women from anorexia reveals totally the effect of the disorder and uses powerful words – *stripped* and *bare* – often associated with modelling.

Things that we need to understand do not always come easily and so we had to make an effort here.

As you find some confidence things will get easier.

Next – questions about questions.

CHAPTER TEN

CLARIFYING AND COMMUNICATING WHAT WE UNDERSTAND

Questions and answers — uses to which English can be put.
Artificial intelligence.

"What do two and two make?"

If the response to this question is, "Five, miss," we would probably assume that someone had yet to learn to add up. The answer is perfectly clear; two and two can only make four. Or are things really that simple?

There is of course the possibility that a student is teasing a teacher by pretending not to know, but that would depend on that student knowing the right answer before deliberately giving a wrong one.

How Can We Answer Honest Questions?

Years ago, when smoking was still permitted on the London Underground, I watched a child of about four, sitting with her mother, opposite a couple who were both smoking.

"Mummy, why are those people smoking?"

The little girl was obviously unaware that personal questions about people can be very embarrassing and are better asked when they are not present. As she asked the question the little girl was clinging to her mother's neck and looking around at the couple who could not have been more than three feet/a metre away. She seemed concerned or anxious about the couple, as if she had been told that smoking was a bad thing to do and was surprised that these adults were prepared to harm themselves.

Her mother's reaction was to hold the child more tightly and to attempt to catch her eye so that she could communicate her motherly disapproval of a question asked in this direct way. In this context, in this situation, the mother felt unable to explain to her daughter that, although smoking is foolish and people should not do it, it was not illegal. Social convention, however, would not allow her to acknowledge the smokers' folly here.

What would you have done were you the child's mother, or one of the smokers sitting opposite?

All communication requires two parties; one person who speaks or writes something and another person who hears or reads the message. Sometimes it is impossible to ignore a voice or a text message: *Your house is on fire!* Sometimes it is easy to ignore the message: *You look awful today.*
Some questions, however, can be much more demanding:

Why did you throw ice cream at me?
Because it tastes horrible.
You're wearing your best suit.
I was bored.
The colour matches your shirt.

The important thing about a question is that it contains clues as to what is required or expected in the answer. The question about two and two asks about the combining of two numbers and so the answer will come in the form of another number. A question can also put you on the spot, making you think about an answer even if you do not want to give one.

In some circumstances – standing outside the headmistress's office at the age of five and yes, I can still remember playing firemen in the boys' toilets – the anticipation of questions that you will have to answer, and the consequences of your answers are worrying. Then there are the questions which trouble you while you are waiting to be interrogated by the police as you travel abroad. Which answer might you choose? Do you really want to tell the truth? Which answers do your interrogators want? How easily will they be able to check your answers?

The harder you try to answer your own questions, the more you are burdened by further questions.

Questions really do put us on the spot, but we should remember the importance of the truth, not only when we are answering questions, but also when we are asking them.

Fortunately, there are other things that we do with sentences.

Before You Begin the Next Exercises

The first three exercises are demanding and increasingly difficult; be prepared to take a break between them if you find them hardgoing.

The fourth section is more straightforward and practical. Each question requires just a moment's thought and is intended to get you to identify key aspects of any question quickly and effectively.

EXERCISE THIRTY-SEVEN

For each of these questions decide what else you might want to consider before making an answer. (For example, in answer to the previous question about two and two, you might want to give a straightforward answer, *four*, to show that you can add or because you might want to avoid upsetting the teacher or in order to bring to an end a boring conversation.)

a. Which flavour ice cream do you prefer?
b. Why's that?
c. Where has Daddy gone?
d. Why has Daddy gone?

EXERCISE THIRTY-EIGHT

Now consider another four questions.

a. Why have I got to do my homework?
b. Why have I got to do my homework now?
c. How did you get that mark on your face?
d. Why don't you come home on Tuesday evenings?

As we consider how we might respond to these questions we become more aware of the context in which they are asked and the audience to whom they are addressed. (The person we are speaking to.) Addressed to a teacher, question a. seems to challenge the idea that students should do additional work away from school. b. might be addressed to a parent to challenge a matter of timing.

> ### Audience
>
> Teachers sometimes forget to set homework. Why draw their attention to this?
>
> Sometimes parents don't understand the system, but if they find out you've misled them…?

Question b. is more obviously one asked by a teacher or some sort of supervisor with responsibility for the student's immediate activity. In c. *how* seems to imply an explanation of the way in which something happened, but often this type of question is used to get beyond the event to the reasons behind it which may be embarrassing, or worse.

A key word in d. is *home*, which suggests a shared residence and domestic life in which consideration for others is important. People who share a home are also likely to know about each other's comings and goings. To ask someone to account for their whereabouts depends on being close to them and entitled to feel let down at least if not informed about these matters. This is the context in which this question is to be answered.

Context

At school there are rules and regulations and people who check on these things – *pass your homework to the front of the class.*

At home there are distractions – *Mum, I think the cat's going to be sick.*

EXERCISE THIRTY-NINE

Questions That Control Conversations

Five questions now. This time try to consider how you might keep control of the conversation. Think about what the questioner wants to do and what you might want to achieve.

a. What else do you know?
b. Do you really expect us to believe that?
c. Do you expect the president to win the next election?
d. Do you expect, Mr President, to win the next election?
e. Prime Minister, would you like to respond to your deputy's call for your resignation?

The point of all this attention to questions is their challenging nature, the way that they make us think about what we are going to do or say next. Considering questions like this can help to show just what it is that we can do with language, with other types of sentence.

Closed and open questions

Closed questions expect simple answers – *yes, no* or an indication that an answer cannot be given.

Open questions allow the respondent to reply as fully as they wish or are able. Their key words, such as *what, why, when, who, which, how* and *where* provide clues for an answer.

EXERCISE FORTY

For each question identify its type (open or closed) and its key idea(s).

a.   Do you have a driving licence?
b.   Do you have the time?
c.   What is it about ice cream that pleases him so much?
d.   Which route do you prefer?
e.   Why do you go that way?
f.   Who threw that?
g.   How did that happen?
h.   Would you like to sit down?
i.   Do you think we should tell the judge?
j.   Would you like to make a statement?

What Questions Work in Other Ways

What? A request for clarification or amplification: explain what you mean, or speak louder.

What do you mean? Rather than the statement, *I don't understand*, which would suggest that you are incapable of understanding whatever has been

> said. This question suggests or implies that the speaker has failed to convey his or her message clearly
>
> *What do you think you're doing?* By ignoring the fact that people usually know what they are doing, the speaker is suggesting that you don't know and that you are somehow less normal or less intelligent. You might know that you should not be doing this, or you might not, but the speaker does not wish to accuse you directly. Whatever you are doing, the speaker has put you in a position where you have to explain yourself.

Last thoughts about questions – at least for the time being

It is said that a philosophy student at Cambridge opened a finals examination paper and read the first question, which was, *Is this a question?* For a few moments he sat quietly pondering the matter and then took up his pen and wrote:

If this is a question then this is an answer.

Then he replaced the cap on his pen, stood up and walked out with over two hours of the examination remaining.

It is also said that he was awarded a first-class degree, the top grade.

Whether we believe that by looking someone directly in the eyes we can be sure of hearing the truth, or whether we rely on truth drugs or lie detectors, we are keen to hear the truth. Behind much of our asking questions there lies this concern.

A thousand years ago, when our Anglo-Saxon forebears were required to answer questions in court, they could take with them an oath-helper, someone of good standing in the community who would vouch for their honesty so that the court would be more inclined to believe their evidence. The Saxon word for answer was *answerian* and both words contains the elements of *swear*, the manner in which we promise, on oath, to tell the truth in court.

Later, in medieval times, it was claimed that the barbarity of trial by ordeal would reveal the truth.

Now we put a deal of trust in references – both personal, for job applications for example, and academic, to validate truths upon which academic work is based. We hear frequently about closed circuit television, electronic monitoring, ID verification and security checks; such is our concern to receive truthful answers to questions.

Artificial Intelligence and Automated Communications

By means of artificial intelligence and automated communications all sorts of organisations use computer programmes called algorithms to monitor traffic from our computers and to contact us automatically.

Because they use our language to do this we need to be alert. Already in the book we have dealt with:

Fact and opinion (abusing our trust).
Questions and answers (evasion, distraction and manipulation).
Passive and active verbs (blame shifting).
Open and closed questions (controlling a conversation).
Subject and predicate/précis (focus on the matter in hand).

We also need to look out for the following:

Invitations with a hidden purpose – that lie.
These accompany a picture, of a celebrity for example, with words such as, *See More* or *Learn more.* When you click on the picture, expecting to see or learn more you are shown a sequence of advertisements that have nothing to do with the subject of the picture. The programmers of such sequences use your interest and the impulse that follows to lead your attention away from whatever you are doing to whatever they want you to see. Wardrobe "malfunctions", the failure of clothes to cover things, are often used to "hook" the viewer.

Feelings behind automated correspondence – which are false.
Oh, I would so like to show you something or *do join us for…*

There is of course no such enthusiasm. Someone has programmed a computer to deliver words to you in an attempt to manipulate you, to get you to do what they want you to do.

The avoidance of direct conversation – avoiding your questions.

Conversation allows us to ask for clarification and for direct and immediate answers. At the end of a good conversation we know exactly where we stand. We have obtained answers to our questions. Many organisations do not bother to publish their phone numbers so that we cannot talk to them. Then, if we contact them in writing, we must make it very clear that we expect them to meet our needs.

Visual "communication" – distraction and poor attention

The importance of written statements is well known. Properly written they provide a permanent record, one that can be analysed and explained. To be written properly, and to be fully understood, statements of any sophistication or significance require concentration and freedom from distraction so that our chains of thought are not broken.

Out of the blue advertising arrives on your computer. It concerns something you were looking up not long ago. Cookies allow companies to spy on you, to respond to your online activity with selected advertising, with you as the target. Bear that in mind before you respond.

If you are writing with any pictures around the screen, especially moving ones, take extra care to check your writing thoroughly.

Remember too, that artificial intelligence can be very helpful. As I type these words a spell-checker is monitoring my progress.

ANSWERS TO THE QUESTIONS
IN CHAPTER TEN

EXERCISE THIRTY-SEVEN

Which flavour ice cream do you prefer?

a. *Strawberry.* A single word might provide sufficient information. Several flavours might be suggested, requiring several words – I always try vanilla as a way of finding out whether a manufacturer can produce a good basic product, but I can always be tempted by *panna cotta* (Italian now – the phrase means cooked cream), *coffee* and *chocolate.* You might be tempted to add words of explanation for your preference.

Why's that?

b. How do you explain a preference? *I simply prefer chocolate. I don't know why.* This is a fact about you, which might be explained – your grandparents had an ice cream shop – but does not have to be justified. Asked about their favourite singer, some people might think they had to justify their preference – *Well, my mates all like her.*

Where has Daddy gone?

c. The answer might involve straightforward information – *next door* – or an explanation – *he's got bored with television and gone back to work.*

Why has Daddy gone?

d. The answer might involve a simple exclamation – *he's gone to borrow a phone charger* – or something more complex – *he's gone to buy your little sister's birthday present.* It might involve another question – *Well, what do you think?* – to suggest that a little more thought should have been given before asking such a silly question or perhaps to indicate a reluctance to discuss the topic.

a. and c. require simple pieces of information: a flavour or a place. Anything in addition is there because the respondent chose to include it. *Which* and *where* are the key words.

b. and d. require something more. In each case the key word is *why* which indicates that an explanation of some sort is required, a more demanding expectation.

EXERCISE THIRTY-EIGHT

a. *Why* – such a terrible word. You might want to explain the good reasons for doing homework – *the importance of education, the need to pass examinations or the benefits of establishing good work habits early in life* – to a son or daughter who wants to listen to an explanation. In other circumstances you might simply want to avoid the nightly row – *so that you can go out with your friends at the weekend/so that I will let you go out with your friends at the weekend.*

b. *Now.* Not later, not tomorrow, not next week. Not when your mum gets home or when this fascinating television programme is over. No, this very minute you must get started unless, by some miracle, you can come up with a good reason not to. The immediacy of all this is double – an immediate answer is required and then, if there is no immediate reason not to get started with your homework then you will have to begin, right now.

c. Are you questioning a child, or another adult? What is the relationship between the two parties? Is the questioner really interested in how the mark came to be there, or why it's there? There may simply be an innocent explanation – a playful pet perhaps, the result of bullying or something that the person with the mark was not aware of – make-up that was not completely removed. The word *how* may simply be doing its own job – seeking to know the manner in which the mark came to be there, or it may be leading the questioner towards a question with *why?* This may well require an answer that is more difficult.

d. It doesn't sound as if the questioner is anticipating a simple, straightforward answer – *You remember – I now have to work late on Tuesdays, so I stay with a colleague overnight.* The questioner might be a puzzled child or a suspicious wife. A child could well accept a straightforward answer, accompanied perhaps by a reassurance – *I'm sorry, I know you like to visit the local football club on Tuesdays.* A suspicious wife may well have intended the question as an accusation requiring a confession or a promise of better conduct in future.

EXERCISE THIRTY-NINE

a. *Else* indicates that previous answers may not have satisfied the questioner. Notice how the questioner appears to assume that there is more information that you could give. You have not been asked, *"Is there anything else you could tell us?"*, to which you could simply respond, *"No,"* and bring a potentially embarrassing conversation to an end. You might be left alone to ask yourself if a friend is going to stick to the story you have made up. You might feel disappointed that you cannot contribute any further to some sort of enquiry. The word *please* is not used, and this makes the question more of a command rather than an invitation such as, *"Would you like to tell us anything more?"*

   To avoid staying behind after school, or longer in the cells, this might be a good time to remember something helpful.

b. Your answer to a previous question was obviously not what was wanted or expected. This question is less a demand for information in the ordinary sense, but more a way of warning you that you have failed to satisfy your questioners and will have to try harder.

   You might decide to confess and take the punishment – picking up litter in the playground after school tomorrow, or a longer, indefinite spell in a country that has just broken off diplomatic relations with your country. Might it help to extend, elaborate or embellish (decorate or make beautiful) your original story? You were there, but only by coincidence. You didn't want to be noticed so you hid until the guilty parties, who you cannot identify, went away.

c. Imagine a reporter, microphone in hand, faced with a crowd of people, all eager to have their say. Like the previous question, this one seems to require a single-word answer: *yes* or *no*. Will you try to add to that?

   On the other hand, if we do not have an answer, if we really do not have an opinion, then what we are entitled simply to say is something like: *I don't know.* Like its predecessor, this question wants a simple answer, without the further complications that earlier questions invited. If you want to add further complications – *I don't know and I don't care* – that is something that you will have to decide.

d.   Replace a definite article – of course you remember – *the* – with a proper noun – the president's title, *Mr President*, and things have changed. There is no one else to whom the reporter is speaking; only the president can answer this question. Here we can sit back in front of the television and watch the game of politics played out in plain English.

Really, did I say *plain* English?

Like the three previous questions this one requires a simple answer, but do our politicians give simple answers when there is an opportunity to say more? No, of course they don't, and you realise that I have smuggled another closed question into our conversation.

What sort of answers might we consider, as a head of state facing an election? (Another question for you I'm afraid, this time an open question.)

No politician is likely to say, *I don't know*, however hard they try to be honest. You, Mr President, will not want to cause the slightest doubt about your approaching victory so you will feel obliged to answer *yes*. Here you are trapped, not by the inadequacies of your English, but by politics.

e.   As prime minister you know that you must respond to this challenge, whether you want to or not. You might want to respond, you might want to ignore the call in the hope that others will not take it seriously either, so you will answer *yes* or *no*. However, this bit, the basic answer to a basic question, will not be left by any politician. Before the interviewer has a chance to draw breath, you, Prime Minister (capitalised here because this is now a proper noun, the title by which you are addressed) will follow up with something like, *and you won't be surprised to hear me announce his replacement later today* or *but I will have something to say at tomorrow's press conference*.

Only one of the five questions here is straightforward and we have to consider what the words convey indirectly and directly about the context of the questions and about the questioner's purpose. Besides, *else* in a., *really* in b. suggests raised eyebrows and a pause while you await the next question. In d. that pause into which *Mr President* is inserted emphasises that this question is only for you to answer and emphasises your loneliness as president. In e. the words *would you like* form an invitation rather than a request, suggesting to you, Prime Minister, that it would be no trouble to you to provide an interesting response for this reporter who may be hoping that you will say more than you intended.

Three of the questions here are closed (Do you…, Will you…, Have you…) but you will probably not want to treat them as closed. You will want to open them out with a more substantial answer.

EXERCISE FORTY

a. Do you have a driving licence?

Closed. Nothing complicated here – you either have one or you do not. If, however, you happen to be driving without one then more questions are likely to follow. The context here is important – who is asking the question and in what circumstances? (A police officer who has just stopped you?)

b. Do you have the time?

This appears to be a closed question, but of course we never use this as a closed one. (Imagine what you would say if you received the answer, "*Yes, I have,*" from someone who walked away immediately.) By convention the question is usually a request for information functioning as an open question. In some circumstances a similar question, "*Do you know what the time is?*" could simply provide a sarcastic way of embarrassing or humiliating someone.

c. What is it about ice cream that pleases him so much?

Open. The answer might be short – *the flavour* – or long – *the sound of the last piece of the cone crunching between his teeth.* In either case the person who answers the question is constrained; his or her answer must contain at least a reference to something that might please someone about eating ice cream, a simple fact or an explanation.

d. Which route do you prefer?

Open, like c. *Which* indicates a choice between possibilities. Your answer might indicate a selection and be short – *via the north* – or long – *we could go round by the lake or, as an agreeable alternative, we could walk past the ice cream shop.*

e. Why do you go that way?

Open. *Why* – a word much loved by children who do not want to go to bed and teenagers who want to stay out late. *Why* delays the carrying out of an instruction and challenges the source of authority – usually a parent. Then, later in life, these young people may become politicians.

Why requires an explanation. An explanation could be based on a reason – *we wanted to buy an ice cream on the way* or on a preference – *That way is prettier.* It could be based on a simple fact – *the alternative route was blocked.*

f. Who threw that?

Closed. There is a very limited range of answers – either you know the identity of the person who threw whatever was thrown, or you do not. *Who*, the personal pronoun, indicates that the questioner expects to hear the name of the offender, or be told another way of identifying him or her – *the one with the ice cream in his hand.*

Very often the requirements of this type of question are ignored. People who fear the next question – *Was it you who threw that?* or *Did you throw that?* – will provide an answer before the question is asked and cry out, *It wasn't me, sir.* At this point a good teacher will change direction with, *Why are you so anxious to tell me something I was not asking for?*

g. How did that happen?

Open. *How* indicates that an explanation of some sort is required and *happen* obviously refers to an event, which you may well prefer to refer to as an accident. Of all the questions in the world, this one is least likely to elicit, evoke or provoke the correct answer: *It was my fault.*

Good answers will indicate an acceptance that something has happened and that the speaker is in a position to contribute an explanation.

The answer *I don't know*, which may be tempting, is likely only get you into further trouble.

h. Would you like to sit down?

Closed. This is an invitation which you might or might not like to accept. It's a gesture, inviting or encouraging you to relax. You might decide that relaxing and putting yourself at ease with the speaker would make you more vulnerable, more likely to accept the next invitation which might be more dangerous – *Would you like to tell us just what your friends have been doing?*

This, of course, is another closed question which is intended to put you at your ease and encourage you to tell your interrogator more than you intended.

i.   Do you think we should tell the judge?

Closed. *We* tells you that this is a decision to be shared. If you do not agree with the answer you may well have to launch a discussion with an open question such as *Why?* or *What else can we do?*

The word *judge* suggests that there are other questions involved, to which answers will probably be demanded.

j.   Would you like to make a statement?

Closed. This apparent invitation might simply convey an opportunity, to deny something perhaps. It might be an indication or a warning that your questioner is becoming impatient and would like you to confess without further delay.

On the other hand, if this really is an invitation, then a simple *no* would be perfectly acceptable as an answer.

The point of examining questions in this chapter has been to show how we use the language to get at the truth, by answering questions. A question demands at least the consideration or preparation of an answer. Meeting this challenge shows what the language offers when we begin a dialogue, or a conversation, and need to construct an answer.

Now we can move on and look more widely at what we can choose to do with English.

CHAPTER ELEVEN

SENTENCES – HOW THEY FUNCTION

Indicative, interrogative, imperative and subjunctive moods.
Statements, questions, instructions and exclamations.
Implicit and explicit meaning.
Passive and active voices.
Fact and opinion.
You will love all this.

We will start this chapter by sorting some sentences into groups. Sort out the following sentences into five groups. You do not have to explain anything – just read through them first and then sort them into groups in the way that you think they should be grouped.

a. Good luck!
b. This is a test.
c. Think carefully.
d. I move that the chairman be suspended.
e. How are you getting on with this test?
f. How easy!
g. You are doing this test on paper.

h.   May they rest in peace.

i.   Try to keep going.

j.   Do you think you will be able to finish this test?

k.   There.

l.   I am no longer using punctuation marks at the end of these sentences

m.   Decide which punctuation marks I should have used

n.   Long live the president

o.   Would you like me to make this more difficult

p.   Arrange questions so that students are more likely to give correct answers

q.   So, I have changed the order in which I ask different types of question

r.   Serves you right

s.   Were they to understand, things would be better

t.   When it gets dark buy me an ice cream

u.   Great

v.   I really like vanilla ice cream

w.   Do you like ice cream

x.   This is the end of the test

Group One

These are **indicative** sentences which indicate something, that this is a test… etc.

This type of sentence has a simple pattern which you can recognise – *subject* followed by the *verb*. For example, *I* + *do like* or *This* + *is*.

They are statements, which may or may not be true. What matters is that they appear as the revelation of something that seems to be true.

b.   This is a test.

g.   You are doing this test on paper.

l.   I am no longer using punctuation marks at the end of these sentences.

q.   So, I have changed the order in which I ask different types of question.

v.   I really like vanilla ice cream.

x.   This is the end of the test.

> **Statements provide information, facts.**
>
> I like cheese. *A fact.*
> This cheese is tasty. *An opinion.*

Group Two

These are **imperative** (think of *imperial*) sentences, otherwise known as **instructions**. Once you have identified the verbs you will see how sentences of this sort work; look at the initial word of each sentence.

The clue lies with the verb which stands out at the start of four of these sentences:

c. Think carefully.
i. Try to keep going.
m. Decide which punctuation marks I should have used.
p. Arrange questions so that students are more likely to give correct answers.
t. When it gets dark buy me an ice cream.

The fifth of these instructions begins with a subordinate clause, an adverbial clause of time – *When it gets dark*. Then we find the main clause which begins with the main verb – *buy*.

You may have noticed that these sentences do not include the subject, the doer or agent of the action. That is because the agent is the person who is being addressed or spoken to. When it is not clear who the agent is then a noun or a pronoun is used; *Charlie, buy me an ice cream please* or *You – pass me your ticket.*

Group Three

Interrogative sentences. Here we have one open question followed by three closed questions.

e. How are you getting on with this test?
j. Do you think you will be able to finish this test?
o. Would you like me to make this more difficult?
w. Do you like ice cream?

Questions are formed in two ways.

In j. and w. *Do* is placed before a statement and this turns the statement into a question.

In e. and o. the usual order of **subject** then **verb** is reversed – *are you, would you* – to form a question.

Closed questions, questions j., o. and w. require simple answers: **Yes** or **No**.

The open question, e., is formed in two stages. First there is a closed question formed by reversing the order of subject and verb, *are you.* Then *How* is added at the beginning: *How are you...*

We can also form questions in this way using other words such as: **what, when, where, which, who, whom** (old-fashioned but still in use) **whose** and **why**.

What, which, who, whom and whose are interrogative pronouns, related to things.

> *What do you want to do? What are you doing?*
> *Which do you want to choose? Which ice cream have you chosen?*
> *Who gave you that? Who did you want to see?*
> *Who did you insult? Who have you met today?*
> *Whose picture did you take? Whose place will you take tomorrow?*

How, where and why are interrogative adverbs, related to actions.

> *How do you do that? How are you going to do that?*
> *Where do you meet? Where are you meeting this week?*
> *Why did you buy me a chocolate ice cream? Why are you such a pain?*

Group Four

Here we have the **subjunctive** mood of the verb, where hopes or wishes are expressed. Often these are expressed in the much more common indicative mood, but sometimes we use the subjunctive.

d. I move that the chairman <u>be</u> suspended. *(A suggestion.)*

h. <u>May they</u> rest in peace. *(A wish.)*

n. <u>Long live</u> the president. *(It looks like an instruction but is a wish.)*

s. <u>Were they to understand</u>, things would be better. *(A possibility.)*

Group Five

Back to basics – how on earth can four of these groups of words
be sentences when they have no verb?

a. Good luck!
f. How easy!
k. There.
r. Serves you right.
u. Great.

Think of them as parts of sentences from which sections that are easily
understood are omitted.

a. May I wish you <u>good luck</u>!
f. <u>How easy</u> that must have been!
k. <u>There</u> – I didn't really mean it!
r. (It) <u>serves you right</u> for tripping him up!
u. That was a <u>great</u> moment for women's football!

They are exclamations. The word comes from the Latin *clamare* which means
to call out. *Ex-clamo* suggests a noise escaping from me. (The words *claim* and
clamorous have the same origin.)

When we want to express good wishes, to react to something, when we are
surprised in some way, we use as few words as possible; think of the word you
use if you hit your thumb with a hammer or catch a finger in a door.

So, exclamations have the very heart of a sentence about them, without
all the other words that we need when we want to communicate accurately.
If someone nearby is not looking but simply hears your one word you may
be asked, *What have you done?*, and you will reply more fully: *I hit my *******
thumb with the ****** hammer.

These are the five basic ways in which words can be assembled to form
sentences, or exclamations, the basic units of communication. It's just a
reminder of the five basic things that we can do with a sentence. The first three
are very straightforward.

Ways That Sentences Work

The indicative mood – to make statements *to indicate.*

The imperative mood – to issue commands *imperial – emperor.*

The interrogative mood – to ask questions *interrogate.*

The subjunctive mood – to express wishes and possibilities.

Exclamations – false or pseudo sentences conveying quick reactions.

Indicative Sentences

We use these to inform other people. We tell them facts and opinions, we describe things and explain things, all with indicative sentences.

Imperative Sentences

We use these to issue commands or instructions: what to do, how to do something, procedures to follow.

Interrogative Sentences

You know all about questions now so you're not getting another word out of me here.

Sentences with the Subjunctive Voice

We use these to suggest possibilities or ideas or wishes, but not facts.

"May the Force be with you."

These are the words of one General Dodonna who has just explained the Death Star attack plan to the Rebel pilots in *Star Wars Episode IV*.

In 2005 the line was actually chosen as number 8 on the American Film Institute list, AFI's 100 Years… 100 Movie Quotes!

What is this all about? Forget the film – we have six words to consider.

The general is wishing someone the best of luck, but the wish is *implied*, not made *explicit* in an ordinary statement. He could have said something along the lines of:

I hope that you will survive whatever is in front of you.

This long-winded way of expressing a wish lacks the drama of the six words he actually used. The general has two things to convey: <u>hope</u> and <u>uncertainty</u>. He is telling his companions that he hopes that they will come through safely and, implicitly, he is warning them of uncertainty and danger ahead.

There are other languages where the subjunctive is used more frequently.
Spanish – Viv<u>e</u> España – indicative – *Spain lives.*
              Viv<u>a</u> España – subjunctive – *Long live Spain* – or – *May Spain live.*
French – Honni <u>soit</u> qui mal y pense – *Shame on he who thinks evil.*
(These words are found on Britain's royal coat of arms, with *honi* misspelt.)

Three More Ways of Looking at Sentences

1. The active and passive voices.
2. Explicit and implicit communication.
3. Fact and opinion.

---

1. The active and passive voices – is the subject doing the action?
Compare the two sentences that follow. You might like first to look again at Chapter Six, at the early section about clause analysis, about subject, verbs, direct and indirect objects.

> *Shelley built the house.*
> *The house was built by Shelley.*

Identify the subject, object and verb of each sentence and we find this:

> *Shelley* (subject) *built* (verb) *the house* (direct object).
> *The house* (subject) *was built* (verb) *by Shelley* (indirect object).

The word *Shelley*, the agent, the person who carried out the action, who did the building, moves from the beginning of the sentence, where it stood out and was first to catch our attention, to the end as something of an afterthought as part of an adverbial phrase.

The house, the object of the verb, moves to the start of the second sentence, as the subject, the centre of attention. This is important; the agent of the action is replaced by the receiver of the action. So, instead of concentrating on who or what did the action, we pay attention to who or what the action was done to. This is crucial.

This change is brought about by a change to the second element of the sentence, the verb *built*. Consider two more short sentences.

> *Fred conquered.* We don't know what or who he beat, but he won.
> *Fred was conquered.* We don't know by whom he was bested, or why, but he was completely finished.

The mechanics of the second sentence is that the verb *to be* is added as an auxiliary verb with *conquered*. (Like *built* and *was built* in the previous sentences.) Instead of being active verbs, *built* and *conquered* become passive verbs. With the verb *to be* added they are treated like adjectives – describing words – and tell us what happened to the house – **it was built**, and to Fred – **he was conquered**. Neither the house nor Fred did anything; things happened to them.

Now that we can see how easily the change is made between active and passive verbs we must spend a few moments looking at the effects this useful change can have.

Have you ever found yourself trying to avoid blame for something? Has anyone ever asked you, "How did you get to the front of the queue?"

> Did you answer, *"I pushed in."* (Active) I did the action and am responsible for it. Honest, but likely to cause you trouble. Well, return to the back of the queue then.
> Or, *"I was pushed."* (Passive) I did nothing; someone or something pushed me and I am not responsible. Misleading, there seems to be no one to blame. But you had better go to the back of the queue all the same.

Teachers are rather like that, aren't they?

Listen to Politicians

Intentions are usually expressed in the active voice:

We will bring down the price of ice cream. (Trust us!)

Explanations are often expressed in the passive voice:

The price of ice cream has risen because world wholesale prices have been increased. (Don't blame us.)

EXERCISE FORTY-ONE

In which of the following sentences is the verb active and in which is it passive?

a. He was helped across the road.
b. He was amazed by her smile.
c. They helped him across the road.
d. She told him that he had an amazing smile.
e. The ducks helped themselves to the old man's sandwiches.
f. They were driven away by the storm.
g. "Serves them right," said the old man.
h. They were served by the head waiter.

2. Explicit or implicit? How open or hidden is the meaning?
Compare the two sentences, a. and b., which follow.

a. *When her boyfriend rang the doorbell she swooped down like a bird of prey.*

What is she being compared with here? Are we actually told what it is? Is there a way that we can be sure of this?

Now ask yourself the same questions about the next sentence.

b.   *When her boyfriend rang the doorbell she flew down to greet him.*

Responses

In a. she is compared with *a bird of prey.*

   In b. she is compared with something that can fly. It might be a bird, but it might be a bat or a butterfly.

   In a. yes, we are told that it is *a bird of prey.*

   In b. no, we are not told.

   In a. yes, the preposition *like* links her action with *a bird of prey.* The comparison is <u>explicit.</u>

   In b. yes, the word *flew* suggests or <u>implies</u> that it is something that is capable of flight. The comparison is <u>implicit.</u>

   In a. the comparison is explicit; <u>it stands out clearly.</u>

   In b. the comparison is implicit, <u>suggested or hinted.</u>

What has all this to do with a pair of pliers?

Now for a French lesson and the French verb **plier** (sounds like *plea-ay*) which means **bend** or **fold**. We can fold material, to make a **pleated** skirt, for example, with our hands. In ballet we bend our knees – plié. To fold metal we need **pliers**.

When the truth is unfolded, we take words out of a fold – ex-*plié* – so that the truth is clearly seen. (It is *explicit*.)

When the truth is folded up – im-*plié* – it is hidden in the words and we have to look for it. (It is *implicit*.)

Try another pair of sentences.

c.   This ice cream is delicious.
d.   I really like this ice cream.

In c. the meaning is clear; she says that it's delicious so, at least as far as she is concerned, it is delicious. No other words are needed to make things clear. The meaning here is <u>explicit</u>; it is <u>certain</u>.

In d. the meaning is less clear. This person may find the ice cream delicious, **but we are not told this**. He may like this ice cream because it is cheap, or because it contains nuts, but we don't know this. We discuss this further – more words – and we might decide that this preference probably does come about because the ice cream is delicious.

The meaning here is <u>implicit</u>; it is <u>less than certain</u>.

EXERCISE FORTY-TWO

Decide which of these sentences involves explicit meaning and which implicit meaning.
For each implicit sentence indicate which words bring uncertainty with them.

a.   I trust him completely.
b.   I have never known him do anything wrong at work.
c.   If the deal goes ahead we can arrange something.
d.   There is no interest to pay on the loan.
e.   You look great.
f.   What are those things that you've got on your feet?
g.   Those shoes must have cost you a fortune.

Now we need to look at some short paragraphs to see how the meaning can be hidden, or made clear, in a group of sentences. Remember, we are looking at the passage as a whole and not at individual sentences.

> *The bungalow stands alone in attractive surroundings. It was constructed with substantial materials and requires little maintenance. The present owners are selling it after enjoying many years in this comfortable family home.*

This sounds like an advertisement; the bungalow is for sale and we are told of its *attractive surroundings, substantial construction, low maintenance requirements, comfort and suitability as a family home.* We are not provided with details; they are implied. For example, we are not told about the surroundings – rural or suburban? Or the materials – wood, brick or stone?

For most of us, buying a house requires an inspection so estate agents (property realtors or real estate dealers) have to make something sound attractive enough to encourage viewers. Explicit detail might discourage people; the thought of green tiles on the roof might put off people who would find the views from the living room absolutely stunning. The details of the bungalow's desirability have to be implied or hinted at to encourage people in the hope that a visit will make explicit the property's real worth.

Explicit or Implicit?

What do we need to ask?

What seems to be the writer's purpose? What is the writer trying to bring about?

What are we not told? Which details are hidden, which details are out in the open?

Why is this?

How then is the language folded or bent? Is the meaning wrapped up in the words?

EXERCISE FORTY-THREE

Here we have a notice or advertisement of some sort and a brief piece of narrative.

For each item identify its purpose then list information that is explicit and information that is implicit.

a. Applications are invited for places in the school for children between the ages of eleven and sixteen. The school has an enviable record of success in public examinations and its students make their way to top universities.

b. She looked back over her shoulder and smiled. Then she shook her head, causing him to ask himself questions again. He wondered why he bothered and then it was over.

3. Fact and Opinion

Consider two sentences.

America is the most powerful country in the world.
America is the best country in the world.

These two sentences could easily start off a long political argument. Which of them do you find easier to deal with?

The first sentence might involve ideas about military power, the numbers of ships and planes and soldiers at the disposal of the United States and other large countries. It might involve arguments about economic power, about economic resources and productivity, about imports and exports, or it might involve arguments about political power, about the influence the US can use in its dealing with other countries, about other governments' willingness to listen to the US.

All rather complicated perhaps, but some sort of idea could emerge about American power. But how are we likely to respond when someone claims that their country is best? "Well, they would say that, wouldn't they?"

I would imagine that the first sentence would be more widely accepted than the second; the idea of a country's power can much more easily be examined and considered than its place in a league table of good countries.

Now for something a little easier.

Best bananas – pound a kilo!

If you visit a traditional street market in England you are likely to hear somebody call out something like this. Would you believe them?

Well, what is being said? Two statements:

These bananas are the best.

They cost a *pound a kilo.* (Be careful not to confuse the pound sterling, the UK's unit of currency with the old-fashioned, imperial weight of a pound, usually abbreviated *lb.*)

Which of these statements is more reliable? Why?

Comparing all the bananas in the world would be even more nonsensical than comparing all the countries of the world. Perhaps the person on the stall simply believes that the bananas are good bananas, just as someone who waves a flag and calls their country the best simply believes that it is a good country.

And the price of bananas? So long as the stallholder's actions match his or her words, so long as they give you the right change, then there is no difficulty here.

> **Facts** can be checked or verified. We can check the price of bananas by asking the stallholder and by watching the change.
>
> **Opinions** have to be argued for, by examining the colour and softness of the bananas, for example, or by considering a whole range of complicated facts about many countries. This is how we form a judgement.
>
> We might be persuaded to change our opinion, perhaps when the stallholder offers us a banana to taste, or when some historical fact about a country is pointed out, but that does not create a fact, only a different opinion.

The Mechanics of Fact and Opinion
How then are words chosen and assembled to form opinions rather than present facts?

We know about the basic structure of a sentence: subject, verb, object or complement. (Complement here with the verb <u>to be</u>.)

X is a singer. (Subject – *X,* verb – *is,* complement – *a singer.*)

This is a fact – X is a singer.

Try adding a pair of adjectives, to the sentence, to tell us more about this singer – *my favourite. X is my favourite singer.* Now this tells us another **fact**.

Now try adding a different adjective – *good. X is a good singer.* This time the speaker has made a judgement about the singer and conveys to us an opinion. We don't know why X is judged to be a good singer so we cannot make any judgement ourselves. Here the speaker is simply stating an **opinion**.

The important thing to remember is that the same kind of sentence can be used to convey either a fact or an opinion. Facts and opinions will seem virtually the same unless we read or listen carefully.

> X is my favourite singer.

> *If you say so, if you really mean this, this is true.* **Fact.**
>
> X is a good singer.
>
> *Your claim or assertion that X is a good singer does not make X a good singer. This sentence may be true but without more facts and argument it is simply an* ***opinion***.

What then would you make of this sentence?

In my view X is a good singer.

Here the speaker is making it clear that the statement concerns his or her opinion rather than a statement of fact. It is a more honest sentence, because the main clause – *X is a good singer* – is qualified by the adverbial phrase, *in my view*.

(Now you can see why it is important to appreciate how sentences are built up.)

> **Don't be taken in by opinion masquerading as fact.**

When people are having a row, or are very excited, or are trying to sell you something, or just having a lively discussion perhaps, it is easier for them to shout with the minimum of words – *X is the greatest*.

But when someone does this it is more difficult to think about what we are hearing.

This is when we need time to consider whether we are faced with a fact or an opinion.

When cold-callers try to rush me with a special offer I simply ask them to put it in writing and email it to me. They never do of course because they cannot easily disguise opinions as facts when they have to write them down.

Now some practice for you.

EXERCISE FORTY-FOUR

Consider each of these sentences and indicate whether it conveys a fact or an opinion.

Indicate key words and comment upon them if you can.

a. Smith is the best candidate.
b. I will vote for Smith.
    (Revision thrown in here. The <u>implication</u> here is that Smith is the best candidate; the intention to vote for him is <u>explicit</u>.)
c. Two and two make four.
d. The old maths book was easier to use than this one.
e. Sodium chloride dissolves in water.
f. I enjoy chemistry lectures.
g. Demonstrations are better, especially when they go wrong.
h. I enjoy vanilla ice cream. (I know – you've heard all this before.)
i. I prefer coffee ice cream.
j. Strawberry-flavoured ice cream is best for the flavour lingers in the mouth.
k. Raspberry ice cream is the best, because it has a stronger flavour.
l. Chocolate ice cream is definitely superior.

Finally, a reminder, some things that we do with sentences

Accuse	*Congratulate*	*Hint*	*Lie*
Acknowledge	*Conspire*	*Humiliate*	*Mock*
Allege	*Contribute*	*Imagine*	*Praise*
Avoid	*Demand*	*Imply*	*Promise*
Boast	*Describe*	*Indicate*	*Reassure*
Challenge	*Disturb*	*Inform*	*Reveal*
Clarify	*Enquire*	*Insist*	*Satirise*
Command	*Exclaim*	*Instruct*	*Suggest*
Complain	*Excuse*	*Invent*	*Warn*
Confess	*Explain*	*Invite*	

Impressive, isn't it?

This chapter has been tough, complete with a short chemistry lesson thrown in. It is an important section because it will help you to be aware of the different ways that English can be used, sometimes in an attempt to mislead you or get you to do something that you would not usually do. When people want to take control over other people they misuse language.

(Read George Orwell's 1984 *in which he imagines a world dominated by politicians who control the way language is used.)*

This section of work will make you more aware of such attempts; you will ask why certain things are being said.

ANSWERS TO THE QUESTIONS IN CHAPTER ELEVEN

EXERCISE FORTY-ONE

Active – c., d., e., g.
Passive – a., b., f., h.

EXERCISE FORTY-TWO

a. Explicit.
b. Implicit – *at work* – he might be a burglar at weekends.
c. Implicit – *something* – just what exactly can be arranged?
d. Explicit
e. Explicit
f. Implicit – *those things* – we are told nothing about them, or the reaction they cause.
g. Implicit – *must have* – they might not have cost a fortune.

EXERCISE FORTY-THREE

a. Purpose – inviting or encouraging applications for places in a school.
Explicit – an age range of eleven to sixteen years old. Students take public examinations and apply to universities.
Implicit – good examination results, the number or proportion of students getting into "top" universities, the identity of these so-called top universities.

b. Purpose – To tell of the ending of something between a male, who has doubts about something, and a female.
Explicit – her actions and his thoughts.
Implicit – her feelings; her smiling and her shaking of her head suggest

a number of feelings. His giving up, accepting the end – is he relieved or disappointed?

In b. you are now looking at language used in a literary way, in fiction where we can do additional things with the language.

EXERCISE FORTY-FOUR

a. Smith is the best candidate. **Opinion** – *best – someone's opinion.*

b. I will vote for Smith. **Fact** – *test the intention – does it happen?*

c. Two and two make four. **Fact** – *use your fingers – the only possibility.*

d. The old maths book was easier to use than this one. **Opinion** – *easier – might not be everyone's view.*

e. Sodium chloride dissolves in water. **Fact** – *demonstrate this fact. (Sodium Chloride – NaCl – common salt.)*

f. I enjoy chemistry lectures. **Fact** – *so long as we believe the speaker.*

g. Demonstrations are better, especially when they go wrong. **Opinion** – *better – you might not share this view of demonstrations.*

h. I enjoy vanilla ice cream. **Fact** – *so long as we believe the speaker.*

i. I prefer coffee ice cream. **Fact** – *so long as we believe the speaker.*

j. Strawberry-flavoured ice cream is best for the flavour lingers in the mouth. **Opinion** – *a stronger opinion because it is accompanied by an argument.*

k. Raspberry ice cream is the best, because it has a stronger flavour. **Opinion** – *a stronger opinion because it is accompanied by an argument.*

l. Chocolate ice cream is definitely superior. **Opinion** – *definitely superior? Really? Obviously the speaker has never tried vanilla. It's a weak opinion; definitely is simply an adverb used to intensify superior. The writer offers no evidence or reasoning to support the opinion.*

Statements, questions, commands, wishes and reactions.

Coming next – Using the language.

PART THREE

USING THE LANGUAGE

CHAPTER TWELVE

SENTENCES – ASSEMBLED AND PUT TO WORK

Application and purpose.
Information, description, discussion.
Organising sentences.

Imagine that we have arrived home and found a note on the kitchen table.

I've taken the box of chocolates to work – no time to get Stephanie's present, now – and they look delicious.

Three sentences have been thrown together here:

I've taken your box of chocolates to work.
(I have done this because) I had no time to get Stephanie's present.
(And) they look delicious.

They are all indicative sentences, the most common type, and yes, I have just checked, in the six books lying closest on my desk.

In the first there is information – what are we told?

In the second there is an explanation – why were the chocolates taken?

In the third sentence there is a description – did they look good enough to be given as a present?

Here you can see the main type of sentence used in most of what you read, and most of what you will write. (In the next chapter!)

Generally speaking, writing a narrative or providing information is easiest, then comes description and, finally, discursive writing in which we use reasons, arguments and explanations.

There are very good reasons for this.

Narrative or informative writing involves facts about which you know something, events you have seen perhaps. This makes up much of children's early writing when they recount things in a simple story form – *this happened and then something else happened and then another thing happened*. When we explain things facts become more involved.

From writing about simple facts, things that we have seen, we can move on to describing things, trying to convey to the reader what something looks like or sounds like. Here we are beginning to use our senses as a source for our writing.

Finally there is discursive writing. (Think of *discussion*.) Now we need to consider matters more carefully, to think in abstract terms and to use reason, example and argument.

Sometimes it is clear that we are using just one of these three basic ways of writing, sometimes we combine two or three of them. In the middle of the story of the deer in a Kyoto park, on the next page, I include a description of the creature's reaction to tea-flavoured ice cream, a description which might help a discussion about the proper treatment of animals.

EXERCISE FORTY-FIVE

Decide whether each sentence is informative, descriptive or discursive, or includes a mixture of these characteristics.

a. Cows can eat grass, silage, hay or straw.
b. Grass takes the form of individual green leaves, silage is brown and smelly, and straw is pale yellow and very dry.
c. Cows have four stomachs so they can digest the fibres in these feedstuffs.

d.   Cows do not eat ice cream.

e.   Ayrshire cattle have red and white coats and distinctly curved horns.

f.   We should be kind to cows.

Exercise Forty-Five should have been very straightforward – enough to accustom you to new ideas perhaps. Now try something rather more involved, more like an ordinary piece of writing, in this case a narrative.

EXERCISE FORTY-SIX

Decide whether each sentence is informative, descriptive or discursive and explain your answers.

a.   I once fed a tea-flavoured ice cream to a deer in a park in Kyoto, Japan.

b.   I had taken the first bite and was so disgusted by the unexpected flavour that I was happy to try out this strange ice cream on the deer.

c.   The deer took only one bite before allowing the remains of my ice cream to fall to the ground.

d.   My wife and I had taken our son to stay with our daughter in Japan, a fascinating and delightful place to visit.

e.   The deer was now coughing and retching, its sides heaving violently every time it was forced to expel yet more breath and from its mouth a piece of ice cream cone fell away.

f.   To remind them that deer too should be able to enjoy delicious, smooth vanilla ice cream, people who feed tea-flavoured ice cream to animals should be forced to eat tea-flavoured ice cream every day for a month.

You will notice from the answers that there is no particular order for the different aspects of a sentence. In the next chapter I will get you to write your way through this evolution so that you can see it for yourself and understand how we move from telling stories, to describing things and then to discussing and explaining things.

Organising Sentences – Making Ideas – Flow
Read the following sentences **aloud** then see whether you can reorder them to produce a more effective paragraph.

It was a warm day, and he had a long way to go. It began at the tip of his nose and trickled all through him and out at the soles of his feet. It was just as if somebody inside him were saying, "Now then, Pooh, time for a little something." He hadn't gone more than half-way when a sort of funny feeling began to creep over him.

Now read the original which was taken from *The Pooh Birthday Book* by A.A. Milne (Methuen London, 1978, pp10/11).

It was a warm day, and he had a long way to **go**. *He hadn't* **gone** *more than half-way when a sort of funny* <u>feeling</u> *began to creep over him.* <u>*It*</u> *began at the tip of his nose and trickled all through him and out at the soles of his feet.* <u>*It*</u> *was just as if somebody inside him were saying, "Now then, Pooh, time for a little something."*

Commentary

I have highlighted the words that provide links from one sentence to the next. Think of them as stepping stones across which the reader can make progress. Try putting the final sentence at the start of the paragraph. Do you think this works satisfactorily?

EXERCISE FORTY-SEVEN

Highlight the link words in the paragraphs that follow.

a. *(Informative or narrative – A friendly honeybee pays a flying visit.)*
    The bees were rushing in and out of the hive now. Only last year her father had been stung by a bee that, foolishly, had strayed into the house. They had felt his pain and embarrassment and watched their mother hurry into the bathroom to find something to reduce his discomfort. One of the bees settled on her arm. Fortunately she remembered what the neighbour had told them and she kept very still then blew on the insect until it decided to fly away. Then she could relax.

b. *(Descriptive – A spark/sparking plug.)*

In front of him the components were lined up in rows. There were four round-shaped items with white ceramic tops that narrowed to a point where a circular collar or nut gripped the top. The other end of each of these items was formed of a steel base at the end of which a tiny strip had been welded then turned down across the steel base which appeared to have been hollowed out. He noticed that this strip almost touched a pin which rose from inside the hollow section. From the crowded rack above the bench he removed a rusty box spanner and took a deep breath.

c.   *(Discursive – Cyclists as seen by pedestrians and motorists.)*
From time to time the local press reports complaints that cyclists are becoming a menace. Pedestrians want them confined to the roads so that they can walk on the pavements without the risk of being knocked down. Parents fear for young children. On the other hand, motorists see cyclists as a nuisance, holding up their progress and not being required to carry identification or be insured. They often complain that cyclists ignore traffic regulations and take unnecessary risks.

Paragraphs – Groups of sentences – Linking ideas
We seem already to have formed paragraphs that grow out of a flow of ideas and words and sentences. In the next chapter we will look at the formation of paragraphs. But first, let me remind you how much you already understand about starting new sentences and linking ideas.

Which of these two versions of the same paragraph do you find easier to read and understand?

1.   He felt sorry for his pet rabbit. It was a buck rabbit. It lived a solitary life in the back garden. It would surely be more fun for him to be surrounded by a family. The girls next door also had a pet rabbit. It was a doe. He could tell by the ruff. It stuck out from under her chin. How then could he introduce them? Suddenly the neighbours were to go on holiday. All four of them were going. Would he look after Fluffy while they were away? Now, at last, here was his chance. It was not online dating but he would be doing his pet a favour.
2.   He felt sorry for his pet rabbit, a buck rabbit, which lived a solitary life in the back garden. It would surely be more fun for him to be surrounded

by a family. The girls next door also had a pet rabbit, a doe; he could tell by the ruff which stuck out from under her chin. How then could he introduce them? Suddenly the neighbours were to go on holiday, all four of them. Would he look after Fluffy while they were away? Now here was a chance; not quite online dating but his pet would be really chuffed.

Not sure? Well, read them again, **aloud**.

Just as we have to consider our readers with our handwriting, our grammar, our punctuation and spelling, so we have to consider them when we arrange whatever it is that we want to say in sentences and paragraphs.

ANSWERS TO THE QUESTIONS
IN CHAPTER TWELVE

EXERCISE FORTY-FIVE

Informative – a, c, d.
Descriptive – b, e.
Discursive – f.

EXERCISE FORTY-SIX

a. Informative – *I once fed a deer*. Descriptive – *tea-flavoured*.
b. Descriptive – *so disgusted by the unexpected flavour*. Discursive – *that*.
c. Informative – we are told what the deer did. Descriptive – *only*, *allowing*, *remains* and *fall* all suggest something more than simple actions.
d. Informative – *had taken our son*. Discursive – *to stay with our daughter in Japan*. Descriptive – *a fascinating and delightful place*.
e. Descriptive – *coughed, looking resentfully*. Discursive – *until*.
f. Discursive – *To remind them that deer too should... – people who feed tea-flavoured ice cream to animals should be forced to eat vanilla ice cream every day for a month*. Descriptive – *tea-flavoured vanilla ice cream*.

EXERCISE FORTY-SEVEN

Your answers will almost certainly be slightly different from mine. Do not let this worry you unless they are completely different. The main thing is that the ideas can be seen moving through each paragraph.

a. The bees were rushing in and out of the hive **now. Only last year** her father had been **stung** by a bee that, foolishly, had strayed into the house. They had felt his **pain and embarrassment** and watched their mother hurry into the bathroom to find something to reduce **his discomfort.** One of the bees **settled on her arm**. Fortunately **she remembered** what the neighbour had told them so she kept very still and blew on the insect until **it decided to fly away**. **Then** she could relax.

b. In front of him **the components** were lined up in rows. There were **four round-shaped items** with white ceramic **tops** that narrowed to a point where a circular collar or nut gripped the top. **At the other end** each of these items was formed of a steel base at the end of which **a tiny strip** had been welded then turned down across the steel base which appeared to have been hollowed out. **He** noticed that this **strip** almost touched a pin which rose from inside the hollow section. From the crowded rack above the bench **he** removed a rusty box spanner and took a deep breath.

c. From time to time the local press reports complaints that **cyclists** are becoming **a menace. Pedestrians** want **them** confined to the roads so that they can walk on the pavements without the risk of being knocked down. **Parents** fear for young children. **On the other hand, motorists** see **cyclists** as **a nuisance,** holding up their progress and not being required to carry identification or be insured. **They** often complain that **cyclists** ignore traffic regulations and take unnecessary risks.

> **We have finished with sentences.**
> **Now we must consider how we can**
> **arrange sentences into paragraphs.**

CHAPTER THIRTEEN

PARAGRAPHS – ASSEMBLED AND PUT TO WORK – ORGANISING IDEAS

Articles, contracts, essays, letters, manuals, reports, stories, textbooks. Advertising, agreement, assertion (claim), autobiography, description, discussion, enquiry, entertainment, explanation, information, instruction, invitation, narration, persuasion, warning.

Here I want you to think about the way other people write so that you can assess the writing I shall ask you to do very soon. Remember – I can't sneak up behind you to check what you are writing. You will have to check your work yourself.

Think of paragraphs as the grouping of sentences together to help us move along with a sense of purpose.

Stepping stones within paragraphs – sentences that lead the reader from one idea to the next, that keep us moving along, one step at a time.

A bird's eye view from outside the paragraphs, that gives us an overall sense of where we are going.

Here you will find paragraphs in examples from a travel book, a contract, an essay, two letters, a manual, a report, a short story and a textbook.

Here you will find writers who are advertising, setting out an agreement, writing an autobiography, a description, conducting a discussion, reporting an enquiry, trying to entertain us, explaining something, informing us about something, setting out instructions, inviting us to something, trying to persuade us to do something or issuing a warning.

Exercises

These are now to be transformed, for the time being, and most of them will take the form of your own commentaries. You will not have many model answers to check against your own answers. You will have to think through ideas and, if possible, discuss them with anyone else who can help.

Each item is presented initially without paragraphing. Before looking at the original, decide where you would start new paragraphs. For each piece of writing here, ask yourself what is going on? What is the writer trying to do? How is the material organised in the paragraphs?

I have highlighted words that I find significant here.

1. From Greene (*The Destructors* in *Complete Short Stories*, pub Pen. London, 2005, pp. 9/10). It's a story that entertains us and makes us think about the power of young people.

A gang of boys has decided to demolish a house while the owner is away. Blackie, who has just been replaced as leader, is one of the last to arrive. The story is set just after the Second World War.

There was no sign of anybody anywhere. The outside toilet stood like a tomb in a neglected graveyard. The curtains were drawn. The house slept.

Blackie lumbered nearer with the saw and the sledge-hammer. Perhaps after all nobody had turned up: the plan had been a wild invention: they had woken wiser. But when he came close to the back door he could hear a confusion of sound hardly louder than a hive in swarm: clickety-clack, a bang bang, a scraping, a creaking, a sudden painful crack. He thought: it's true, and whistled. They opened the back door to him and he came in. He had at once the impression of organization, very different from the old happy-go-lucky ways under his leadership. For a while he wandered up and downstairs looking for T. Nobody addressed him: he had a sense of great urgency, and already he could begin to see the plan. The interior of the house was being carefully demolished without touching the walls. Summers with hammer and chisel was ripping out the skirting boards in the ground-floor dining-room: he had already smashed the panels of the door. In the same room Joe was heaving up the parquet blocks, exposing the soft wood floorboards over the cellar. Coils of wire came out of the damaged skirting and Mike sat working hard with an inadequate child's saw on the banisters – when they saw Blackie's big saw they signalled for it wordlessly. When he next saw them a quarter of the banisters had been dropped into the hall. He found T (the newly elected leader of the gang) at last in the bathroom – he sat moodily in the least cared-for room in the house, listening to the sounds coming up from below. "You've really done it," Blackie said with awe. "What's going to happen?" "We've only just begun," T said. He looked at the sledge-hammer and gave his instructions. "You stay here and break the bath and the wash-basin. Don't bother about the pipes. They come later."

> **You decide where you think new paragraphs should begin.**

*There was **no sign of anybody** anywhere. The outside toilet stood like a tomb in a neglected graveyard. The curtains were drawn. The house slept. Blackie lumbered nearer with the saw and the sledge-hammer. **Perhaps after all nobody had turned up:** the plan had been a wild invention: they had woken wiser. But when he came close to the back door he could hear a confusion of sound hardly louder than a hive in swarm: clickety-*

clack, a bang bang, a scraping, a creaking, a sudden painful crack. He thought: it's true, and **whistled**.

They **opened** *the back door to him and he came in. He had at once the impression of organization, very different from the old happy-go-lucky ways under his leadership. For a while he wandered up and downstairs looking for T. Nobody addressed him: he had a sense of great urgency, and already* **he could begin to see the plan**. *The interior of the house was being carefully demolished without touching the walls. Summers with hammer and chisel was ripping out the skirting boards in the ground-floor dining-room: he had already smashed the panels of the door. In the same room Joe was heaving up the parquet blocks, exposing the soft wood floorboards over the cellar. Coils of wire came out of the damaged skirting and* **Mike sat happily on the floor clipping the wires**.

On the curved stairs **two of the gang** *were working hard with an inadequate child's saw on the banisters – when they saw Blackie's big saw they signalled for it wordlessly. When he next saw them a quarter of the banisters had been dropped into the hall.* **He found T** *(the newly elected leader of the gang) at last in the bathroom – he sat moodily in the least cared-for room in the house, listening to the sounds coming up from below.*

"You've really done it," Blackie said with awe. **"What's going to happen?"**

"We've only just begun," T said. He looked at the sledge-hammer and gave his instructions. **"You stay here** *and break the bath and the wash-basin. Don't bother about the pipes.* **They come later***."*

352 words

Commentary Five Paragraphs

1. Blackie's initial disappointment – *no sign* – turns to hope when he hears the sounds of the gang at work, described as – *a confusion of sound…*

2. An explanation – *The interior of the house…* is followed by a further description of the boys' purpose – *heaving up the parquet blocks.*

3. Drama – *when they saw Blackie's big saw they signalled for it.* Now Blackie has made a contribution and he finds T, the new leader.

4/5. Dialogue – more drama with Blackie's exclamation and the order from the new leader – *You stay here…*

2. From Danziger (*Danziger's Travels*, pub. Grafton London, 1987, pp. 1/2).
    An introduction to an autobiographical account of his travels, to inform
    and describe.

In 1982 the photojournalist Nick Danziger had applied for one of fourteen
Winston Churchill Fellowships in order to travel. There had been eight
hundred applications. Nick was about to face an interview.

*I'd left Art School eighteen months before, and since then had spent a good
deal of time applying for grants, fellowships and scholarships. This process
had been punctuated by a successful exhibition of my work at Riverside
Studios in West London, which had provided me with the means to journey
to Central America. For a long time I had been fascinated by the Mayan
civilisation, led there by my own art works: paintings, drawings, sculptures
and constructions based on mathematics and assembled in a vast web
of geometrical and architectonic patterns. From an early age I had been
mesmerised by adventure and foreign travel, but it was not to the great
explorers or travellers that I had looked but to Hergé's fictional hero Tintin.
I sought a Central America of ancient monuments jutting out of a sea of
trees and swamps, swarming with snakes, monkeys, vampire bats and hordes
of insects. A continent beset by political turmoil that offered the challenges
of pitting oneself against the elements, of survival, discovery, especially of
past and present peoples, customs, cultures and civilisations; if danger was
involved it would as a consequence rather than a prerequisite. I thought
with exhilaration of the people I would meet. For to me the essence of travel,
especially to remote places, is precisely that you are on your own. There are
no printed guides and maps to help you, and so the only way to see the place
you are visiting is through the eyes and with the help of the people who live
there. True travel doesn't involve visiting a place, and seeing its monuments;
it involves getting to know its inhabitants.*

*It was during my first visit to Central America that I had begun to develop
the idea which formed the basis of my application to the Churchill Memorial
Trust: I wanted to return to Guatemala, fell my own tree, build a dugout
canoe, and in it try to retrace the trade routes of the Mayan civilisation along
the rivers that cut through the jungle. "Will you go anyway, even if you don't
get a Fellowship?" the other secretary asked me, as if she'd been reading my*

thoughts. I was so tense that for a moment I wondered if the question might have been a ploy – a sounding-out of my resolve. "Of course I will," I replied, returning her smile. In truth though, without funding my project would be impossible to realise. I put the thought to the back of my mind and tried to concentrate on what I would say to the people sitting round the table behind that polished mahogany door. But it was too late. The door was opening.

*

I'd left Art School *eighteen months before, and since then had spent a good deal of time applying for grants, fellowships and scholarships. This process had been punctuated by a successful exhibition of my work at Riverside Studios in West London, which had provided me with the means to journey to Central America. For a long time I had been fascinated by the Mayan civilisation, led there by my own art works: paintings, drawings, sculptures and constructions based on mathematics and assembled in a vast web of geometrical and architectonic patterns. From an early age I had been mesmerised by adventure and foreign travel, but it was not to the great explorers of travellers that I had looked but to Hergé's fictional hero Tintin.* **I sought** *a Central America of ancient monuments jutting out of a sea of trees and swamps, swarming with snakes, monkeys, vampire bats and hordes of insects. A continent beset by political turmoil that offered the challenges of pitting oneself against the elements, of survival, discovery, especially of* **past and present peoples, customs, cultures and civilisations***; if danger was involved it would as a consequence rather than a prerequisite.* **I thought with exhilaration of the people** *I would meet. For to me the essence of travel, especially to remote places, is precisely that you are on your own. There are no printed guides and maps to help you, and so the only way to see the place you are visiting is through the eyes and with the help of the people who live there. True travel doesn't involve visiting a place, and seeing its monuments; it involves* **getting to know its inhabitants.***

It was during my first visit to Central America that I had begun to develop the idea which formed the basis of my application to the Churchill Memorial Trust: I wanted to **return to Guatemala***, fell my own tree, build a dugout canoe, and in it try to retrace the trade routes of the Mayan civilisation along the rivers that cut through the jungle.*

*"Will you go anyway, even if you don't get a Fellowship?" the other secretary asked me, as if she'd been **reading my thoughts**. I was so tense that for a moment I wondered if the question might have been a ploy – a sounding-out of my resolve.*

*"Of course I will," I replied, returning her smile. In truth though, without funding my project would be impossible to realise. I put the thought to the back of my mind and tried to **concentrate on what I would say to the people sitting round the table** behind that polished mahogany getting to know its inhabitants*

*But it was **too late**. The door was opening.*

447 words

Commentary Five Paragraphs

1. Aims to return to the people of Guatemala. Description – *fascinated by the Mayan civilisation*. It's a long paragraph and I would be tempted to start new paragraphs with – *From an early age...* – where Danziger explains something from a much earlier time in his life, and possibly at – *For to me...* – where he sets out (explains and describes) a view of travel that arose from his early years.
2. Explanation – *the basis of my application*.
3. Resolve – *questioned*.
4. Drama – his response and *concentration on what he would say*.
5. Drama – *it was too late*.

3. From the *Los Angeles Times, Letters: Age difference and marriage legitimacy. Re "Trying to prove their love," Column One.
    April 7, 2013*

Your poignant story about Gerardo Herrejon and Ana Verdin-Hernandez – who fell in love when he was 63 and she was 22, but whose marriage is under question by U.S. immigration officials because Ana is an undocumented immigrant – brings to mind one of the most famous romances of the 20th century. After three failed marriages, acclaimed actor Charlie Chaplin met the love of his life – Oona O'Neill, daughter of the playwright Eugene O'Neill – when he was 54 and she was 17. They had eight children and she never married after he died. Research shows that age difference is a poor predictor of success in a marriage; who you marry is far more important than the age of that person.

*

Your **poignant story** *about Gerardo Herrejon and Ana Verdin-Hernandez – who fell in love when he was 63 and she was 22, but whose marriage is under question by U.S. immigration officials because Ana is an undocumented immigrant –* **brings to mind** *one of the most famous romances of the 20th century.*

After three failed marriages, acclaimed actor Charlie Chaplin met the love of his life – Oona O'Neill, daughter of the playwright Eugene O'Neill **– when he was 54 and she was 17. They had eight children** *and she never married after he died.*

Research shows **that age difference is a poor predictor of success in a marriage***; who you marry is far more important than the age of that person.*

118 words

Robert Epstein, Vista – *The writer is senior research psychologist at the American Institute for Behavioral Research and Technology.*

Commentary Three Paragraphs

1. Information to introduce the topic, age differences in marriage, to report an official opinion – *whose marriage is under question* – and introduce a famous marriage.
b. Information – some details of that romance.
c. Discursive – a contrary opinion to that implied in the opening paragraph – *who you marry is far more important…*

> ### "Rules" for Paragraphs
>
> Could you now set out guidance for paragraphing? You have already learnt to assemble the smallest components of our written language, words, into sentences. How should we go about assembling these larger components to form paragraphs?

4.   How might you react if you received the following letter?

Now Consider a Letter of Invitation

Spring Ice Cream Fair

Dear Customer,

We do hope that you will be able to join us this year at our spring ice-cream fair on Saturday, April 1st. After last year's exciting event over fifty companies have asked to join us this year with the very best of their products and we are expecting larger crowds than ever. Surely, you will not want to miss this great occasion. In order to ensure that all our guests have a great time we would appreciate your completing the form below and indicating the following: your flavour preferences, any special provision that would help you to enjoy your day with us – high chairs for the kiddies, a crèche, wheelchair access, indigestion pills and anything else you can think of. And afterwards – send us the best of the pics that you take at the fair and we will enter them in a competition. The winning picture will be displayed on our website and, by return there will be an enormous 1-litre tub of your favourite ice cream delivered to your door.

Hope you can make it.
Flossie *– your favourite brand*

*

Dear Customer,

We **do hope that you will be able to join us** *this year at our spring ice cream fair on Saturday, April 1st.*

After last year's exciting event over fifty companies have asked to join us this year with the very best of their products and we are expecting larger crowds than ever. **Surely, you will not want to miss** *this great occasion.*

In order to ensure that all our guests have a great time we would appreciate your **completing the form below** *and indicating the following: your flavour preferences, any special provision that would help you to enjoy your day with us – high chairs for the kiddies, a crèche, wheelchair access, indigestion pills and anything else you can think of.*

And afterwards – send us the best of the pics that you take at the fair and we will enter them in **a competition**. *The winning picture will be displayed on our website and, by return there will be one of our* **enormous 1-litre tubs of your favourite ice cream delivered to your door**.

Hope you can make it.
Flossie *– your favourite brand*

184 words

(Now there's a thought. How do you brand ice cream? The word *brand* means burn. In the States cattle were branded, marked permanently to discourage theft, with red-hot irons. In German the word *Brand* means *fire*.)

Commentary Four Paragraphs

1. An invitation, a mixture of persuasion and instruction – *we do hope...*
2. Discussion – persuasion – a suggestion that you would be foolish not to attend – *Surely, you will not want to miss...*
3. A request, a subtle instruction – *we would appreciate...*
4. A further invitation – to involve yourself further – by offering the chance of a prize – *an enormous 1-litre tub...*

5. From Andrew Clegg *IGCSE Chemistry* (pub Heinemann, Harlow, 2009, p35.) A textbook which informs and explains.

A Pattern of Elements – the Periodic Table

Before scientists can think up useful scientific theories to help us understand the universe around us, they have to make a lot of observations and collect data. This was what many chemists were busy doing a hundred and fifty years ago; they collected a lot of information about the properties of elements and the kind of compounds they form when they join together. By around one hundred and fifty years ago scientists had discovered many elements and had also been able to calculate their atomic masses (even though they only had a very simple idea of what an atom was like). Then some chemists began to look for patterns in all the data. It was from the patterns they found that they could devise the theories that explained the observations they had made. A German chemist called Johann Döbereiner was the first to find a pattern. He realised that many elements could be grouped together in threes. The elements in each group were very similar. Lithium, sodium and potassium formed one group; they were all very reactive metals. Chlorine, bromine and iodine formed another group, this time of reactive non-metals. One group that had been known of for a long time was copper, silver and gold. In 1864 an Englishman called John Newlands realised that if he arranged the elements in a list in order of their relative atomic masses, each element was often very similar to the one eight places above it. Later still, in 1869, the Russian Dimitri Mendeleev took all these ideas and produced his famous Periodic Classification of the Elements. This combined the ideas of Döbereiner and Newlands and it has proved to be very useful. It has helped us to understand much more about the elements that matter, the significant elements from which the universe is made. The modern Periodic Table is based on Mendeleev's original one.

*

Before scientists *can develop useful scientific theories to help us understand the universe around us,* ***they have to make a lot of observations and collect data****. This was what many chemists were busy doing a hundred* *and fifty years ago; they collected a lot of information about the properties of elements and the kind of compounds they form when they joined together.*

By around one hundred and fifty years ago *scientists had discovered many elements and had also been able to calculate their atomic masses (even though they only had a very simple idea of what an atom was like). Then some chemists began to look for* **patterns in all the data**. *It was* **from the patterns they found that they could devise the theories** *that explained the observations they had made.*

A German chemist called Johann Döbereiner was the first to find a pattern. He realised that **many elements could be grouped together in threes**. *The elements in each group were very similar. Lithium, sodium and potassium formed one group; they were all very reactive metals. Chlorine, bromine and iodine formed another group, this time of reactive non-metals. One group that had been known of for a long time was copper, silver and gold.*

In 1864 an Englishman called John Newlands realised that if he arranged the elements in a list in order of their relative atomic masses, **each element was often very similar to the one eight places above it**.

Later still, in 1869, the Russian Dimitri Mendeleev took all these ideas and produced his famous **Periodic Classification** *of the Elements. This combined the ideas of Döbereiner and Newlands and it has proved to be very useful. It has helped us* **to understand much more about the elements that matter**, *the significant elements from which the universe is made. The modern Periodic Table is based on Mendeleev's original one.*

311 words

Commentary Five Paragraphs

1. Information – explanation – *they have to make…*
2. Information – historical development of scientific understanding – *began to look for patterns…*
3. Information – an important example, with a little description – *grouped together in threes – all very reactive metals…*
4. Information – another important step – each element was often very similar to the one eight places above.
5. Information – to explain the significance of this achievement (the Periodic Table of the Elements) – *to understand much more about the elements that matter.*

6. This essay tries to set out some of the arguments for and against smacking a child.

Many parents use physical punishment to discipline their children: others prefer different methods. This essay addresses some of the arguments that are found in discussions about the physical punishment of children. Many people claim that physical punishment damages children in later life. Opponents of corporal punishment claim that the children who are subject to physical punishment will grow up to become delinquents or even use violence and the threat of violence against their wives. However, many happily married adults were smacked when they were younger but are never violent towards their spouses. Another criticism of physical punishment is that it teaches children that you can use violence to force others to do whatever you want them to. In fact children raised well soon learn that violence by itself is nothing – it must be linked to moral right. Finally, some people say that smacking a child will damage the relationship between the child and the parents. This is clearly wrong. Children who appreciate rules, who understand them, will be happier than children whose parents fail to explain these things. There are specific concerns about physical chastisement. Some parents are unable to control their tempers and inflict injuries on their children, sometimes causing bruises or even breaking bones. Other parents inflict violence excessively or, sometimes, as the sole means of discipline. In this case, the child will fail to learn to distinguish right from wrong because they are injured, in pain, fearful and anxious. Judging the fitness of the punishment is also an important aspect of all this. It is one thing to smack a small child who is having a temper tantrum, it is another to hit an adolescent whose timekeeping is poor. Finally, corporal punishment can be a useful method of discipline, but as a last resort. Ultimately, if children are to become responsible adults, we must start when they are young with the intention that we should help them to become responsible individuals in a world of responsible people, whatever our particular views about disciplining children.

*

*Many parents use physical punishment to discipline their children: **others prefer different methods**. This essay addresses some of the **arguments** that are found in discussions about the physical punishment of children.*

*Many people claim that physical punishment **damages** children in later life. Opponents of corporal punishment claim that the children who are subject to physical punishment will grow up to become delinquents or even use violence and the threat of violence against their wives. **However**, many happily married adults were smacked when they were younger but are never violent towards their spouses. Another criticism of physical punishment is that it **teaches children that you can use violence** to force others to do whatever you want them to. In fact children raised well soon learn that violence by itself is nothing – it must be linked to moral right. Finally, some people say that smacking a child will **damage the relationship between the child and the parents**. This is clearly wrong. Children who appreciate rules, who understand them, will be happier than children whose parents fail to explain these things.*

*There are specific concerns about physical chastisement. **Some parents are unable to control their tempers** and inflict injuries on their children, sometimes causing bruises or even breaking bones. Other parents **inflict violence excessively** or, sometimes, as the sole means of discipline. In this case, **the child will fail to learn to distinguish right from wrong because they are injured**, in pain, fearful and anxious. Judging the **fitness of the punishment** is also an important aspect of all this. It is one thing to smack a small child who is having a temper tantrum, it is another to hit an adolescent whose timekeeping is poor.*

*Finally, corporal punishment can be a useful method of discipline, but **as a last resort**. Ultimately, if children are to become responsible adults, we must start when they are young with the intention that we should help them to become responsible individuals in a world of responsible people, whatever our particular views about disciplining children.*

337 words

Commentary Four Paragraphs

1. Informative – introduces the topic, a discussion – *arguments that are found in discussions about the physical punishment of children.*
2. Discussion – reasons underlying opinions – *However – clearly…*

3. Further discussion – *Some – Others – Judging…*
4. Final discussion point – tries to bring together both views under a more important argument – *Ultimately…*

7. This item deals with safety procedures that should be observed before starting a chainsaw. (From Husqvarna's *Operator's Manual – 128RJ.*)

Each paragraph in the final version deals with a particular aspect of starting a chainsaw.

The complete clutch, clutch cover, and shaft must be fitted before the machine is started, otherwise parts could come loose and cause personal injury. Always remove the machine away from the refueling area before starting. Place the machine on a flat surface. Ensure the cutting attachment cannot come into contact with any object. Make sure no unauthorized persons are in the working area, otherwise there is a risk of serious personal injury. The safety distance is 15 meters.

*

The complete clutch, clutch cover, and shaft **must be fitted** *before the machine is started, otherwise parts could come loose and cause personal injury.* (A **passive** verb – it must be fitted, by someone.)

Always remove *the machine away from the refueling area before starting. Place the machine on a flat surface.* **Ensure** *the cutting attachment cannot come into contact with any object.* (An **active** verb – you must always remove the machine.)

Make sure no unauthorized persons are in **the working area,** *otherwise there is a risk of serious personal injury.* (<u>You</u> are responsible for this.) **The safety distance** *is 15 meters.*

78 words (excluding brackets)

Commentary Three Paragraphs

1. An instruction – *must be fitted* and an explicit warning – *otherwise.*
2. Two instructions – *Always remove… Ensure…*

3. Information (an implied warning) – *The safety distance…* which is required to carry out the final instruction – *Make sure…*

"Rules" for Paragraphs

Would your list of "rules" include any of the following?

1. A change of topic? Moving on from one idea to the next?
2. A change of purpose, to inform, to describe or discuss?
3. A change of direction, to follow one character and then another?
4. A parallel idea, something to help explain something?
5. A contrast, something rather different to help you understand?
6. A pause, part-way through a lengthy passage – remember the suggestion made about the paragraph in the extract from *Danziger's Travels*?
7. A new paragraph is required for each new speaker.

You could think of paragraphs like the courses of a meal. Imagine that you are about to finish a plate of your favourite savoury dish, fish and chips perhaps, a steak, a curry or a special pizza. Two mouthfuls to go and, suddenly, someone is dumping spoonfuls of your favourite dessert alongside these remaining savoury mouthfuls: ice cream, fruit salad, Black Forest gâteau, apple pie.

Yes, these things are all delicious, but not mixed up together. To be enjoyed they have to be eaten separately and in the right order.

**If we're feeling really confident about paragraphs we could move on.
If not we really should try two more exercises.**

8. What would you make of these versions of two sections of a contract for the recruitment of a Foreign Domestic Worker (FDW) in Singapore?

(From: http://www.lucky.com.sg/contract/contract.htm)
NB. In the first version the words of the contract are set out in two ordinary prose paragraphs: complete sentences, clearly punctuated.

The first paragraph deals with the appointment of the agency to recruit a foreign domestic worker on behalf of a client. The second deals with the matter of replacing a foreign domestic worker. The link words, that carry the subject from one sentence to another throughout the paragraphs, have been highlighted. The subject of each sentence is indicated by capitals.

The Employer hereby appoints the Agency to secure the services of a Foreign Domestic Worker (FDW) (set out in the Services & Fees Schedule) for a contract for service on the terms and conditions that appear below. The period of this contract of service shall be from the date of signing this contract, to the last day of employment of the last FDW provided by the Agency for the Employer, within the FDW's employment duration of two years. The Agency shall hand over the FDW to the employer within _____ day(s)/ month(s) after obtaining the in-principle approval by the Ministry of Manpower.

The Employer may request a replacement after the FDW has worked for the Employer at least _____ days/weeks but before the expiry of the replacement period which was agreed (set out in the Services & Fees Schedule). The grant of replacement is subject to the following: The Employer agrees to transfer the FDW to a new employer specified by the Agency and will not in any way prevent or jeopardize the FDW's transfer or opportunity to seek re-employment with another employer, unless the employer can show to the satisfaction of the Agency that the FDW is medically unfit to work as a domestic worker or has committed a criminal offence in Singapore. For request of transfer, the Employer must sign the Consent to Transfer Form from the Work Permit Office to allow the FDW to seek employment with the new Employer. In the event of any fines or penalties imposed by the Immigration and Checkpoints Authority (ICA) and/or the Ministry of Manpower (MOM) if the FDW overstays due to any delay resulting from either the Employer's or the Agency's failure to complete the transfer of the FDW to the new Employer, the party at fault shall bear the costs. The Agency will bring the replacement (FDW) into Singapore only when the existing FDW is successfully approved by the Work Pass Division for transfer to the new Employer. In the event that the FDW seeks the protection of the Embassy of her home country, the Agency shall not be held responsible for the FDW's action. The Agency reserves the right to arrange for a replacement subject to the selection of a new FDW by the Employer, in the event of delay or non-arrival of the FDW due to death, injury, sickness, civil unrest, war or any acts of God or other circumstances beyond the agency's control. THE EMPLOYER reserves the right to reject **the intended replacement** *and terminate this Agreement if the replacement does not fulfil the Employer's selection criteria (based on the original selection criteria).*

438 words

In these two paragraphs there is no simple link between sentences, apart from the subjects of the sentences, in most cases the two parties to the contract, the employer and the agency.

The original version of the contract which follows here is very different and sets out clearly the requirements of each party. Essentially, a contract simply sets out a list of things that two or more parties have agreed to do (Latin – *Contractus* – pulling or drawing together).

So, we could say that these paragraphs provide instructions to each party, clear lists of the things that are to be done.

Appointment of Services

- The employer hereby appoints the Agency to secure the services of a Foreign Domestic Worker (FDW) (set out in the Services & Fees Schedule) for a contract for service on the terms and conditions that appear below.
- The period of this contract of service shall be from the date of signing this contract, to the last day of employment of the last FDW provided by the Agency for the Employer, within the FDW's employment duration of two years.
- The Agency shall handover the FDW to the employer within _____ day(s)/ month(s) after obtaining the in-principle approval by the Ministry of Manpower.

Conditions for Replacement/Transfer

- The Employer may request a replacement after the FDW has worked for the Employer at least _____ days/weeks but before the expiry of the replacement period which was agreed (set out in the Services & Fees Schedule). The grant of replacement is subject to the following:

- The Employer agrees to transfer the FDW to a new employer specified by the Agency and will not in any way prevent or jeopardize the FDW's transfer or opportunity to seek re-employment with another employer, unless the employer can show to the satisfaction of the Agency that the FDW is medically unfit to work as a domestic worker or has committed a criminal offence in Singapore.

- For request of transfer, the Employer must sign the Consent to Transfer Form from the Work Permit Office to allow the FDW to seek employment with the new Employer.

- The Employer must release the FDW to the Agency for _____ days for her to be interviewed and re-deployed. During this period, the employer shall bear the cost of providing the FDW with food and accommodation (at a rate of $_____ per day, (if applicable), in addition to the levy payable. Thereafter, the Agency shall bear the costs, until it finds a new employer for the FDW.

- In the event of any fines or penalties imposed by the Immigration and Checkpoints Authority (ICA) and/or the Ministry of Manpower (MOM) if the FDW overstays due to any delay resulting from either the Employer's or the Agency's failure to complete the transfer of the FDW to the new Employer, the party at fault shall bear the costs.

- The Agency will bring the replacement (FDW) into Singapore only when the existing FDW is successfully approved by the Work Pass Division for transfer to the new Employer.

- In the event that the FDW seeks the protection of the Embassy of her home country, the Agency shall not be held responsible for the FDW's action.

- The Agency reserves the right to arrange for a replacement subject to the selection of a new FDW by the Employer, in the event of delay or non-arrival of the FDW due to death, injury, sickness, civil unrest, war or any acts of God or other circumstances beyond the agency's control.

- The Employer reserves the right to reject the intended replacement and terminate this Agreement if the replacement does not fulfil the Employer's selection criteria (based on the original selection criteria).

524 words

The sub-heading for each "paragraph" and the numbering of each sentence make it much easier to find our way around the information than words alone, even when organised into sentences and ordinary paragraphs. This is the distinctive and helpful nature of a well-written contract.

You should also note that of the twelve sentences here, nine begin with the subject and this makes clear immediately who is responsible for each of the agreed actions.

Be aware that lawyers will refer to each of these numbered sections as a clause, not in the grammatical sense that we explored earlier, but as a statement, a separate item in a contract.

9.   This item was published in *The Spectator*, a British political journal.

From "The ungovernable Co-op could become the last customer of its own funeral service". Martin Vander Weyer. April 19, 2014.

The writer foresees the end of a business whose owners were once its customers.

'Care, respect, clarity and reassurance' are what the Co-operative funeral service says it offers the bereaved, and the parent Co-op Group may soon find itself in need of just such support to help it come to terms with the resolution of the Co-op Bank. 'Resolution' is modern banking jargon for an orderly burial, involving powers vested in the Bank of England to transfer all or part of a troubled bank's business to a private-sector purchaser, or into temporary public ownership, or to ensure that depositors are either paid out by the Financial Services Compensation Scheme or are transferred to healthier banks. These last rites have not yet been publicly contemplated, but it is hard to see how else the story can end. Knocked off course by its disastrous takeover of the Britannia Building Society, fatally distracted by the purchase of Lloyds branches that never happened, the bank has a huge black hole in its balance sheet and scant hope of returning to profit. Its 'ethical' status has been dented by its record of mis-selling payment protection insurance. Following a recapitalisation last year, it is 70 per cent owned by a curious collection of US hedge funds whose only interest is to make a fat turn as swiftly as possible, while the Co-op Group itself, as a 30 per cent shareholder, is left with diminished influence over the bank

which so dangerously bears its name. And that stake will reduce again if the parent (which has other problems of its own, notably in the aftermath of its acquisition of Somerfield supermarkets) cannot come up with its share of an additional £400 million capital call made by the bank last month. The distinctly non-ethical consortium of banks to which the Co-op Group is heavily indebted – Barclays, RBS and Lloyds to the fore – are no doubt ready to swallow Co-op Bank's 4.7 million retail customers between them as part of a wider settlement. All this will come into even sharper focus with the confirmation of record group losses this week. Meanwhile in the board game of corporate survival, 'Lord Myners parachuted in to overhaul your governance' was probably more of a snake than a ladder* in the first place; but 'Myners' shock resignation' is a big, slippery, hissing PR disaster, confirming as it does what departing chief executive Euan Sutherland said last month about the group being 'ungovernable'. Myners – the multi-millionaire former Labour minister for the City, was never likely to hit it off with the representatives of provincial Co-operative movements who make up the group's bloated and unbusinesslike board. Those directors are now locked in a defensive mindset which makes intervention by the Bank of England and the Treasury all the more likely in the end. The walk-on part of Lord Myners is, I fear, no more than a sideshow in the slow procession towards the crematorium of this once great institution.

The darker script indicates main ideas and the dark capitals, the links between the beginning of a paragraph and an item or items in the previous paragraph.

__'Care, respect, clarity and reassurance'__ are what the Co-operative funeral service says it offers the bereaved, and the parent Co-op Group may soon find itself in need of just such support to help it come to terms with the __resolution__ of the Co-op Bank. 'Resolution' is modern banking jargon for __AN ORDERLY BURIAL__, involving powers vested in the Bank of England __to transfer all or part of a troubled bank's business__ to a private-sector purchaser, or into temporary public ownership, or to ensure that depositors are either paid out by the Financial Services Compensation Scheme or are transferred to healthier banks.

__THESE LAST RITES__ have not yet been publicly contemplated, __but it is hard to see how else the story can end.__ Knocked off course by its *disastrous takeover of the Britannia Building Society, fatally distracted by the purchase of Lloyds branches that never happened, the bank has **a huge black hole in its balance sheet** and scant hope of returning to profit. Its 'ethical' status has been dented by its record of mis-selling payment protection insurance. Following a recapitalisation last year, it is 70 per cent **owned by a curious collection of US hedge funds** whose only interest is to make a fat turn as swiftly as possible, while the Co-op Group itself, as **A 30 PER CENT SHAREHOLDER**, is **left with diminished influence** over the bank which so dangerously bears its name.*

*   **AND THAT STAKE** will reduce again if the parent (which has other problems of its own, notably in the aftermath of its acquisition of Somerfield supermarkets) **cannot come up with its share of an additional £400 million CAPITAL CALL MADE BY THE BANK** last month. The distinctly non-ethical consortium of banks to which the Co-op Group is heavily indebted – Barclays, RBS and Lloyds to the fore – are no doubt **ready to swallow Co-op Bank's 4.7 million retail customers** between them **AS PART OF A WIDER SETTLEMENT.***

*   **ALL THIS** will come into even sharper focus with the confirmation of record group losses this week. **Meanwhile** in the board game of corporate survival, 'Lord Myners parachuted in to overhaul your governance' was probably **MORE OF A SNAKE THAN A LADDER**[1] in the first place; but 'Myners' **shock resignation**' is a big, slippery, hissing PR disaster, confirming as it does what departing chief executive Euan Sutherland said last month about the group being **'ungovernable'.***

*   **MYNERS** – the multi-millionaire **former Labour minister** for the City, was **never likely to hit it off** with the representatives of provincial Co-operative movements who make up t**he group's bloated and unbusinesslike board**. Those directors are now locked in a **defensive midset** which makes intervention by the Bank of England and the Treasury all the more likely in the end. The walk-on part of Lord Muners is, I fear, no more than **a sideshow in the slow procession towards the crematorium** of this once great institution.*

506 words

---

1   *Snakes and ladders*, a board game in which ladders lead players up towards their target, and snakes lead them down, away from it. *Snake* suggests treachery.

Commentary Five Paragraphs

1. The bank needs the kind of support it used to offer the customers of its funeral service as it is likely that the government will have to intervene in its business.
2. It's difficult to see any other outcome; it has enormous debts, is largely owned by hedge funds which want to sell it as soon as possible and has little power to control the situation.
3. The Co-op parent group must find £400m to pay off the banks to which it owns money or they will simply swallow up its customers.
4. Record group losses and the sudden resignations of two leaders have worsened matters.
5. The idea of Myers getting on with unbusinesslike board members is a bit of a joke as the organisation moves slowly towards its own funeral.

Well Done

You have been paying close attention – I hope – and, in this chapter especially, I have worked you very hard indeed.

So, it's time for a story.

Once upon a time some fifteen-year-olds were in class waiting for the last bell of the afternoon. It was hot and it was Friday and they were tired and Mr Inson was droning on about something.

For one of them it was all too much and he let his head slide onto the lid of his desk, and fell asleep. Still Mr Inson droned on. Then Mr Inson came to a pause and looked around at the class. Slowly, he reached over to one side and then wrote these words on the board: *When the bell rings please make sure that you leave as quietly as possible. It would a pity to wake him up.*

There were some smiles; when the bell rang the boy's classmates left as quietly as mice. Forty-five minutes later, as the sounds of life drained out of the school, Mr Inson met him, head hunched down in his shoulders, half way across the playground.

"Why didn't you wake me up, Sir?"

"You didn't bother to ask me if you could sleep during my lesson, did you? How was I supposed to know how long you wanted to sleep? What if I'd woken you up too soon?"

It was the easiest after-school detention that he had ever arranged.

Want to test yourself further, or practise on paragraphs?

For any of the items that you have been working on in this chapter, simply write a heading for each paragraph. Compare them with the suggestions here.

1. From *The Destructors*.

   a. Blackie arrives
   b. He looks for T.
   c. He finds T.
   d. He questions T.
   e. T replies.

These headings follow the drama between the old leader of the gang and the new one. The highlighted sections show what Blackie discovers and provide a background, a context for the drama here.

2. *Danziger's Travels*

   a. Danziger's reasons for travelling.
   b. His reasons for applying for a fellowship.
   c. The possibility of failure.
   d. An attempt to ignore that possibility.
   e. Attempt halted.

3. Letter – age in marriage

    a. Chaplin's marriage introduced.

    b. Details of that marriage.

    c. Conclusion about age in marriage.

4. An invitation to an ice cream fair

    a. Fair announced.

    b. An event not to be missed/excitement anticipated.

    c. Application urged.

    d. Excitement to be continued.

5. *IGCSE Chemistry*

    a. Observation and data collection for scientific theory.

    b. Patterns in the data lead to theories.

    c. A theory concerning the grouping of elements.

    d. The significance of relative atomic mass.

    e. A better understanding of important elements.

6. An essay on physical punishment of children

    a. Opinion on the physical punishment of children.

    b. The effects of smacking.

    c. Excessive or inappropriate punishment.

    d. Over-riding aim – responsible individuals.

7. Husqvarna's *Operator's Manual*

    a. Before starting/safe machine.

    b. Safety checks/safe operating.

    c. Keep others away/safety of others.

8. A contract for the recruitment of a Foreign Domestic Worker (FDW)

This item most closely follows the Husqvarna's *Operator's Manual*, where three separate instructions are found. They match the two section headings in this contract.

9. *The ungovernable Co-op…*

    a. Its death looms ahead.
    b. It's lost control of its situation.
    c. Its creditors will willingly destroy it.
    d. Further losses and resignations.
    e. Boardroom troubles – a joke.

Paragraphs – assembled and put to work – organising ideas

Advertising, agreement, assertion (claim), autobiography, description, discussion, enquiry, entertainment, explanation, information, instruction, invitation, persuasion, warning.

Here you have had much to read – I do like to encourage you to read – and a great deal to think about.

Once I have cheered you up about those unmentionable matters, spelling, punctuation and grammar, you will be getting on with your own writing.

CHAPTER FOURTEEN

BOGEYMEN

Things that we might get wrong.
Things that might trouble us.
Things that we can understand.
Things that we can improve hugely.

SPaG – Spelling, punctuation and grammar.

Spelling and Punctuation – Their Importance

Spelling and punctuation provide visual clues that help someone to read what we have written. Most of us read about three times faster than we speak. When we do anything at speed it is much easier to go wrong – if something is not written clearly we hesitate, like a cyclist about to swerve when someone steps into the road, or when someone wrong-foots us in tennis or dodges round us in football.

So clear spelling, punctuation, and grammar too, are ways in which we make it easier for a reader to understand what we have written. We must never forget this important truth; if we don't bother with these things, other people may not bother with what we have to say and we have wasted our time as well as theirs.

> **Make it easier for your reader with clear spelling,**
> **punctuation and grammar.**

EXERCISE FORTY-EIGHT

Read the passage that follows aloud and as quickly as you can. Count the number of times that you hesitate, or get someone else to count for you. Try to identify the cause of each hesitation.

> *all write then they would have lam for supper she carried it upstairs holding the thin bone end of it with both her hands and as she went through the living room she saw him standing over by the window with his back to her and she stopped*
>
> *for god's sake he said hearing her but not turning round don't make supper for me I'm going out at that point Mary maloney simply waked up behind him and without any pause she swung the big frozen leg of lamb hi in the air and brought it down as hard as she could on the back of his head she might just as well have hit him with a steal club she stepped back a pace wating and the funny thing was that he remayned standing their for at least four or five seconds gently swaying then he crashed to the carpet*

Clarity

Without punctuation it is difficult to know when to pause or stop and words that are actually spoken (*direct speech*) are not clear. *All write*, with the wrong spelling of *right*, looks like an instruction, but as soon as the words are spoken the meaning becomes clear.

> ### Just what is grammar? A little revision.

First, try this short exercise.

EXERCISE FORTY-NINE

a.   Arrange these words so that they make sense.

> *Cat mat sat the on the.*

> This should not trouble you and you will probably arrive at this sentence:

The cat sat on the mat.

Then try to explain how you came to arrange the words in this order –
you were doing something similar back in Chapter Two.

b. Try rearranging these words to make sense of them.
    bull cows meets the the.

c. *and at bus driver end got man of off old road stopped the the the the the.*

Now then, how many rules do you think were involved in all the choices and
decisions we had to make in Exercise Forty-Nine?

The question a. uses rules for placing the article in front of the noun to which
it is related, about the nature of the things in the sentence, the cat and the mat
and which of them is able to sit. Other rules concern the placing of the subject
before the verb and the object afterwards. A least four, I would say.

How many more then for c.? No, don't even think about it.

Grammar is simply the way in which words relate to one another to convey
meaning. We hear or see this in three ways: **word order**, **word choice** and
alterations to a word.

1. The order in which we use words, which we saw in (a) and (b) above.
2. The choice of words: pairing the definite article, *the*, with a noun in (a),
    and pairing *cat* with *sat*.
3. Changes to a word – *inflections* – that change meaning.

Singular or plural	*cat or cats*
Present or past	*speak or spoke*
Adjective or adverb	*a <u>gradual</u> change or changing <u>gradually</u>*
Noun or participle	*a gradual <u>change</u> or <u>changing</u> gradually*

So long as you understand these three principles, these three simple ideas, and
remember to check what you have written, you will have a sufficient grasp of
the rules of grammar to be able to write well. You may also come across the
word **syntax**, which simply means the ordering of words and phrases.

Do not be put off by serious-looking books about grammar. They are very interesting and helpful to people who wish to study further the business of language and writing, or who want a thorough explanation of some aspect of English. You have built-in grammar that you use when you speak and which should help you when you write.

Rules

Life is much easier when there are simple rules to follow – turn taps to the right to stop the water and flick the switch upwards to turn off the light. Press the green button to call a number, the red one to end the call. Without these rules there would be confusion, possibly danger. Sometimes our consistency, our sticking to these rules can save lives, by driving on the same side of the road as everyone else, for example. These rules follow decisions.

Grammar rules are different, they are like the rules of nature that help us to understand how natural forces work, why the roots of a plant will grow towards a source of water – *hydrotropism*.

They are not like the rules or laws by which we organise ourselves. These laws are set out in legislation as guides and instructions about the way we lead our lives – if we want to drive we must pass a driving test.

Grammar rules ensure that the relationship between the words we speak or write is clear and that what we mean is readily understood. They are rules that we follow, not in order to avoid punishment, but in order to communicate effectively.

We follow them as we learn to speak. We may never learn them as we learn the rules of the highway code, but we appreciate them, and use them instinctively, just as most of us cycle instinctively without ever studying the laws of physics.

Only when we need to discuss our language is it sometimes helpful to consider, for example, rules about the position of subject and object relative to the verb of a sentence.

In much the same way, the rules of spelling – *i* before *e* except after *c* unless the sound produced is *a* – can help with *receive* and *weigh*, for example, but not with an exception – *seize*.

Remember – these rules can only be a guide and that there are a number of exceptions to them.

Now, if you haven't already done so, stop worrying about rules.

How to Improve Our Spelling, Punctuation and Grammar

For the moment we must put spelling to one side – we will deal with it a little later in this chapter. Grammar you have already mastered, at least as far as spoken English is concerned, and punctuation is an extension of this. If you had not already mastered grammar you would not be following this now. You might not be able to recite the rules of grammar but grammar is already installed in your brain.

Now we come to writing and the twenty-six shapes from which we can choose to represent the sounds we use when we speak. Speech is the basic form of a language and it is only very recently, in historic terms, that most of us have been able to read and write. Speaking comes naturally to all of us and, by the time that most of us can think about these things we are already competent speakers.

Reading and writing are different. Most of us can remember early reading and writing lessons because reading and writing do not come naturally to us and have to be learnt and cultivated – encouraged and worked on.

Fortunately, we can use our understanding of the spoken language to help us when we write, and that is why I was so insistent about reading work aloud in earlier chapters. It is with our ears, which pick up spoken words so quickly, that we can check the punctuation and grammar of what we write.

So, be grown-up about this matter, read your work aloud so that you can check it and, if necessary, make improvements.

Comfortably sitting you are?

Once his grandchildren had heard him read their favourite stories a number
of times my father-in-law would reorganise the words and begin each story
with,

"Time upon a once"

The children would roar with laughter and encourage him to continue the
story in the same way, starting to read at the end of each sentence instead
of at the beginning. They loved telling him that he was a silly old grandad
and had got things wrong, but they could not have done this had they not
understood first what he should have said.

Spelling

Spelling, like punctuation and grammar, does not trouble us until we start to
write – no, not the wild lettering that we spread across our bedroom wallpaper.
No, the serious stuff at school, with corrections and, once upon a time, red ink!
How could we think about spelling until we learn to write? It is then that
our teachers insist that we make an effort to get things right because they
know that if our spelling is inconsistent – look back at the first exercise in this
chapter – it will be difficult to read easily what we have written. And where do
we first meet the business of spelling? When we read, of course, and, just as
deaf children find it very difficult to learn to speak, so do people who read little
find it difficult to write well.

So, remember the advice about reading.

**Why on earth don't we just modernise or simplify
or regularise (UK) or regularize (US) our spelling?**

The heading here provides part of the answer; which version would we
adopt, *regularise* or *regularize*?

Changes in spelling, or punctuation, like mistakes with these matters, surprise or disturb readers who want to get along as quickly as possible with things that are familiar.

This is why spelling is very slow to change. Sometimes there are historical reasons; words from classical Greek keep reminders of their Greek letters: the letter *phi* in *photograph* – the word means *write with light*. Sometimes it's because the pronunciation of a word such as *light* has changed and no longer sounds like its German cousin – *Licht*. The *h* here is sounded in the throat as in our *loch*. *Cwen* was our spelling of *queen*, but the letter *w* troubled the French when they arrived in England, in 1066, and has done so ever since.

Now that our eyes have come into play we have to help them remember the appearance of words, especially the ones that we find difficult to spell.

These are practical things we can do to help ourselves. We can use:

- A notebook to record spellings that trouble us.
- Information about words that are troublesome for us. (Look at the way I have dealt with the twenty words on the list below. Use an etymological dictionary which will tell us about the history and origins of words.)
- Cover and copy methods to practise spelling difficult words. (Look at a word then cover it while you try to write it correctly.)
- Any scraps of information which remind us of the correct spelling. (For example, when I am faced with *vehicle*, where the *h* is almost silent, I remember learning that its Latin ancestor is *vehiculum* – pronounced *wayhiculum*; English students soon learn to make a joke of the word and pronounce it *vee-hickle* so that they remember the *h*.)
- Lists of words that are commonly misspelt.

My keys to help you remember twenty most frequently misspelt words:

1. Separate   Two e's separated by two a's which keep them apart.

2. Definitely   You have already met *finis* – end. At the end things are more certain, more definite. (More finished, more complete.)

3. Manoeuvre   Blame French spelling. Manoover yet hors d'oeuvres – oar-derv.

4. Embarrass   Stress – second syllable so double r. Unpleasant experience so double ss.

5. Occurrence   Pronounce it Ock-cur-rance. Double r to avoid the sound of cure.

6. Consensus   Con – with, and sensus – sense or feeling. Having the same feeling about something – agreement.

7. Unnecessary   Double n to avoid a magic e and une as in fortune, and to show that un, a prefix, not, has been joined to necessary. Necessary also needs to be learnt. Two c's might well cause the word to sound like neck-sessary. If it helps you can blame again the French who spell this word's cousin: necessaire. And another suggestion from a friend: a shirt is always necessary – one collar and two sleeves.

8. Acceptable   Double c to separate (again) the first two sounds or syllables, ack and septable.

9. Broccoli   Double c to separate two syllables.

10. Referred   Prefix re added to ferr (from ferreo – I carry in Latin. Mod. English ferry) or just remember ferry or say something daft such as I referred him to the ferry master.

11. Bureaucracy   The key problem is having two letter u's close together. Even the Americans, who like to get rid of an unnecessary u when they can, cannot change this French word!

12. Supersede   Literally sit above. Sitting – sedentary as in sedentary occupation.

13. Questionnaire   Rhymes with millionaire but takes a double n. Alphabetically, millionaire comes first and takes on one n. Questionnaire comes second and takes two n's.

14. Connoisseur   Two n's to keep the first o short. The second o when the sound is more like an a is puzzling and just has to be learnt.

15. Allot   Misspelling of this word is a grammar mistake really – a failure to recognise a word, lot, which means a large

number or amount, or an item which has been allocated or allotted (note the double ll) in an auction, perhaps.

16. Entrepreneur — Entre-nous – between ourselves – helps with the first part. The word looks French, is French and this can be off-putting. We pronounce it French fashion, the first sound down the nose and the second r rolled. Just remember the final u to maintain its French appearance.

17. Particularly — Pronounce all five syllables and this word will be easier to spell. It is often spoken as partickuly. The suffix ly has been added to an adjective, particular, to form an adverb. (Remember, details in Chapter One.)

18. Liquify — The suffix fy indicates that something has been turned into the state indicated in the first part of the word. Words formed in the same way include: terrify and electrify.

19. Conscience — Learn to spell science first, then add con.

20. Parallel — It's the double ll that is the trouble. Think of parallel bars.

> **Spelling – Over to You**

EXERCISE FIFTY-FOUR

Here is a reminder to help with words that produce different sounds with the same group of letters. How many sounds are represented here by the letters *ough*?

Though the ploughman thought the borough rough he coughed his way through.

Make up your own reminders for any of the following words that you find difficult to spell.

Look up the meaning and origins in dictionaries, try online searches and try using the difficult words in nonsense sentences. All this will help your visual memory.

accomplish	determination	opposition
accustom	diminish	ornament
applaud	disappoint	parliament
artificial	disease	patient
association	disguise	persevere
athletic	engineer	pretence
acquaintance	exception	privilege
boundary	experiment	quaint
business	extremely	quarry
camera	fulfil	resign
cancel	fragment	ridiculous
capable	genuine	rumour
ceremony	grateful	sacrifice
choir	heir	scissors
cleanliness	immediately	seize
column	immense	slaughter
commit	industrious	soothe
condemn	introduction	stationary – at rest
conqueror	leisure	stationery – envelope
contempt	manageable	suspicious
curiosity	mischievous	traitor
deceitful	nourish	variety
decision	obedience	ventilation

Final thoughts on SPaG – spelling, punctuation and grammar:

DON'T GIVE UP

Remember that in conversation either party can ask immediately for an explanation of something that has been said, or can challenge something that has been said, and the matter can be pursued immediately, until it is resolved. It is rare for us to be able to question the writer of anything that we have in front of us. Writing started off as a way of making records that would last a long time. If writing is to be effective, whether on paper or in some electronic form it usually requires a much higher degree of precision than speaking.

Remember too that, as we get older, habits become more entrenched and new ones are more difficult to establish. Then the older reader may find that a special effort is required, especially with the memory and matters such as spelling. On the other hand, I would hope that the wisdom or cunning that comes with age might help some people to cope well in other ways.

Finally, a note of hope for people who are troubled by dyslexia. Someone I know, who has struggled for years with dyslexia, recently bought a Kindle, which has a dyslexic font. Now, for the first time in his life, he has read and enjoyed a whole novel, and now that he can enjoy reading he will almost certainly read more. Then he will become much more familiar with good spelling and his writing will improve as will his confidence. Then there will be something more in life for him to enjoy.

Words That Are Abused, That Are Used to Mislead Us

Have you ever noticed what is written on the doors of police cars in your area? Cycling to work in Lancashire, in the north of England, I took the trouble to read the words on the door of a police car: *Lancashire Police. Serving the people of Lancashire.*

Fancy that, I thought. I would never have imagined them doing that. Suddenly I had a vision of local police officers turning out of the police garage in Lancaster or Preston and one of them saying to the other, *To hell with Lancashire today. Let's go and serve the people of – Yorkshire.*

Using slogans like this in an attempt to impress people is a form of dishonesty and it's a waste of our time reading them. The police force of Lancashire has no business to do anything other than serve the good people of Lancashire. The force is doing no one a favour; it is merely doing its duty to its employers. This slogan is really a claim for our approval which insults the reader's intelligence and wastes time.

Education is often said to be delivered, as if it is a physical commodity. This suggests control over education to match our control over physical objects upon which we can lay our hands. This suggests a promise that we will deliver or provide them. This, of course, is impossible with education, which is a service or an activity, or an achievement, not a product. It is something that takes place in our heads and cannot arrive on the back of a lorry.

Convince/persuade. To convince someone is to put them in a position where they believe something. Having listened to your argument, someone might believe that something should be done. To be convinced of this the person would have to <u>believe</u> that it was right. If I have a large enough wad of banknotes, or a sufficiently heavy stick, I might well <u>persuade</u> you to do something, even if you thought it wrong.

Even the BBC now does not bother to make this important distinction, between believing that something should be done, and doing something simply because somebody else wants you to do it. If you are convinced that something should be done then you will try to do it. If you have been persuaded to do something and the person responsible withdraws the money, or puts away the stick, then you are likely to stop.

If we abuse the words entrusted to our care, we also abuse whoever it is who is listening to us or is reading something that we have written.

Ask what these words are meant to achieve.

Some words are simply overused, either because it is easier to seize upon words or expressions that are constantly heard, or because they are thought to impress. Consider:

> *Wembley Stadium (England's national football/soccer stadium) is* **iconic***.*
> *So too are various birds and animals, buildings, and leisure and sporting*
> *activities.*

Do these speakers really mean that all these things are pictures or images of something special, or representative of something?

> **Going forward** *we will ensure that this does not happen again.*

What do the words *going forward* add to this sentence? They seem related to the future, but the future is covered anyway by the use of the future tense of the verb, *will ensure.*

Brilliant!

This word serves currently as a general purpose reaction to a statement of any sort, as a general approval of whatever has just been said. It means *bright* or *shining*, so the idea of a brilliant performance can make sense. However, over-use has robbed the word of its capacity to make the things to which it refers stand out.

*Then she **goes**, "It's great." So I **go**, "Oh no it ain't."*

Exclaim, respond, rant, holler, scream, remark, observe, object, shout, cry, gasp, whisper, moan, breathe or remark.

Ask why words such as *go* are used when there are alternatives that are more precise. Sometimes it's because a speaker is in a hurry to get the words out, whereas a writer has more time to choose words carefully.

Redundant Words – Words that have nothing to say

1. We will learn our lessons from this unfortunate incident *and ensure that nothing like it happens again.*

If the lessons have been learnt then precautions against a repetition of the incident will surely be taken. It is understandable that the speaker wants to reassure listeners but the transformation of a simple statement into a compound sentence suggests that a second important action – *ensure* – will occur. It suggests that there is more that can be done, when this is not the case. *We will* apply *the lessons of this unfortunate accident* would be more reassuring. It's more compact, more forthright, and promises the application of the lessons, an important step beyond simply learning them.

The words in the second clause of the original sentence – *and ensure that nothing like it happens again* – offer little information and serve only to intensify the emotion of the first clause.

Put another way, ensuring is part of the learning, not additional to it; the second clause is redundant.

2. He was arrested on suspicion of a racially aggravated *Section 4a* Public Order *Act* offence and *currently* remains in custody at the West London *police station.*

Here the offending words, which have been identified above, serve to load a simple statement: a man suspected of committing a racially aggravated public order offence remains in custody in west London.

Sometimes, when we are anxious not to omit anything of importance, we give little thought to the material with which we are troubling our reader. In this case the details of the particular act, the excessive precision of *currently* and the false precision of *the West London police station* – is this a reference to a particular police station, at Shepherd's Bush or Acton perhaps, or just a way of assuring us that the suspect is well and truly "banged up"? All this conjures up a picture of a police officer in front of a bench of magistrates, glancing at his notebook and making clear that all the proper procedures have been followed.

Perhaps the writer of the news statement has simply taken a police press release and not bothered to translate it into ordinary English.

Twenty-six words instead of seventeen, an additional fifty per cent of unnecessary words, a considerable additional burden for the reader.

Ask what these words contribute.

Handwriting

And of course if you can't read the words in the first place…

(Adapted from Heinemann. English First Language. Peter Inson. pub 2011, p. 193.)

Examiners and others sometimes complain about the problems caused by poor handwriting. Here is an easy way for you to analyse and improve your handwriting. Write out this sentence three times on ordinary lined paper, as follows:

(The fourth line is to be left blank to start with.)

The quick brown fox jumps over the lazy dog.

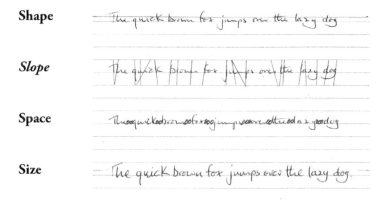

Shape	
Slope	
Space	
Size	

Remember – four S's – shape, size, slope and space.

Pencil in:

First and last lines of writing – a line 3mm above the base to indicate how well the letters are <u>shaped</u> and <u>sized</u>.

Second line of writing – lines extending parts of letters that should be formed with straight lines.

Third line of writing – insert the letter *o* as many times as you can between the words.

Aims

1. Letters touch both lines and letters are recognisably shaped – e.g. g and y.
2. Stems that are parallel.
3. Spaces between words that can accommodate only one *o*.
4. Draw a construction line, as in line 4, write the sentence then erase the extra line. (The remains of the construction line can be seen at each end of the sentence.)

Practise – little and often. Don't expect sudden or dramatic results. In time you can modify bad habits.

A handwritten note is often useful, and handwritten cards or letters are much appreciated on special occasions.

ANSWERS TO THE QUESTIONS
IN CHAPTER FOURTEEN

EXERCISE FORTY-EIGHT

All right then, they would have lamb for supper. She carried it upstairs, holding the thin bone end of it with both her hands, and as she went through the living room, she saw him standing over by the window with his back to her, and she stopped.

"For God's sake," he said, hearing her, but not turning round. "Don't make supper for me. I'm going out."

At that point, Mary Maloney simply walked up behind him and without any pause she swung the big frozen leg of lamb high in the air and brought it down as hard as she could on the back of his head.

She might just as well have hit him with a steel club.

She stepped back a pace, waiting, and the funny thing was that he remained standing there for at least four or five seconds, gently swaying. Then he crashed to the carpet.

> *(From Lamb to the Slaughter in Roald Dahl*
> *Collected Short Stories pub Pen.1992)*

EXERCISE FORTY-NINE

a. *The cat sat on the mat.*

Each definite article – *the* – needs to accompany a noun and we can find *cat* and *mat*. The verb, *sat*, is clear and this action is not something a mat does to a cat so the only version that makes sense is the one you have picked, isn't it?

b. *The bull meets the cows.*

This time the singular verb, *meets*, makes clear that it is the singular noun which must be the subject of the sentence, which precedes the verb and the object.

c.   *The driver stopped the bus at the end of the road and the old man got off.*

Two verbs – *stopped* and *got off.*

Two possible subjects – only drivers and old men stop things or get off things and only buses can be stopped – the object – so we have:

The driver stopped the bus and the old man got off.

(It could have been the old man who stopped the bus and the driver who got off.)

Now we are left with the words, the phrase, *at the end of the road.*

We might try *The driver stopped the bus and the old man got off at the end of the road*, but as the first action, stopping, must have happened so that the old man could get off, it makes more sense to tell us where all this took place, *at the end of the road*, as soon as possible in the sentence.

Good manners – considering other people

We are all of us at least slightly lazy and sometimes find it hard to make an effort with something that does not come easily to us, whether it's our spelling, our punctuation, our grammar or our choice of words.

When we write we have to remember the other people who will also want an easy time, especially when they come to read what we have written.

In some ways writing well is simply an extension of good manners. Two things matter: saying what we want to say to best effect, and making it as easy as possible for our reader to grasp this.

A final thought – the effect of reading on the way we speak. When we write we are forced to take far more care with our words than when we speak. If we persist with our efforts then we will find our ability to speak effectively will also improve as will our confidence when we have to address an audience.

And at last, in the next chapter, you are going to put this into practice.

CHAPTER FIFTEEN

PUTTING IT
DOWN IN WORDS

Organising your words. Writing for a variety of purposes.

Getting you to write.
Getting you to write confidently.
Getting you to write well.

Making sure that you check your work.

Someone has been helping you to learn to ride your bike. They have run alongside you, given you advice, steadied you by holding on to the saddle stem, picked you up off the ground when you have not paid attention and fallen off, and got you going again and managed not to lose their temper when you have failed to listen.

This time they have not turned up for a lesson and your bike is waiting there and you have to decide, either to wait and see whether they turn up eventually, or to set off on your own.

Writing is rather like riding a bike – chaotic when you begin, graceful once you have got the hang of it. Once learnt, not forgotten.

Just to Get You Started

Here are some pieces of dialogue. Write out each one as reported or indirect speech, as something that might be found in a letter, a report, a newspaper or magazine article, a piece of fiction or as sub-titles for television news. The first one has been done for you as a guide.

1. "Well, I really do want the job. I love anything to do with electronics. I've got loads of qualifications. I've done this sort of work before."

Dear Sir,

I have read the advertisement for the job in electronics and would like to apply.

I spent two years at college studying this subject and passed all my qualifications. (Normally you would state exactly what any qualifications were.) I have spent several holidays gaining experience in electronics with a local firm. (Normally you would name such a firm.)

2. "Norman Stanley Fletcher I hereby sentence you to a term of four years in prison for the theft of four tons of ice cream."
3. "That's it then. Shan't be seeing you anymore."
4. "I didn't see where they came from. Suddenly they were just there, in front of me."
5. "And now we go over live to the national stadium, where (choose your favourite team) have just beaten (choose your friend's favourite team)."
6. "Find the green wire first, that's the earth, for safety, that's it. Right, now you've fastened that one find the red wire, that's right, this is old wiring, yes, fix that over to the right, yeah, then get that black one and insert the end in here, over to the left."
7. "Now just remember that you need to follow these instructions very carefully if you are to make really good ice cream. First of all find a really nice-looking bowl and six eggs – white or brown. Then break them, one at a time, into the bowl."

So, you're on your own, writing your own material.

Now the pace of your work is going to change. Rapidly you are going to find your feet with the three basic types of writing: information, description and discussion.

You are going to use three pieces of writing to find ideas about which you will write in several different ways, checking your work for yourself as you progress. In effect you will condense the work of several years into a period of months, possibly only weeks. You are able to do this with an understanding of the ideas about which you will write, unlike a child in primary school who may be an enthusiastic writer but who will not have your range of knowledge and understanding.

Before you write you will need an idea of what you are going to write about, and what you are going to say about it. The idea might be something simple, ready to hand, like the things that you have been writing about as you have made your way through this manual.

As you write you will jot down ideas, reminders of a rough plan. You can glance at these as you go and modify them as new ideas emerge and as you think of new ones.

When you have written a paragraph perhaps, or a page, you will check what you have written by reading it aloud.

First Words

Trying them out. Testing them. Building confidence.
Making notes. Planning a piece of writing.

These fourteen words formed my plan for the last three paragraphs above this box, starting with *Before* and amounting to 108 words.

Getting Started – Writing a Narrative
From *To Kill a Mockingbird* by Harper Lee (Pub Penguin, 1963).

An important event in a life, an important event in the narrative, her first day at school. This famous story tells of a motherless family in the southern state of Alabama. Here Scout, the narrator, remembers joining her older brother Jem at elementary school.

From the start of Chapter Two:

Dill left us early in September, to return to Meridan. We saw him off on the five o'clock bus, and I was miserable without him until it occurred to me that I would be starting school in a week. I never looked forward more to anything in my life. Hours of wintertime had found me in the tree-house, looking over at the school yard, spying on multitudes of children through a two-power telescope Jem had given me, learning their games, following Jem's red jacket through wriggling circles of blind man's buff, secretly sharing their misfortunes and minor victories. I longed to join them.

Jem condescended to take me to school the first day, a job usually done by one's parents, but Atticus (the children's father) had said Jem would be delighted to show me where my room was. I think some money changed hands in this transaction, for as we trotted around the corner past the Radley Place I heard an unfamiliar jingle in Jem's pockets. When we slowed to a walk at the edge of the school yard, Jem was careful to explain that a during school hours I was not to bother him, I was not to approach him with

requests to enact a chapter of Tarzan and the Ant Men, to embarrass him
with references to his private life, or tag along behind him at recess and noon.
I was to stick with the first grade and he would stick with the fifth. In short,
I was to leave him alone.

"You mean we can't play anymore?" I asked.

"We'll do as we always do at home," he said, "but you'll see – school's
different."

It certainly was. Before the first morning was over, Miss Caroline
Fisher, our teacher, hauled me up to the front of the room and patted the
palm of my hand with a ruler, then made me stand in the corner until
noon.

319 words

Written Responses

Carry out the following responses to the passage. As you finish each one, check
it and see whether you could improve it before moving on to the next response.

1. Write a single-sentence introduction to the passage.
2. Explain in a maximum of four sentences the most important things that
    happen during the course of this passage.
3. Write a passage of some three hundred words about an early episode in
    your life such as your first day at school.
4. Scott looks forward to joining her brother at school but it's not until the
    final short paragraph that she discovers what school is like. Write a short
    sequence in which you anticipate something and then finally find out what
    it is really like.

Speech into Writing and Writing into Speech

Finding ways of conveying ideas – you have just hit your thumb with a hammer
– again.

"S***" or "B******" or maybe just, "Damn!"

How many seconds between the arrival of the hammer and the sound of
the word?

No time, no need to think. We shout out what we hear others shout out
on these occasions.

Then the pain is loosening its hold and a friend calls out.

"What's the matter?"

"Hit my thumb."

"You all right?"

"Will be when I do something about this mess."

The sound of the speaker's very first word had been followed by the sound of breaking glass.

As witnesses we would have heard nineteen words spoken. In a witness statement we might have written:

Charlie was trying to mend the window frame when he struck his finger with the hammer and broke the glass.

20 words

Or we might have written:

I could see the man and an accomplice trying to break into the house.

14 words

Or we might have written this:

Charlie told me that someone had distracted him by asking him if he would like an ice cream.

17 words

Here you can see the greater choice of words that we have when we have the time to write or to think about the words we use. Try to identify the words in the sentences above which represent important choices – commentary below.

When people are asked to speak publicly, at a meeting perhaps or a wedding, they usually make notes to help them, or even write out the speech, word for word, like a script. Essentially, they take time to choose their words carefully.

With these writing exercises you will find it helpful to start off with ideas and words that you could speak about, ideas that come into your mind when you are thinking about these things, and then setting them out in writing. This would provide a first draft, which you can then improve if necessary.

Commentary – chosen words: *mend, struck, broke, accomplice, break into the house, distracted.*

Now read this – from *The Bookseller of Kabul* by Åsne Seierstad (pub Virago, 2004, pp. 125/6).

Mansur is dozing in his uncle's bookshop when a young woman comes in and asks for a copy of Advanced Chemistry. Mansur can detect the woman's beauty and tells her that he only has copies at home and promises to bring one to the shop the next day. She fails to arrive the next day, but the day following she is back again.

The sound of light footsteps and the rustling of heavy material wake him out of his sombre mood. She stands, like the first time, in the middle of a ray of sun that makes the dust from the books frolic around her. Mansur takes care not to leap up with joy and puts on his bookseller's look.

"I was expecting you yesterday," he says, professionally friendly! "I have the book at home, but I did not know which edition, which binding or what price you wanted to pay. The book has been published in so many editions that I could not bring them all. So if you would like to come with me and choose the one you want?"

The burka looks surprised. She twiddles her bag with an air of uncertainty. "Home with you?"

They are quiet for a moment. Silence is the best persuasion, Mansur thinks, quivering with nerves. He has issued a daring invitation.

"You need the book, don't you?" he asks in the end.

Wonder of wonders, she agrees. The girl settles in the back seat, positioned so she can look at him in the mirror. Mansur tries to hold what he thinks is her gaze while they talk.

"Nice car," she says. "Is it yours?"

"Yes, but it's not much," Mansur answers casually. This makes the car even more wonderful and him even richer.

He drives aimlessly round the streets of Kabul with the burka in his back seat. He has no book at all, and anyhow, at home are his grandmother and all his aunts. It makes him nervous and excited to be so close to someone unknown. In a moment of boldness he asks to see her face. She sits for a few seconds, absolutely stiff, then lifts up the front piece of the burka and holds his gaze in the mirror. He knew it; she is very beautiful with beautiful, big, dark, made-up eyes, a few years older than him. With the aid of the most exceptional capers, insistent charm and the art of persuasion he makes her forget the chemistry book and invites her to lunch in a restaurant. He stops the car, she creeps out and up the steps to The Marco Polo restaurant, where Mansur orders the entire menu: grilled chicken, kebab, mantu – Afghan noodles filled with meat and pilau rice with large pieces of mutton and, for dessert, pistachio pudding.

402 words

Written Responses

1.   Write an introduction to this passage of one sentence.
2.   Write the next one hundred words (approximately) of this story.
3.   Describe a meeting with someone you find either attractive or repulsive.
4.   Write the section of the story where the young woman realises that Mansur does not have a copy of *Advanced Chemistry*. Make the passage about as long as this extract.
5.   Try writing a short story which begins with "a daring invitation". It could involve the police and the law, politics, a place of work, the media, a social gathering or any other suitable setting.

Don't forget – check each of your responses before starting the next one.
   And how will you check each section?

Next – Descriptive Writing
From *Slide Rule*, the autobiography of Neville Shute, author of *A Town Like Alice* (pub. Vintage, 2009, pp. 101/2).
   Shute, an aeronautical engineer, was involved in the construction of one of the first great airships at a time when it was believed that airships, rather than airplanes, were the future of flying.
   R. 100 flew at an altitude of between fifteen hundred to two thousand feet (500–700 metres).

I think that it was during this flight that I went outside on the top of the ship for the first time. R.100 had a little cockpit on top at the extreme bow, forward of the first gasbag and reached by a ladder in the bow compartment; this was for taking navigational sights with a sextant. From this cockpit a walking way ran aft on top of the ship along one of the girders; this was a plywood plank a foot (30cm) in width with the outer cover stretched over it. To give courage to the inexperienced it had a rope lashed down along it every two feet (60cm) or so, to serve as a handhold. This walking way ran the whole length of the ship to the rear of the fins, where another hatch was provided behind the last gasbag. The slope of the hull at the bow cockpit was about forty-five degrees, which made the first part a little tricky to climb, and personally I always went from bow to stern because the rush of air pushed you up the first climb and you didn't have to look down. When the ship was cruising at about sixty miles an hour (100kph), as soon as you got to the top, or horizontal, part of the hull you were in calm air crawling on your hands and knees; if you knelt up you felt a breeze on your head and shoulders. If you stood up the wind was strong. It was pleasant up there sitting by the fins on a fine sunny day and whenever I went up there I would usually find two or three men sitting by the fins and gossiping. We kept a watch up there in daylight hours to keep an eye on the outer cover, and the riggers (technicians responsible for checking and repairing the fabric of the airship) got so used to it that they would walk upright along this little catwalk with their hands in their pockets, leaning against the wind and stepping over my recumbent body as I crawled on hands and knees. Burney (a colleague) lost his wrist watch up there one evening; it lay on top of the ship all night and was found by one of the riggers at dawn next day, and returned to him.

387 words

At the time "flying circuses" had performers strapped to the wings of aircraft. Imagine what it must have been like, wandering about on that shape, like the edges of Ayers Rock – Uluru – in Australia, that fall away in front of you.

Written Responses
Don't forget to check each one before going on to the next one.

1. Describe your initial response to this passage in one sentence.
2. For each of the descriptive points here write a sentence of your own.
3. Write a brief description of the room where you are at the moment. (A single paragraph.)
4. Write a longer description of the place where you would like to be right now.

Commentary
Descriptive Points
The cockpit
The walking way
Another hatch
The slope of the hull
The top of the hull
The riggers

Finally – Discursive Writing
From *The Times* – 'The not-the-slightest-bit-great Train Robbery'. Ben Macintyre, March 22, 2013

Some people regarded these robbers as heroes because, for some time, they managed to outwit the police. Ben Macintyre sees things differently.

The British penchant for romanticising crime has turned the heist of 1963 into an orgy of moral hypocrisy. (Penchant – literally leaning – inclined to do something. Hypocrisy – pretended beliefs or values.)

Ronnie Biggs, a Great Train Robber in his wheelchair, sticks two trembling fingers up at the ranks of photographers and British history stands still. It is 1963 again and the cheeky chappies who robbed the Glasgow to Euston mail train are still cocking a snook at authority, still on the "lam".

The funeral this week of Bruce Reynolds, the ringleader of the heist, was an opportunity to celebrate, once again, something that never happened, a robbery that was never great but has become so in the telling and the retelling. This single act of thievery has long ceased to be merely an event in history; it is a cultural legend, sentimental shorthand for a society long gone. The mythology of the Great Train Robbery has outstripped and eclipsed the reality faster and more completely than any episode in modern times.

Biggs, 83, can no longer speak, because of a series of strokes, but a statement was read out on his behalf, written in the standard language of criminal obituary. Reynolds, said Biggs, was a "good man" (not in 1963: he was greedy crook); the robbery was "an adventure" (not for the train driver, it wasn't). The robbers were "the most infamous rogues in British criminal history" and "gentlemen thieves". (No they weren't:

they were a bunch of fairly incompetent, second-rate gangsters, who got spectacularly lucky, briefly, and then spent a very long time in prison.) Bruce Reynolds was "an artist at heart", the mourners were told. "The Great Train Robbery was his Sistine Chapel." These "artists" were armed with coshes, iron bars and an axe; they could not work the brakes of the train and played Monopoly with the stolen money while munching tins of pork luncheon meat in their hideout, leaving behind a mass of fingerprints for the grateful police. Those who got away were fleeced by brighter crooks, or manipulated by Fleet Street. The train driver, Jack Mills, was beaten about the head so violently that he never recovered, and died seven years later.

But no amount of fact can stand up to the myth, which took root almost from the moment, on August 8, 1963, when the robbers escaped with £2,631,684 (Now equivalent to £300 million) in what was then Britain's largest cash robbery. The Great Train Robbery still grips the British imagination like no other crime, a peculiar amalgam of nostalgia, rebellion and a willing moral hypocrisy that is part of the national character.

The robbery is a period artefact, standing somewhere between the arrival of the miniskirt and winning the World Cup, between a deferential postwar world and the disobedience of the 1960s. It coincided with a wave of anti-Establishment feeling provoked by the Profumo scandal and the advent of Beatlemania. In the 1965 film Help!, *John Lennon turns to a policeman in Scotland Yard and asks acidly: "Great Train Robbery, how's that going?"*

The authorities failed to grasp the sneaking public sympathy for the robbers and the antipathy towards the police and courts. As one newspaper editorial observed: "In private many are thinking: 'for they are jolly good felons'." As in the Lady Chatterley trial three years earlier, the language of the judge when the robbers came to trial reflected an Establishment out of touch, outraged at the robbers' effrontery.

Mr Justice Edmund Davies thundered against the "impudence and enormity" of the crime and warned: "Let us clear out of the way any romantic notions of daredevilry" – thus ensuring those notions became ingrained in the public imagination forever. Even the thieves bought into the idea that they were not robbers, but rebels. Reynolds offered this hilarious assessment of his crime: "We had thrown down the challenge and the Establishment had picked it up." Any would-be iconoclast looking for validation turned to the robbers: Ronnie Biggs sang with the Sex Pistols in The Great Rock 'n' Roll Swindle.

What had begun its life in headlines as the "Cheddington Train Robbery" became "Great" because the press, the public and popular culture imbued it with a significance that was irresistible, if almost entirely synthetic.

In his book about the robbery, Piers Paul Read suggested that "poetically one might describe the train robbers as Saxons (the Germanic people who ruled Britain after the Romans until the arrival of the Normans from Northern France) still fighting the Normans". Poetic, but wrong. These were the sort of crooks who avoided battle but robbed the goods wagons afterwards.

As Alan Ayckbourn pointed out, the gap between the brutal truth and the artificial fable reflected a twisted set of priorities: "We live in a world where the Great Train Robber is a star and the poor old train driver who got hit on the head and subsequently died is forgotten." The robbers have been immortalised in more than 20 books, as well as films, music and television; a 50th anniversary BBC dramatisation is coming later this year. The sole memorial to the battered driver is a scale model of a Class 40 locomotive, named after him two years ago, which runs on a miniature railway in the Avon Valley.

Judge Davies said he hoped the train robbery would be "the last of its kind", and so it was. As British crime became ever more brutal, sophisticated and international, the Great Train Robbers came to represent a romanticised and very British era of crime, when diamond geezers guzzled bubbly after a caper, thieves did not grass on each other and everyone wore his moniker with pride: Leonard "Nipper" Read and "Slipper of the Yard" on one side, Bruce "Napoleon" Reynolds and Freddie "Brown Bread Fred" Foreman on the other.

The counterpart to the British capacity for hysterical public moralising is a private affection for bad people. Dick Turpin, the Krays, Professor Moriarty, the Lavender Hill Mob, all are quintessentially British, for we celebrate crime and the hidden wickedness in us all more than any other nation. Dr Jekyll and Mr Hyde could not have been written by a Frenchman.

So we will continue to glorify the Great Train Robbery as accomplices after the crime. Such thieves are now a dying breed: when the last of the robbers is brought in for questioning by Saint Peter, a strange chapter in British cultural history will be over and we should raise a cheery two-fingered salute by way of farewell.

1084 words

Some Key Points That You Should Consider:

1. Memories of the famous mail train robbery, which was carried out in 1963, provoke moral hypocrisy.
2. The funeral of the ringleader is a reminder of what has become a myth.
3. A fellow robber said of him that he was "a gentleman thief" and that the robbery was "an adventure".
4. The robbers were armed with coshes, iron bars and an axe; the train driver, Jack Mills, was beaten about the head so violently that he never recovered, and died seven years later.
5. The Great Train Robbery, nostalgia, rebellion and a willing moral hypocrisy – part of the British national character.
6. Sneaking public sympathy for the robbers and the antipathy towards the police and courts.
7. The British seem capable of private affection for bad people; Dr Jekyll and Mr Hyde could not have been written by a Frenchman.
8. Australia had Ned Kelly and in the States Bonnie and Clyde are remembered.

Written Responses

1. Your initial reaction to this article.
2. Contrast the public interest in the robbers with the public interest in the driver of the train.
3. What reasons can you find for admiring the robbers?
4. In your opinion, how should violent robbers be treated? Give reasons for your opinions.
5. Explain how you think people in your country would react to a robbery on such a grand scale.

6. Describe any outrageous criminal act that has occurred in your country and explain your reaction to it.

Now, if all you have learnt from all this is that you should always check your writing, either by reading it aloud, or by imagining that you are reading it aloud, then both of us – you and I – can be pleased. However, I hope that you can do rather more than that now and that your English really has improved.

Narrative, **descriptive** and **discursive** writing, in ascending order of difficulty. That's what you have achieved.

You have reached the end of Part Three.

You have covered the essential understanding and skills to write clearly and effectively, to check your work and make further progress. **Well done!**

MAIN GLOSSARY

Items marked with an asterisk * are taken from the current UK national curriculum. They are included here to help the reader who may well encounter them elsewhere. Other items can be found by reference to the list of contents or to a dictionary.

Abstract	To do with understanding and ideas rather than with things that can be seen, heard, touched, tasted or smelt. The latter are said to be tactile or concrete, recognised by our senses. See also US usage with précis and summary in Chap 7.
Agent	In grammar, the person or thing that carries out an action, often the subject of a verb.
Ambiguity	Unclear in meaning – literally meaning both things.
*Antonyms	Words with opposite meanings. *Weak* is the antonym of *strong*.
Apposition	Repeating information with different words, usually for emphasis. e.g. Grandad, the silly old fool, was trying to climb onto the roof. *Silly old fool*, a noun phrase in apposition.
Articulate	Able to handle words.

Categorise	To sort items into groups by which we can identify them.
Clause	A group of words, including a finite verb, which forms only part of sentence.
Clarity	Clearness.
*Cohesion	In writing the business of connecting or linking words and ideas appropriately within sentences or within a whole piece of writing. *She was angry because he had borrowed her ice cream.* The word *because* connects the idea of her anger with his borrowing her ice cream. The word *cohesion* is linked to *adhesive*; think of things that are stuck together.
Complement	Forms a sentence with a subject and the verb to be. e.g. *She is* <u>clever</u>.
Composing	Putting words together – writing.
Compound	Word, *football* – two words together make a third word.
Compound	Verb, *has eaten*.
Consonants	The letters b–d, f–h, j–n, p–t, v–z.
Convention	An unspoken agreement about the way things should be done.
Defining	And non-defining constructions – see Chap 4.
*Diagraph	Two letters which, when combined, represent, a single sound, such as ph or th.
Dismissive	Rejecting something.
*Ellipsis	The omission of a word where its omission is obvious.
Emphasis	Ways of expressing ourselves more strongly.
*Etymology	The study of the history and origins of words. For example, *mother* and its German equivalent, *Mutter*, and *maternal* with its Latin ancestor, *mater*, which means mother.

Explicit	See Chap 11.
Express	To say or write something, e.g. *He expressed his delight in words that could be heard on the other side of town.* or *She expressed her anger with carefully chosen words that she left on social media.*
Expression	Something brief, spoken or written. e.g. *Look out!* or *an early bath.*
*Grapheme	A unit of writing which represents a sound from a language. For example the *t* in *it*, or the letters *ight* in *bright.*
*Homophones	Words that sound the same but have different spellings and meanings – *so* and *sow* (seeds) and *sew* (with a needle), *threw* and *through.*
Implicit	See Chap 11.
Interjection	A word or words thrown into a conversation. e.g. *Wow* or *Rubbish.*
*Modal verbs	Auxiliary verbs.
*Morphology	the composition of a word, its root and prefixes and suffixes. For example, *health* (root), *health*y (plus suffix) *and* un*healthy* (plus prefix).
Object	Direct and indirect – see Chap 6.
Parsing	See Chap 2.
Parts of speech	Different kinds of words – see Chap 1.
*Perfect tense	See tense.
Phrase	A group of words that does not include a finite verb.
*Phoneme	The basic unit of sound. Alone, and in combination they make up the words of a language.
Precis	A summary – see Chap 7.
Predicate	What we are told about the subject of a sentence.
*Received pronunciation	Clear spoken expression, without regional

Redundancy	Identity, intended to be understood easily. redundant words which make no contribution to communication. See Chap 14.
*Register	The nature of the language used in particular contexts, with varying degrees of formality. A change of register involves a variation of word choice and grammar.
*Root word	See morphology.
Sentence	A group of words that contains a finite verb and which makes complete sense. See Chap 5.
Setting	The circumstances or background to something that is expressed, spoken or written.
*Standard English	The form of English used in more formal situations by educated speakers.
Subject	The thing or person that a sentence is concerned with.
Suffix	A letter or letters added to the end of a word to change its meaning, e.g. *ly*.
Synchronised	Timed together.
*Synonyms	Words that have the same meaning, e.g. *closed* and *shut*.
Syntax	The arrangement of words, the ordering of words. See Chap 14.
*Tenses	Verbs – past, present and future – see Chap 1.
*Transitive and intransitive verbs	See Chap 1.
Verb	The word which denotes the action of a sentence. See pages 16 and 37.

Supplement
UK National Curriculum Key Stages 3 and 4
Subject Content – Links to Key Chapters in *What, How and Why*

Reading	Intro and Chap 2
Understand increasingly challenging text.	Chaps 5–8
Understand and critically evaluate text.	Chap 13
Read critically	Chaps 5 and 6
Writing	Chaps 2, 5, 13 and 15
Plan, draft and edit.	Chap 15
Paying attention to accurate grammar, punctuation and spelling.	Chap 14
Revise and edit.	Chap 3, 4, 14, 15
Write accurately, fluently, effectively and at length for pleasure and information.	Chap 11, 13, 15

Grammar and vocabulary	
Analysing some of the differences between spoken and written language.	Chap 2
Knowing and understanding the differences between spoken and written language.	Chap 1
Studying the effectiveness and impact of the grammatical features of the texts they read.	Chaps 2, 5, 6

Items from the National Curriculum Glossary

These items are dealt with in Chap 1:

Article	Past tense
Auxiliary verbs	Progressive (continuous)
Compound verbs	Plural
Conjunction	Preposition
Consonant	Pronoun
Determiner	Suffix
Infinitive	Tense
Modify	Vowel
Noun	Word

These items are dealt with in other chapters:

Active voice	Chap 11	Passive voice	Chap 11
Apostrophe	Chap 3	Phrase	Chap 2
Clause	Chap 2	Possessive	Chap 3
Complement	Chap 2	Prefix	Chap 14
Coordinating conjunction	Chap 6	Present tense	Chap 5
Ellipsis	Chap 3	Punctuation	Chaps 3 and 4
Finite verbs	Chap 2	Sentences	Chaps 2, 5, 11 & 12
Fronting (word order)	Chap 14	Stress	Chap 3
Future	Chap 5	Subject	Chap 2
Inflection	Chap 14	Subjunctive	Chap 11
Object	Chap 2	Subordinate clause	Chap 2
Participle	Chap 6		

Other items from the National Curriculum glossary will be found in the glossary of WHW.

ESSENTIALS (GUIDANCE) FOR TUTORS – AN INTRODUCTION

Our students may be unhappy at school, struggling with essays at university, hoping for promotion at work or simply trying to find a job.

- **Make sure they understand why literacy is important.**
- **Show them that we are on their side.**
- **Reassure them that they will make progress.**
- **Point out the need to keep going when the going gets tough.**
- **Share jokes with them whenever possible.**
- **Do anything legal to get them reading regularly.**
- **Remind them that their mates who mock them now will not be around to offer them jobs in a few years' time.**

When I started teaching I remembered a few bad lessons I had suffered at school so I always tried very hard to help students who had given up. Seeing them get started again was one of teaching's greatest joys.

So long as our students can read and write we can get started.

Treat them as young adults, friends who need a helping hand. Listen to what they have to say. Tell them what you think, directly, honestly – disguising unpleasant truths makes them all the more unbearable. ***Show, Explain, Encourage*** should be your motto.

Tell them that failure at school, with their first exams, is not the end of the world. Ten years after failing English literature at school I finally passed, was offered a place at Cambridge and then went on to become an examiner of the subject.

Do not let our students worry about:
Spelling There are lots of ways they can help themselves.

Punctuation Two early chapters will help them deal with this.

Grammar We use it without thinking about it whenever we speak.

How the Book Is Organised
The first section explains words and how these "components" are assembled as sentences. The second section shows how we put together sentences for a variety of purposes: contracts, explanations, essays, articles and stories. The third section looks at the language assembled and put to work.

This manual is designed to help students understand the way that we use our language so that they read and write effectively. Much encouragement is given to get students reading, to expose them to the written language so that they pick up vocabulary and a wider range of expression.

Material from the book could be presented for use in class, as a teacher's reference book and for private students. With electronic publishing this could be achieved at the press of a button.

Responses to *What, How and Why*
Material from this manual has been tried out successfully in schools, in the Army's Military Correction Centre, with school "failures", with private tutors and private students.

It has been presented to three educational charities, all of which were impressed by the quality and usefulness of the material.

A fifteen-year-old who had been out of school for two years spoke of an imaginary classroom where there were no bullies or disruptors and where he could rely upon a friendly and encouraging teacher.

A mother-and-son team has used it successfully.

A neighbour's son was predicted a fail grade for GCSE English. In six lessons we worked through chapters 1–6 and he passed with a C.

ESSENTIALS FOR TUTORS – CHAPTER ONE

Words and Their Work 1 – the jobs done by individual words. These basic jobs done by words have to be understood before our students can look at the way they work together when they speak and write.

Nouns label things, give them an identity or show what sort of thing they are, individual things, groups of things, particular things or things that cannot be detected with our senses but with our understanding: ***dogs***, ***teams***, ***Aukland*** and ***excitement***.

Adjectives qualify nouns: ***black*** ice cream, ***friendly*** teachers, ***clever*** liars. The word ***qualify*** requires careful explanation. In practical terms it means to add information about something, the colour of the ice cream, etc.

Verbs – The Most Important Word in a Sentence

You must make clear that without a verb there is no sentence, that without a verb nothing is said because, grammatically speaking, nothing has happened. Without a verb all you will have done is draw attention to something without saying anything about it.

You may mention your favourite musician, school mate, neighbour or even politician, but until you have used a verb, you have said nothing. "Elvis Presley," you shout. "What about Elvis Presley?" I reply. Until someone has said something such as, "Elvis ***lives***," we have said nothing.

Adverbs qualify verbs and adjectives. They can tell us more about an action: how do we whisper? We whisper ***loudly***. They can also tell us more about a quality of something: how can you notice the ice cream shop? It's **brightly** coloured.

Pronouns stand in for nouns. Each time we meet a name we check it mentally. If it is one that we have only just checked, the flow of information is interrupted while we check it again. This is a nuisance so we use pronouns to refer to identities that we have already met.

Pippa walked up to Billy. **She** smiled and gave **him** her handbag. **He** could see that **it** was **hers**. This is much easier than: Pippa walked up to Billy. Pippa smiled and gave Billy her handbag. Billy could see that the handbag was Pippa's handbag.

Prepositions simply link nouns, or nouns and verbs, to show how they fit together: We slip **out** of the classroom **to** the seat **in** the park.

Conjunctions join words **and** groups of words. Sometimes they are simply put side by side – rock **and** roll. Sometimes more is indicated: **but** I don't care, **so** I will stay indoors, **then** it poured, **because** it's raining.

Articles make clear the identity of things. **The** girl who threw ice cream at the teacher. (Not any girl. **The** is the **definite** article.) **Some** girls (we don't know which ones because **some** is an **indefinite** article) wished they had thrown ice cream at the teacher and **a** girl near the back of the class had just unwrapped a choc ice (**a** girl, one of the other girls in the class – **a** and **an** are indefinite articles).

And Finally

Exclamations – *Wow* – interjections – *Look out!* – and swear words are used in immediate, automatic reactions to things. I encouraged sixth-formers to restrain themselves by saying, "Oh fffff… fertiliser!"

ESSENTIALS FOR TUTORS – CHAPTER TWO

Parsing – showing that each word has a job in a sentence, as part of a phrase, a clause or a sentence. We understand these things when we speak; in writing they are more easily examined. Simply identify each word as a part of speech then show its links to other words.

e.g. A large elephant squeezed through the door which had been left open.

(Here we have a phrase, a verb, another phrase and a clause.)

A (indefinite article – it could be <u>any</u> elephant) large (adjective – qualifies *elephant*) elephant (noun – subject of the verb *squeezed*) squeezed (main verb – action of the sentence) through (preposition of movement – links *squeezed* and *the door*) the (definite article – it is a particular door, the one that was left open) door (noun – indirect object of the verb *squeezed*) which (relative pronoun – links *the door* with the verb *had been left*) had been left (subordinate verb – action of the subordinate clause) open (adjective – qualifies *door*).

Phrases, groups of words that function without a verb but need to be added to other groups of words to work properly, e.g. He sat *under the table* or *on the table* or *beside the table*.

Clauses, groups of words that do include a verb but which do not make complete sense on their own. e.g. *Although they arrived late*, the teacher gave them ice cream. *Because Brer Rabbit begged Brer Fox not to throw him into the briar patch*, Brer Fox did just that.

Without a verb, there can be no sentence and no meaning.

Whether it is a single word – *Stop* (which really means, "You stop.") – or several words – "You *will be stopping*," – one verb is essential in a sentence. Many verbs involve action: kick, walk, flirt, escape, so your job here is to explain that the verb *to be* (I am, you are, he is, we were, they will be) counts grammatically as an action.

Grammar – built in and working even as we learn to speak.

Make clear that without their built-in grammar our students could not ask questions about grammar, or about anything else. Understanding grammar helps them when we explain rules as conventions, when, for example, we explain that the subject (the agent or "doer" of an action) should normally come before the verb of a sentence because that is the order in which we expect to receive information.

Main verbs and subordinate verbs.

The key thing for our students to understand is that every sentence must have a verb, technically a **finite verb**. (You might be able to impress them by explaining that the word *finite* comes from the Latin *finis*, which means *end*. French *fin*.) In the word **finished** there is a sense of completeness which we find in the finite verb in a sentence. A complete or finished verb not only indicates the nature of the action, but also whether it occurred in the past, is happening now, or will take place in the future.

Explain that, besides the main verb, there may well be subordinate verbs, in subordinate clauses which cannot stand alone, e.g.

> *They continued, although it was raining heavily and their feet ached and they knew the teacher would be upset.* Five verbs, but only one main verb: **continued**.

Sentences can have more than one main verb. *The cat sat in the kennel and barked.* The same meaning could be expressed in two separate sentences: *The cat sat in the kennel. The cat barked.*

Subject and predicate – the two basic parts of meaning.

Helping young people to appreciate this is crucial to any understanding of things that are spoken or written. Any utterance has two parts, the **subject** or topic that is being addressed, and the **predicate**, whatever it is that is said about the subject.

Put simply, we need answers to two questions; *who or what is this sentence about?* (Who or what is the subject?) and *what are we told about the subject?* The subject of the sentence is the cat and we are told that it hid in the kennel and barked.

Continue to encourage reading; remember that jokes and short stories often make for easy reading. Reading widens our vocabulary and makes it easier for us to choose the best words to communicate effectively.

ESSENTIALS FOR TUTORS – CHAPTER THREE

Punctuation, capital letters, full stops, question marks, exclamation marks, apostrophes and speech marks, semicolons and colons, but not commas, not until the next chapter.

We must convince our students that good punctuation is an extension of good manners, for by punctuating our writing accurately we make it easier for our readers and this, of course, is self-interest too. To make the point, strip out the punctuation of any written passage and ask someone to read it aloud. Then get them to reassemble the passage, with punctuation.

Good punctuation has to be practised until it is automatic and reading aloud is a good way to improve our sense of the need for punctuation.

Young people have to get over their aversion to making mistakes when reading aloud, especially in the company of other people. They probably feel childish, but then they must go through the process of learning to read well which other people might have coped with earlier. This is the way to better English. Reading jokes aloud can help.

Then remind your student(s) that ignoring the conventions of punctuation is to inconvenience the reader who can easily reject whatever it is that they are trying to say.

Beginning and Ending Sentences

One technique that helps with the placing of stops: full stops (periods in North America), exclamation marks or question marks, is to read aloud to your student(s) and ask them to clap or make some other noise as loudly as they can every time you come to the end of a sentence. Some of them will quite enjoy this.

Apostrophe's. No, No No. Apostrophes

Normally there are only two jobs for apostrophes: to indicate the omission of a letter or possession. *It's time to look at John's homework.*

Semicolons and Colons

The history of semicolons and colons is more varied than that of other punctuation marks. My suggestions come from modern good practice. Semicolons make a smooth connection between two closely related sentences and can separate long items in a list. Colons are best used to introduce evidence: a list of examples perhaps.

Everything Else, Apart from Commas

Writing dialogue for someone else to read can encourage people to work at different kinds of pause. Putting speech or thought balloons on pictures of famous people can be very effective; making them appear undignified or just plain stupid encourages young people to concentrate on getting the pauses right. *Really, George – I couldn't care less. George (why on earth do I bother?), do hurry up.*

Any authority figures – parents, teachers, police officers, judges, politicians and parking wardens – provide targets to encourage writing; writing like this gives young people a chance to get their own back.

Remind them, good punctuation, like clear road signs, makes it easier to make progress.

ESSENTIALS FOR TUTORS – CHAPTER FOUR

First "Rules"

Young people, and some adults, are easily intimidated by talk of the rules of grammar, of punctuation and of spelling. However, we all learn to speak without any knowledge whatsoever of these rules. People who say *We was* instead of *We were* are ignoring convention rather than breaking a rule about singular and plural verbs. In speech they are understandable. It's only in writing that these conventions become more important in aiding clear communication.

The notion of rules is sometimes helpful when we explain what makes some pieces of writing clearer than others, which is what I have been doing here. The same applies to punctuation and spelling. However, an obsession with "rules" is to be avoided.

Commas for Pauses, in Direct Speech, in Lists, in Apposition and to Separate Clauses

Listen to people's pauses, simple pauses, to get someone's attention. *Charlie, look out.*

In speech, to indicate a question at the end of a statement. *This makes sense, doesn't it?*

In direct speech, to introduce or end words which are spoken. *"This teacher's nuts," he whispered.*

Listen to a market trader's list – *cauliflowers, fifty pence each, carrots, seventy pence a pound, ice cream, you must be joking.* Or a waiter's list – *Delicious Mersea oysters, freshly picked mushrooms, soup of the day.* (You can point out here that we do it all the time without so much as giving it a thought.)

Commas separate adjectives so as to make each one as distinctive as possible: *He was unpredictable, uncontrollable, ill-tempered, spiteful and getting closer.*

Apposition – Noun Phrases in Apposition

Commas separate different references to the same identity.

This book, the second textbook that I've written, has taken me longer to write than the first. I try to explain important things, the things that matter, to my readers. Some of my readers, parents or tutors, will help other readers who need to improve their English.

Separating Items

Commas can be used to separate items to prevent them working together.

Ice cream will be delivered daily, and twice on Tuesdays, unless it rains. If it rains there will be no deliveries.

Ice cream will be delivered daily, and twice on Tuesdays unless it rains. If it rains on a Tuesday there will be only one delivery.

Help your student here by substituting *essential components* for *ice cream*. Then ask which version they would insert in a contract with a supplier if they were running a manufacturing business.

Defining and Non-Defining Phrases and Clauses

Try to show that defining phrases and clauses become part of the subject of a sentence, rather than phrases or clauses in apposition.

Spotty feet that trouble walkers should be treated. Only if they trouble walkers.
Spotty feet, which trouble walkers, should be treated. They always trouble walkers.

Remember, rules are best used to help us to appreciate a performance, not to produce one.
By considering examples of writing we internalise the rules or conventions which we then apply automatically when we write.

ESSENTIALS FOR TUTORS – CHAPTER FIVE

So far our students have been dismantling the language. Now we have to encourage them to look at ways of bringing words together effectively.

To do this it is important that they can see how words and groups of words function together. Because we can look at the written language in a permanent form, we can examine it and question how it works; students should be helped and encouraged to do this.

Remember, when something of importance is being said, we write it down: contracts and agreements, court and parliamentary records, and instructions, for example. See if your students can think of other important matters that are spoken and then recorded. Encourage them to make observations about what they read.

Four Ways of Examining Sentences

1. **Bringing words and groups of words together.** Identify the subject (the agent or doer of the action), verb (the action), object (the person or thing to which the action is done) or the complement which completes the sense of a verb – *He was* <u>clever</u>. (Clever, of course is an <u>adjective</u> and its function here is as a <u>complement</u>.)

   These are the basic structures in a sentence. Now there are other words and groups that bring ideas into longer sentences. For example, *He was clever,* <u>but lazy</u>. (an adjectival phrase) or *He was clever,* <u>always</u>. (an adverb).

Remember. The complement completes the meaning of a sentence.

2. **Subject and predicate.** Now it is easier to show just what is being said. Once we have identified the **subject** – who or what the speaker or writer is referring to – then we can see what is said about the subject. We call this the **predicate**. *The dog* (subject) *sat on the mat* (predicate).

3. **Simple, compound and complex sentences – construction.** This way of examining sentences is rather like using a wiring diagram to show how wires are connected to provide power and control in a machine.

   A simple sentence has only one main clause – *The cat sat on the mat.*

   A compound sentence has more than one main clause – *The cat sat on the mat and stared at him* (*and* links the two clauses).

   A complex sentence has at least one subordinate clause – *The cat sat on the mat, which was now filthy, and stared at him* (*which was now filthy* is the subordinate clause. This additional information is inserted between the two main clauses of the sentence and this is what makes it complex).

   You might get students to try inserting this additional information more elegantly – once they have given up you could show them how, by forming two sentences, we can do this: *The mat was filthy. The cat sat on it and stared at him.*

4. **The effect of loose, balanced and periodic sentences – emphasis or force.**

   Here we have to show students how a sentence is given its force, its emphasis on the main idea or ideas. This has to do with a sense of where this lies rather than the sort of mechanical analysis used in 3.

   Verbs are very important here but other words or groups of words can also carry the emphasis which may be found anywhere in the sentence.

   Ice cream was cheap (loose – no particular strong emphasis).

   Ice cream was cheap and (was) consumed in large quantities (balanced – two main verbs and equally powerful ideas).

   Ice cream was cheap and consumed in large quantities, which led eventually to a visit to the doctor's, where he was told never again to touch the stuff (periodic – *never again* adds strength to the final clause).

ESSENTIALS FOR TUTORS – CHAPTER SIX

Here we have to help students to develop two skills in analysing or dismantling sentences.

Clause analysis reveals different ways of assembling words to form sentences. Understanding this will enable our students to write more accurately and more effectively. It will give them greater control over their use of the language.

Identifying the subject and predicate of a sentence helps the reader to develop the habit of identifying the topic of that sentence and what is being said about that topic. This is an important step in understanding what we read.

Clause Analysis

The first step is to identify the clauses, each of which will have a finite verb. (A verb that is complete or finished because it is in the past, present or future tense and has a subject.) Once we have identified them we need to consider their purpose in the sentence.

Main clauses can stand alone, independent and complete, as sentences. For example – *All cows eat grass.*

Subordinate clauses can only function as part of a sentence. For example – *so long as they are standing on four legs.*

We can put the two together. *All cows eat grass so long as they are standing on four legs.*

Here we have a subordinate clause of condition; cows have to stand on four legs if they want to eat. Standing on four legs is the *condition*.

If it rains (subordinate clause, of condition) *we will wear sunglasses* (main clause), or *We will wear sunglasses* (main clause) *if it rains* (subordinate clause, of condition).

When grass grows really tall (subordinate clause, of time) *farmers take their sheep out of the fields* (main clause) *so that they do not get lost* (subordinate clause, of purpose).

Sheep spend most of their time looking for holes in walls and fences (main clause) *which make them really excited* (subordinate clause, qualifying *holes in walls and fences*) *because they can escape through them and look for other sheep* (subordinate clause, modifying the verb *make*).

Help your students here by asking them questions which will lead them to the right answer, for example: *What must cows do if they want to eat grass? They must stand on four legs.*

Subject and Predicate

There are two key questions to help students: *What is the sentence about – who or what is its subject?* Then, *What are we told about the subject – what is the predicate?*

Another useful activity is to give them the <u>first</u> or <u>last</u> word, then ask them to write a long sentence in which the subject or the predicate consists of only one word, e.g.

<u>Marie</u> *longed for really expensive ice cream, running down the cone and forcing her to lick her fingers.*

(All of the words, except the first one, form the predicate and tell us what Marie, the subject, did.)

Henry, covered in sweat from an hour's hard run, and aware of the glass that a friend was about to pass him, <u>fainted</u>.

(All of the words, except the last one, tell us more about Henry, and form the subject. The last word forms the predicate and tells us what he did. He fainted.)

The return to this topic is important. While we are looking at the mechanics of sentence construction we must not lose sight of what any sentence is about.

ESSENTIALS FOR TUTORS – CHAPTER SEVEN

Precis and Summary

This exercise is very important, for it requires a student to show a clear understanding of written material, as well as the skill of summarising its important points clearly and economically. It involves careful reading of the selection of the main ideas expressed in a passage and the setting out of those ideas clearly. It is important because intelligent handling of ideas is important in commerce and industry, in college and university study, in politics and journalism, in religion and the arts, and as part of educated life.

Now we are moving our students away from words, phrases, clauses and sentences to the meanings that they convey, in sentences, in paragraphs and in articles and the chapters of books. This may seem more demanding than looking at the way words are grouped on a page, but summarising a passage is something that is best done methodically, step by step.

- Read the passage three times.
- Identify the main points – reorder them if necessary.
- Draft a sentence for each point into a paragraph or paragraphs.
- Check that all your main points are still present.
- Read through the draft then make any necessary corrections or improvements.
- Write the final draft, which should be approximately one third the length of the original.

Identifying the main points in a passage of writing

Help students to use familiar, mechanical ideas to move towards an understanding. Identify subject and predicate, then verbs and the ideas that accompany them. A dialogue here between tutor and student, about what might or might not be the main point of a sentence will help the student start the sort of internal, private dialogue that we all use when working like this unassisted. In this way our students will learn the questions they will need to ask themselves when working alone – *does this idea, this word or phrase seem to be the most important part of this sentence? What is really important here? Which bits of the sentence can be left out?*

Remind your students that some ideas are developed through a series of sentences. This is why, after a rapid, preliminary reading to form an impression of the passage, it is important to read carefully and methodically to build a confident understanding of the passage with settled conclusions.

Another way of identifying main points – eliminate words that are redundant or of lesser importance. Once the passage has been read thoroughly, students may prefer to eliminate words that make no contribution to the main points of the passage. The remaining words can then be transformed into the list of main points.

Students should be encouraged to try both ways as part of finding out for themselves how they work best.

Writing the summary

Students should check each draft to see that all the main points have been included and that nothing unnecessary has remained. Ask students whether they could improve the way that points are presented, by rewording or re-phrasing sections of their drafts.

Encourage students to check the final draft as they would any written piece, preferably by reading it **aloud.**

ESSENTIALS FOR STUDENTS – CHAPTER ONE

You need to understand that there are several kinds of words and each kind of word has a particular job or jobs. Words are the components of our language.

Nouns name things such as ***dogs***, ***teams***, ***Auckland*** and ***excitement***. There are common nouns – ***dogs***, collective nouns – ***teams***, proper nouns – ***Auckland*** and abstract nouns – ***excitement***.

Adjectives qualify nouns: ***black*** ice cream, ***friendly*** teachers, ***clever*** liars.

Verbs indicate the "action", the heart of a sentence: cats ***purr***, parents ***complain*** and grammar ***puzzles*** us.

Adverbs qualify verbs and adjectives: We slip ***quietly*** out of the classroom, stroll ***coolly*** along the corridor, walk ***boldly*** across the playground and turn ***excitedly*** into the street towards the ***brightly*** coloured ice cream shop.

Pronouns stand in for nouns: Pippa walked up to Billy. ***She*** smiled and gave ***him*** her handbag. ***He*** could see that ***it*** was ***hers***. Pronouns refer back to something already mentioned.

Prepositions link nouns, or nouns and verbs: We slip ***out*** of the classroom ***to*** the seat ***in*** the park.

Conjunctions join words ***and*** groups of words: Rock ***and*** roll, rhythm ***and*** blues. It might rain ***but*** I don't care. It's raining ***so*** I will stay indoors. It rained ***then*** it poured. I will stay indoors ***because*** it's raining.

Articles make clear the identity of things. ***The*** girl who threw ice cream at the teacher. (Not any girl.) ***Some*** girls (we don't know which ones) wished they had thrown ice cream at the teacher and ***a*** girl near the back of the class has just unwrapped a choc ice. (One of the other girls in the class.) ***The*** refers to a particular girl; ***some*** refers to several unspecified girls and ***a*** refers to one of the other girls, but we don't know which one.

Exclamations are words used in immediate reactions to things: ***Ouch!*** That hurt. ***Damn*** – I've forgotten my mobile. ***Wow*** – look at that. So are swear words, but they sometimes give offence.

ESSENTIALS FOR STUDENTS – CHAPTER TWO

Words Join Together to Form Phrases, Clauses and Sentences
These are the components of meaning. Put together they enable us to build up an understanding of something said or written.

> *in trouble (**phrase**), although he was in trouble (**clause**), Although he was in trouble, he escaped (**sentence**).*

The Verb, the Heart of a Sentence
Dogs **bark**. Cats **chase** mice. Ice cream **melts** in the mouth.
Dogs **whistle**. Mice **chase** cats. Ice cream **is** revolting.
Without verbs we learn nothing here about dogs, cats or ice cream.

Grammar – already built in. I can't install it; I can only explain what is already there.
Listen to a baby's words: *Mummy talk*. We are not sure whether the baby is telling Mummy to talk or simply saying that Mummy talks. Once the baby gets this right we know that a bit of grammar has been learnt. This is how we are programmed; this is why you can understand me.

Main Verbs

They **stopped**, although it **was raining** heavily and their feet **ached** and they **knew** the teacher **would be** upset. Five verbs, but there is only one main verb: **stopped**.

Although it was raining heavily and their feet ached and they knew the teacher would be upset, they **stopped**. It doesn't matter where the main verb appears; it is the only main verb, the essential part of the whole sentence.

Subject and Predicate – the Two Basic Parts of Meaning

The dog sat on the mat.

Who or what is this sentence about? **The dog.**

What are we told about the subject? **It sat on the mat.** Yes. The dog sat on the mat.

Learning from Reading

Before we speak words we listen to them thousands of times. So, in order to write well, we must read a lot. Unconsciously, we take over what others say and write. When we speak or write, understanding a wider range of words helps us to gossip, amuse other people, explain things, describe things, discuss things or flirt.

> *Working alone? Puzzled still?*
>
> *DO NOT GIVE UP.*
>
> *Ask someone, at home, online, in a library, at work, down at the pub.*
>
> *Whatever you do,*
>
> *DO NOT GIVE UP, PLEASE.*

ESSENTIALS FOR STUDENTS – CHAPTER THREE

Punctuation helps us to follow what someone has written, just as road signs help drivers to make good progress. Without road signs we are more likely to come off the road and arrive late at our destination. Without clear punctuation our readers become uncertain and hesitant as they struggle to read and may not even complete their journey.

Good manners – writing clearly matters for two reasons.
Writing that is clearly punctuated enables your reader to grasp your meaning more easily, and more sympathetically. Result – better communication.

Beginning and ending sentences.
A sentence provides the basic component of a message, of something you want to say. If the beginning and end of each component is not clearly marked then different parts of the message will become mixed up and unclear. Start with a capital letter and finish with a full stop, a question mark or an exclamation mark.

~~Apostrophe's~~. No, No, No. Apostro<u>phes</u>
Normally there are two jobs for apostrophes: to indicate possession – *the teacher's bicycle* – or the omission of a letter – *the teacher's a cyclist.* The bicycle <u>belongs</u> to the teacher. The teacher <u>is</u> a cyclist.

Some people want to play safe with apostrophes and insert them before the "s" at the end of any word. What would happen on the road if someone erected road signs at random?

Semicolons and colons

Semicolons are useful for connecting two sentences with closely linked meanings; this is what I have done here. They are good for separating long items on a list. Colons introduce evidence: like this.

Everything else, apart from commas

Hyphens join words: semi-detached. Dashes allow the reader to control a pause. We've won – at last. Brackets allow the insertion of additional ideas (Don't turn over the page yet.) without bringing the reader to a halt.

Punctuation should be like good wiring in a car

Careless wiring could result in windscreen wipers coming on when you press the brake pedal. We have to take care with punctuation so that components – words – work together correctly.

Don't forget – puzzled still? Look somewhere else. Do not give up.

ESSENTIALS FOR STUDENTS – CHAPTER FOUR

First "Rules"

Do not worry yourself about rules. The rules of grammar, punctuation and spelling are not laws to be obeyed. They are conventions, unspoken agreements about the ways in which we communicate. They are a helpful way to understand why we do things in certain ways, but we do not have to be able to recite them off by heart. If we break these rules we will not be taken to court, but we may reduce the clarity of our writing. Simply use rules to help you to write well.

Commas for Pauses, in Direct Speech, in Lists, in Apposition, to Separate Clauses

Simple Pauses

To get someone's attention. – *Oi, Fred.*

In speech to indicate a question at the end of a statement which seeks the listener's agreement. For example: – *It's raining, isn't it?*

Direct Speech

In writing, pauses indicated by commas show the start and finish of words that are spoken. *"Stop," he said. He said, "Stop."*

Lists

Commas separate items in a list and help to keep clear their identities.

We cannot resist ice cream, choc ices, vanilla ices, raspberry and parsnip flavoured ice cream, and Japanese tea-flavoured ice cream.

Commas separate adjectives: he was good looking, rich, unattached and a long way away.

Apposition – Noun Phrases in Apposition

Commas separate different references to the same identity.

His boss, John Smith, gave him huge bonus. John Smith, his boss, gave him a huge bonus. My wife, Henrietta, threatened me with a weapon of mass destruction, a melting choc ice.

Separating Items

Commas can be used to separate items to prevent them working together.

Ice cream will be delivered daily, and twice on Tuesdays, unless it rains. If it rains there will be no deliveries.

Ice cream will be delivered daily, and twice on Tuesdays unless it rains. If it rains on a Tuesday there will be only one delivery.

Puzzled still? Ask someone else. Look somewhere else. Do not give up.

ESSENTIALS FOR STUDENTS – CHAPTER FIVE

Assembling the components of sentences (individual words, phrases and clauses) confidently so that you write as effectively as possible.

First examine sentences. Look for subject, object/complement, verb and words that modify these components.

The dog (subject) *chased* (verb) *the cat* (object).

The cat (subject) *was* (verb) *too fast* (complement).

What Is It All About?

His enormous feet (subject) *embarrassed him* (predicate).

Her tiny feet (subject) *enabled her to tip-toe quickly past his large ones* (predicate).

Identifying the subject and the predicate helps us to make sure we understand what is said.

Assembling the Components

Next we look at the results of assembling our sentences in different ways.

The teacher cried (a simple sentence).

The teacher cried and the students feared the worst (a compound sentence).

The teacher, who had already planned things carefully, cried until the class realised that he was teasing them (a complex sentence).

The compound sentence involves the addition of a second clause based on the verb *feared.*

The complex sentence contains additional information that is inserted in two different places.

Just to Make Sure

We can analyse the function of each group of words – the components of the previous sentence.

The teacher (subject), *who had already planned things carefully* (adjectival clause) *cried* (main verb) *until the class realised that he was teasing them* (adverbial clause).

Finally, emphasis. Place the emphasis of a sentence in ways that increase its impact. Now we are looking at the important ideas in a sentence and how they are made to stand out.

The ball landed in the back of the net.

A **loose** sentence; there is no one really important idea here. The ball landed, in the back of the net. A goal presumably, but it doesn't really seem to matter.

At last they had won, for the ball had smashed into the back of the net.

A **balanced** sentence with two strong ideas, winning and smashing.

For months they had pursued the trophy, training hard every Wednesday evening until at last, here, at Wembley, they lifted the cup.

A **periodic** sentence; we build up to the climax, *lifted the cup*, with the words, *for months, pursued, training hard, at last, here, at Wembley.*

Read these examples aloud so that you get a sense of how they work.

ESSENTIALS FOR STUDENTS – CHAPTER SIX

In this chapter I am asking you to look again at ways that words and groups of words fit together. This is important because it will help you to show a clear and accurate understanding of written passages.

First – Clause Analysis – How Is the Sentence Assembled?

What is the job of each clause? Whether the sentence is long or short, every word or group of words has a function, a job to do. Watch this one grow.

> *The quickest way of travelling across the city was by underground, <u>but they caught a bus outside the mainline station</u>* (subordinate clause – underlined).

> *The quickest way of travelling across the city was by underground, but they caught a bus outside the mainline station <u>and sat at the front of the top deck</u>* (another subordinate clause – joined by and to the first subordinate clause).

> *The quickest way of travelling across the city was by underground, but they caught a bus outside the mainline station and sat at the front of the top deck <u>from where they could look down on the streets and see the people there dressed in summer clothes</u>* (an adjectival clause that qualifies top deck).

We need to understand the function of each clause so that we know what it is contributing to our writing.

Next – subject and predicate – again – we need to keep focused on what a sentence is about and what we are told about it – pointers to its meaning and our understanding of it.

> *The quickest way of travelling across the city* (subject) *was by underground* (predicate).
> *They* (subject) *caught a bus outside the mainline station (predicate).*

Now look at the effect we can have if we vary the length of the subject and the predicate:

> *The girl* (subject) *smiled* (predicate). Emphasis on the final action, the smile.
> *The girl* (subject) *smiled at him as if she had forgotten the embarrassment and pain she had caused* (predicate). Emphasis on her causing embarrassment and pain.
> *The girl who had laughed at him when he asked her out* (subject) *smiled* (predicate). Emphasis on the final action, the smile.
> *The girl who had laughed at him when he asked her out (subject) smiled as if she had forgotten the embarrassment and pain she had caused* (predicate). Emphasis on her forgetting the embarrassment and pain she had caused.

> ***Look at the variation in emphasis caused by our selection***
> ***and ordering of words.***

ESSENTIALS FOR STUDENTS – CHAPTER SEVEN

Precis or Summary

What? This exercise requires you to show a clear understanding of written material and the ability to sum up its important points clearly and economically in writing.

How? It involves careful reading, the selection of the main ideas expressed in a passage and the setting out of those ideas clearly in writing.

Why? It is important because the intelligent handling of ideas is important in commerce and industry, in college and university study, in politics and journalism, in religion and the arts, and as part of educated life.

Until now we have concentrated on the way words are assembled, as if were putting together a machine or a piece of equipment. Now we are moving away from words, phrases, clauses and sentences, the components, to see what happens when we start up the machine. Then we will see the achievements of the first word processor, the human brain.

Aim to reduce a piece of writing to a third of its original length without losing its key points

What to do – a check list:

- Read the passage three times.
- Identify **the main points** – make a list then reorder them if this will improve things.
- Draft a sentence for each point into a paragraph or paragraphs.
- Check that all your main points are still present.
- Read through the draft then make any necessary corrections or improvements.
- Write the final draft, which should be approximately one third the length of the original.

Identifying the main points in a passage of writing – the most important part of this process:

- Identify the verbs, the subject and the predicate of each sentence.
- Ask yourself what each sentence seems to be about.
- Ask yourself what is really important in each sentence.
- Ask yourself whether any ideas are dealt with in more than one sentence.
- Do some ideas develop into new ideas as you move from one sentence to the next?

Main points – another way

Eliminate words from the passage that are redundant or of lesser importance. Look for key words among those that remain, e.g.

~~Having seen the~~ ice cream, ~~the~~ dog ignored ~~the~~ cat.

Writing the Summary

Read over each draft a number of times, to be really sure that you have included your main points. Make sure that you have removed words that do not convey main ideas.

Check your draft as you would any piece of writing.
If you possibly can, read it **ALOUD.**

ESSENTIALS FOR STUDENTS AND TUTORS – CHAPTER EIGHT ONWARDS

An Explanation

So far it has been relatively easy to lead students and tutors along separately as we deal with matters of fact – *Is this a noun? What kind of clause is this?* Now we all have to imagine being like a child who has just learnt to ride a bike and has set off knowing that a grown-up is watching but is too far away to prevent a fall. You are in charge of your journey with English now and must take responsibility for yourself, you must bring more of your ideas into your conversation. So, watch out for the next lamp-post.

Comprehension – Chapters Eight and Nine

Use the commentaries provided with the answers to the exercises by testing them, asking yourself whether you find that they make sense. Do be prepared to question them and, if you can, provide alternatives.

Questions – Chapter Ten

"Who are you?" The question starts an exchange of information, and whatever your answer – *"The Pope," "President Regan"* or *"Joan of Arc,"* there is likely to be another question: *"Do you have any ID?"* Questions hold clues about satisfactory answers; in this case it's the word *who*.

Back to the Sentence – Chapter Eleven
Assembling the words, the components, was one thing, now it is important to see the range of things we can get them to do. Hinting at information and revealing it, turning ideas around – *he works hard* or *he is made to work hard* – and distinguishing fact from opinion, are crucial skills in life, not just in an English exam.

Putting Sentences to Work – Chapter Twelve
When we start a piece of writing it is helpful to be reminded that writing about facts is generally easier than writing a description, and that writing a description is usually easier than presenting arguments in writing. It is easy to set out simple facts, but a description requires some organisation and a discussion requires careful expressing and ordering of opinions and argument.

Paragraphs – Chapter Thirteen
Here again there is no simple cut-and-dry way of doing things. It is very helpful to find words – stepping stones – that lead us on when we read and provide help for our readers when we write. Then, when we have finished a paragraph we need to take a bird's eye view and consider where it is taking the reader. Then we can ask ourselves what should come next.

Bogeymen – Spelling, Punctuation, Grammar and Handwriting – Chapter Fourteen
Oh, the hours of broadcasting and the columns of journalism that have been wasted bemoaning people's ignorance of the rules of spelling, punctuation and grammar. If only all these clever people could explain that these so-called rules are simply conventions that help us to communicate effectively. They could remind us that writing clearly is simply good manners; it's consideration for other people that requires us to get these things right. Learning the "rules" may help a bit, but that's all.

Writing – Chapter Fifteen
The more we have read of what other people have written and the more we have examined and thought about other people's writing, the better prepared we are when we start to write ourselves. That was the concern of the first seven chapters of the book. Now I hope that students will have the confidence to join

in the discussions, by asking themselves questions. Now they can check their own work, by reading it and asking themselves how they might improve it.

In a strange sort of way students of this book are lucky for, when puzzled, they have been unable to raise a lazy arm and say, "Please sir, what's a…?" No, you have had to think these things out for yourselves and now you are well on your way with the business of using English well.

REVIEW

Did you ever think that you knew everything about the English language, but came unstuck when you tried to put it into words? Or do you lack confidence in your literacy levels? If so, then read this extremely useful manual on how the English language works. It contains very clear and relevant real-life examples that a range of readers can relate to: from secondary school pupils, to adults and tutors alike. I have not only used examples from this book successfully with KS3, GCSE and A-Level English Language students, but also to refresh my own subject knowledge before teaching grammar in my classroom.

Text boxes highlight key information and asterisks draw attention to main points that you need to remember. The activities and tests enable readers to consolidate their learning, recognise their progress and identify any aspects that they need to look over again. The 'essentials' sections provide quick and easy glossaries of technical terms, again with clear examples. There are lots of other useful tips for retaining learning and making helpful revision notes, with a good mixture of reading and writing tasks throughout. The author has also offered direct links to his website, in order to provide further assistance. His classroom experiences provide not only humour, but also reassurance that these approaches are successful. A super book! *Julia Hayden – teacher.*

Author interviews Julia and Ben, a reformed tearaway: http://www.peterinson. net/teacher-tearaway-praise-the-book/